The DLM Early Childhood Express

Teacher's Edition

Unit 3
My Community

Nell Duke • Douglas Clements • Julie Sarama • William Teale

McGraw Hill **Wright Group**

The McGraw·Hill Companies

Authors

Nell Duke
Professor of Teacher Education and Educational Psychology and Co-Director of the Literacy Achievement Research Center Michigan State University, East Lansing, MI

Douglas H. Clements
Professor of Early Childhood and Mathematics Education University at Buffalo, State University of New York, New York

Julie Sarama
Associate Professor of Mathematics Education University at Buffalo, State University of New York, New York

William Teale
Professor of Education University of Illinois at Chicago, Chicago, IL

Contributing Authors

Kim Brenneman, PhD
Assistant Research Professor of Psychology at Rutgers University, National Institute for Early Education Research Rutgers University, New Brunswick, NJ

Peggy Cerna
Early Childhood Consultant Austin, TX

Dan Cieloha
Educator and President of the Partnership for Interactive Learning Oakland, CA

Paula Jones
Early Childhood Consultant Lubbock, TX

Bobbie Sparks
Educator and K-12 Science Consultant Houston, TX

Image Credits: Cover (roof)Ryan McVay/Getty Images, (wheels)felinda/istockphoto, (all other)The McGraw-Hill Companies; **5** blue jean images/Getty Images; **9** Seth Joel/Photographer's Choice RF/Getty Images; **18-19** Richard Hutchings / PhotoEdit; **19** Mimi Haddon/Getty Images; **24** Jose Luis Pelaez Inc/Getty Images; **25** (l r)Bobbi Tull/Photodisc/Getty Images; **26** Valeria Cis; **30** Comstock/Getty Images; **32** Tom Grill/CORBIS; **36** Eileen Hine; **38** (bl)Hisham Ibrahim/Getty Images, (br)Royalty-Free/CORBIS; **42** Mike Wesley; **44** Jose Luis Pelaez Inc/Getty Images; **48** Steve Mack; **48** Tim Beaumont; **50** Studio DL/CORBIS; **54** Steve Mack; **56-57** Royalty-Free/Masterfile; **57** Ariel Skelley/Blend Images/CORBIS; **62** Daniel Pangbourne/Getty Images; **63** Mitch Hrdlicka/Getty Images; **64** Holli Conger; **68** Brand X Pictures/PunchStock; **70** Mike Wesley; **74** Brand X Pictures/PunchStock; **76** Ingram Publishing/Alamy; **78** 1998 Image Ideas, Inc.; **82** Ingram Publishing/SuperStock; **88** Stockbyte/PunchStock; **92** Melissa Iwai; **94-95** Klaus Lang/Getty Images; **95** India Picture/CORBIS; **100** Royalty-Free/Masterfile; **101** Stocdisc/Getty Images; **103** Radius Images/Alamy; **106** Eileen Hine; **142** Medioimages/PunchStock; **144** Daniel Griffo; **146** Stockbyte; **148** Ariel Skelley/Getty Images; **150** Valeria Cis; **156** Mike Wesley; **162** Jose Luis Pelaez Inc/Getty Images; **162** Melissa Iwai; **168** Eileen Hine; **171** (r)The McGraw-Hill Companies, Inc./Ken Cavanagh photographer; **172** Radius Images/Alamy; **178** D. Berry/PhotoLink/Getty Images; **181** (t)Steve Mack, (c)Ingram Publishing/Alamy, (b)Daniel Griffo; **183** (t)Susan LeVan/Getty Images, (b)Laura Gonzalez; **185** Mike Wesley; **186** (t)The McGraw-Hill Companies, Inc., (b)Eileen Hine; **192** Photodisc Collection/Getty Images; **BackCover** (all wheels)felinda/istockphoto, (pencil)Andy Crawford/Getty Images, (rust wicker)Comstock/CORBIS, (bell)Stockbyte/Getty Images, (webcam)Medioimages/Photodisc/Getty Images, (pencilmirror)Yasuhide Fumoto/Getty Images, (U3roof)Ryan McVay/Getty Images, (elephant)PhotoLink/Getty Images, (looking glass) CMCD/Getty Images, (alligator)Siede Preis/Getty Images, (alligatorbelly)Ryan McVay/Getty Images, (U5traincar)83owl/Getty Images, (toothbrush)Raimund Koch/Getty Images, (U8traincar)Ryan McVay/Getty Images, (brush)Brand X Pictures/PunchStock, (all other)The McGraw-Hill Companies.

The McGraw·Hill Companies

www.WrightGroup.com

Wright Group

Send all inquiries to:
Wright Group/McGraw-Hill
P.O. Box 812960
Chicago, IL 60681

ISBN 978-0-07-658081-1
MHID 0-07-658081-4

2 3 4 5 6 7 8 9 WEB 16 15 14 13 12 11 10

Acknowledgment

Building Blocks was supported in part by the National Science Foundation under Grant No. ESI-9730804, "Building Blocks— Foundations for Mathematical Thinking, Pre-Kindergarten to Grade 2: Research-based Materials Development" to Douglas H. Clements and Julie Sarama. The curriculum was also based partly upon work supported in part by the Institute of Educational Sciences (U.S. Dept. of Education, under the Interagency Education Research Initiative, or IERI, a collaboration of the IES, NSF, and NICHHD) under Grant No. R305K05157, "Scaling Trajectories and Technologies" and by the IERI through a National Science Foundation NSF Grant No. REC-0228440, "Scaling Up the Implementation of a Pre-Kindergarten Mathematics Curricula: Teaching for Understanding with Trajectories and Technologies." Any opinions, findings, and conclusions or recommendations expressed in this material are those of the authors and do not necessarily reflect the views of the funding agencies.

Reviewers

Tonda Brown, *Pre-K Specialist,* Austin ISD; Deanne Colley, *Family Involvement Facilitator,* Northwest ISD; Anita Uphaus, *Retired Early Childhood Director,* Austin ISD; Cathy Ambridge, *Reading Specialist,* Klein ISD; Margaret Jordan, *PreK Special Education Teacher,* McMullen Booth Elementary; Niki Rogers, *Adjunct Professor of Psychology/Child Development,* Concordia University Wisconsin

Table of Contents

Unit 3: My Community

What is a community?
Getting Started 4

Week 1

What are the parts of a community?
Overview, Learning Goals, and Planners 18
  Learning Centers 24
  Day 1 26
  Day 2 32
  Day 3 38
  Day 4 44
  Day 5 50

Week 2

How does a community help me?
Overview, Learning Goals, and Planners 56
  Learning Centers 62
  Day 1 64
  Day 2 70
  Day 3 76
  Day 4 82
  Day 5 88

Week 3

Who helps the community?
Overview, Learning Goals, and Planners 94
  Learning Centers 100
  Day 1 102
  Day 2 108
  Day 3 114
  Day 4 120
  Day 5 126

Week 4

How can I help my community?
Overview, Learning Goals, and Planners 132
  Learning Centers 138
  Day 1 140
  Day 2 146
  Day 3 152
  Day 4 158
  Day 5 164

Assessment 170

Unit Wrap-Up 172

Appendix 175

Getting Started

Getting Started with *The DLM Early Childhood Express*

The DLM Early Childhood Express is a holistic, child-centered program that nurtures each child by offering carefully selected and carefully sequenced learning experiences. It provides a wealth of materials and ideas to foster the social-emotional, intellectual, and physical development of children. At the same time, it nurtures the natural curiosity and sense of self that can serve as the foundation for a lifetime of learning.

The lesson format is designed to present information in a way that makes it easy for children to learn. Intelligence is, in large part, our ability to see patterns and build relationships out of those patterns, which is why *DLM* is focused on helping children see the patterns in what they are learning. It builds an understanding of how newly taught material resembles what children already know. Then it takes the differences in the new material and helps the children convert them into new understanding.

Each of the eight Teacher Edition Unit's in *DLM* are centered on an Essential Question relating to the unit's theme. Each week has its own more specific focus question. By focusing on essential questions, children are better able to connect their existing knowledge of the world with the new concepts and ideas they are learning at school. Routines at the beginning and end of each day help children focus on the learning process, reflect on new concepts, and make important connections. The lessons are designed to allow children to apply what they have learned.

Social and Emotional Development

Social-emotional development is addressed everyday through positive reinforcement, interactive activities, and engaging songs.

Language and Communication

All lessons are focused on language acquisition, which includes oral language development and vocabulary activities.

Emergent Literacy: Reading

Children develop literacy skills for reading through exposure to multiple read-aloud selections each day and through daily phonological awareness and letter recognition activities.

Emergent Literacy: Writing

Children develop writing skills through daily writing activities and during Center Time.

Mathematics

The math strand is based on *Building Blocks*, the result of NSF-funded research, and is designed to develop children's early mathematical knowledge through various individual and group activities.

Science

Children explore scientific concepts and methods during weekly science-focused, large-group activities, and Center Time activities.

Social Studies

Children explore Social Studies concepts during weekly social studies-focused, large-group activities, and Center Time activities.

Fine Arts

Children are exposed to art, dance, and music through a variety of weekly activities and the Creativity Center.

Physical Development

DLM is designed to allow children active time for outdoor play during the day, in addition to daily and weekly movement activities.

Technology Applications

Technology is integrated throughout each week with the use of online math activities, computer time, and other digital resources.

English Language Learners

Today's classrooms are very diverse. *The DLM Early Childhood Express* addresses this diversity by providing lessons in both English and Spanish. The program also offers strategies to assist English Language Learners at multiple levels of proficiency.

Flexible Scheduling

With *The DLM Early Childhood Express*, it's easy to fit lessons into your day.

Typical Full-Day Schedule

10 min	Opening Routines
15 min	Language Time
60-90 min	Center Time
15 min	Snack Time
15 min	Literacy Time
20 min	Active Play (outdoors if possible)
30 min	Lunch
15 min	Math Time
	Rest
15 min	Circle Time: Social and Emotional Development
20 min	Circle Time: Content Connection
30 min	Center Time
25 min	Active Play (outdoors if possible)
15 min	Let's Say Good-Bye

Typical Half-Day Schedule

10 min	Opening Routines
15 min	Language Time
60 min	Center Time
15 min	Snack Time
15 min	Circle Time (Literacy, Math, or Social and Emotional Development)
30 min	Active Play (outdoors if possible)
20 min	Circle Time (Content Connection, Literacy, Math, or Social and Emotional Development)
15 min	Let's Say Good-Bye

Welcome to *The DLM Early Childhood Express.*

Add your own ideas. Mix and match activities. Our program is designed to offer you a variety of activities on which to build a full year of exciting and creative lessons.

Happy learning to you and the children in your care!

Themes and Literature

With *The DLM Early Childhood Express,* children develop concrete skills through experiences with music, art, storytelling, hands-on activities and teacher-directed lessons that, in addition to skills development, emphasize practice and reflection. Every four weeks, children are introduced to a new theme organized around an essential question.

Literature selections and cross-curricular content are linked to the theme to help children reinforce lesson concepts. Children hear and discuss an additional read-aloud selection from the *Teacher Treasure Book* at the beginning and end of each day. At the end of each unit, children take home a *My Theme Library Book* reader of their own.

Unit 1: All About Pre-K
Why is school important?

	Focus Question	Literature
Week 1	What happens at school?	*Welcome to School* *Bienvenidos a la escuela*
Week 2	What happens in our classroom?	*Yellowbelly and Plum Go to School* *Barrigota y Pipón van a la escuela*
Week 3	What makes a good friend?	*Max and Mo's First Day at School* *Max y Mo van a la escuela*
Week 4	How can we play and learn together?	*Amelia's Show and Tell Fiesta/Amelia y la fiesta de "muestra y cuenta"*
Unit Wrap-Up	**My Library Book**	*How Can I Learn at School?* *¿Cómo puedo aprender en la escuela?*

Unit 2: All About Me
What makes me special?

	Focus Question	Literature
Week 1	Who am I?	*All About Me* *Todo sobre mí*
Week 2	What are my feelings?	*Lots of Feelings* *Montones de sentimientos*
Week 3	What do the parts of my body do?	*Eyes, Nose, Fingers, and Toes* *Ojos, nariz, dedos y pies*
Week 4	What is a family?	*Jonathan and His Mommy* *Juan y su mamá*
Unit Wrap-Up	**My Library Book**	*What Makes Us Special?* *¿Qué nos hace especiales?*

Unit 3: My Community
What is a community?

	Focus Question	Literature
Week 1	What are the parts of a community?	*In the Community* *En la comunidad*
Week 2	Hoe does a community help me?	*Rush Hour,* *Hora pico*
Week 3	Who helps the community?	*Quinito's Neighborhood*
Week 4	How can I help my community?	*Flower Garden* *Un jardín de flores*
Unit Wrap-Up	**My Library Book**	*In My Community* *Mi comunidad*

Unit 4: Let's Investigate
How can I learn more about things?

	Focus Question	Literature
Week 1	How can I learn by observing?	*Let's Investigate* *Soy detective*
Week 2	How can I use tools to investiagte?	*I Like Making Tamales* *Me gusta hacer tamales*
Week 3	How can I compare things?	*Nature Spy* *Espía de la naturaleza*
Week 4	How do objects move?	*What Do Wheels Do All Day?* *¿Qué hacen las ruedas todo el día?*
Unit Wrap-Up	**My Library Book**	*How Can We Investigate?* *¿Cómo podemos investigar?*

Unit 5: Amazing Animals
What is amazing about animals?

	Focus Question	Literature
Week 1	What are animals like?	*Amazing Animals* *Animales asombrosos*
Week 2	Where do animals live and what do they eat?	*Castles, Caves, and Honeycombs* *Castillos, cuevas y panales*
Week 3	How are animals the same and different?	*Who Is the Beast?* *Quien es la bestia?*
Week 4	How do animals move?	*Move!* *¡A moverse!*
Unit Wrap-Up	**My Library Book**	*Hello, Animals!* *¡Hola, animales!*

Unit 6: Growing and Changing
How do living things grow and change?

	Focus Question	Literature
Week 1	How do animals grow and change?	*Growing and Changing* *Creciendo y cambiando*
Week 2	How do plants grow and change?	*I Am a Peach* *Yo soy el durazno*
Week 3	How do people grow and change?	*I'm Growing!* *Estoy creciendo!*
Week 4	How do living things grow and change?	*My Garden* *Mi jardin*
Unit Wrap-Up	**My Library Book**	*Growing Up* *Creciendo*

Unit 7: The Earth and Sky
What can I learn about the earth and the sky?

	Focus Question	Literature
Week 1	What can I learn about the earth and the sky?	*The Earth and Sky* *La Tierra y el cielo*
Week 2	What weather can I observe each day?	*Who Likes Rain?* *¿A quién le gusta la lluvia?*
Week 3	What can I learn about day and night?	*Matthew and the Color of the Sky* *Matias y el color del cielo*
Week 4	Why is caring for the earth and sky important?	*Ada, Once Again!* *¡Otra vez Ada!*
Unit Wrap-Up	**My Library Book**	*Good Morning, Earth!* *¡Buenos días, Tierra!*

Unit 8: Healthy Food/Healthy Body
Why is healthy food and exercise good for me?

	Focus Question	Literature
Week 1	What are good healthy habits?	*Staying Healthy* *Mantente sano*
Week 2	What kinds of foods are healthy?	*Growing Vegetable Soup* *A sembrar sopa de verduras*
Week 3	Why is exercise important?	*Rise and Exercise!* *A ejercitarse, ¡uno, dos, tres!*
Week 4	How can I stay healthy?	*Jamal's Busy Day* *El intenso día de Jamal*
Unit Wrap-Up	**My Library Book**	*Healthy Kids* *Niños sanos*

Tools for Teaching

The **DLM Early Childhood Express** is packed full of the components you'll need to teach each theme and enrich your classroom. The *Teacher Treasure Package* is the heart of the program, because it contains all the necessary materials. Plus, the *Teacher's Treasure Book* contains all the fun components that you'll love to teach. The *Literature Package* contains all the stories and books you need to support children's developing literacy. You'll find letter tiles, counters, and puppets in the *Manipulative Package* to connect hands-on learning skills with meaningful play.

Teacher Treasure Package

This package contains all the essential tools for the teacher such as the *Teacher's Treasure Book, Teacher's Editions*, technology, and other resources no teacher would want to be without!

ABC Picture Cards (English and Spanish)

Alphabet Wall Cards (English and Spanish)

Sequence Cards (English and Spanish)

Oral Language Development Cards (English and Spanish)

Photo Library CD-ROM

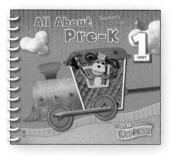

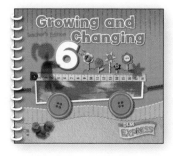

▲ Each lesson's instruction uses a variety of cards to help children learn. **Alphabet Wall Cards** and **ABC Picture Cards** help build letter recognition and phonemic awareness. **Oral Language Development Cards** teach new vocabulary, and are especially helpful when working with English Language Learners. **Sequencing Cards** help children learn how to order events and the vocabulary associated with time and sequence.

▲ There is one bilingual **Teacher's Edition** for each four-week theme. It provides the focus questions for each lesson as well as plans for centers and suggestions for classroom management.

▶ The bilingual **Teacher's Treasure Book** features 500+ pages of the things you love most about teaching Early Childhood, such as songs, traditional read alouds, folk tales, finger plays, and flannelboard stories with patterns.

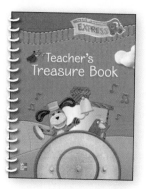

▶ An **ABC Take-Home Book** with blackline masters is provided for each letter of the English and Spanish alphabets.

ABC Take-Home Book (English and Spanish)

▶ Flip charts and their Audio CDs support the activities in each lesson. Children practice literacy and music skills using the **Rhymes and Chants Flip Chart,** which supports oral language development and phonological awareness in both English and Spanish. An Audio CD is included and provides a recording of every rhyme or chant. The **Making Good Choices Flip Chart** provides illustrations to allow students to explore social and emotional development concepts while facilitating classroom activities and discussion. 15 lively songs recorded in both English and Spanish address key social emotional development themes such as: joining in, helping others, being fair, teasing, bullying, and much more. The **Math and Science Flip Chart** is a demonstration tool that addresses weekly math and science concepts through photos and illustrations.

▶ Other key resources include a **Research & Professional Development Guide,** and a bilingual **Home Connections Resource Guide** which provides weekly letters home and take-home story books.

Building Blocks, the result of NSF-funded research, develops young children's mathematical thinking using their bodies, manipulatives, paper, and computers.

Building Blocks online management system guides children through research-based learning trajectories. These activities-through-trajectories connect children's informal knowledge to more formal school mathematics. The result is a mathematical curriculum that is not only motivating for children but also comprehensive.

▶ **DLMExpressOnline.com** includes the following:

● e-Books of student and teacher materials

● Audio recordings of the **My Library** and **Literature Books** (Big/Little) in English and Spanish

● Teacher planning tools and assessment support

Tools for Teaching

Literature Package

This package contains the literature referenced in the program. Packages are available in several variations so you can choose the package that best meets the needs of your classroom. The literature used in the program includes expository selections, traditional stories, and emergent readers for students. All literature is available in English or Spanish.

▶ *My Library Books* are take-home readers for children to continue their exploration of unit themes. (English and Spanish)

▶ *Concept Big Books* are nonfiction selections that introduce the essential questions for each unit and help children make connections between their background knowledge and unit themes. (English and Spanish)

▶ The *ABC Big Book* helps children develop phonemic awareness and letter recognition. (English and Spanish)

▶ The *Big Books* and *Little Books* reinforce each week's theme and the unit theme. Selections include stories originally written in Spanish, as well as those written in English.

▶ The stories in the *Big Books and Little Books* are recorded on the *Listening Library Audio CDs*. They are available in English and Spanish.

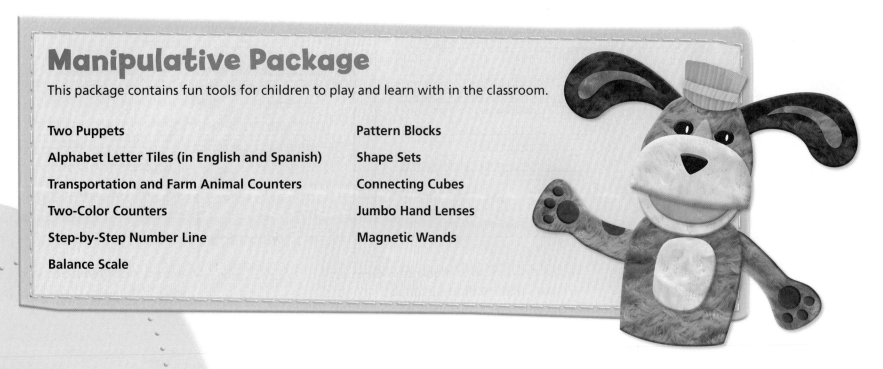

Manipulative Package

This package contains fun tools for children to play and learn with in the classroom.

Two Puppets

Alphabet Letter Tiles (in English and Spanish)

Transportation and Farm Animal Counters

Two-Color Counters

Step-by-Step Number Line

Balance Scale

Pattern Blocks

Shape Sets

Connecting Cubes

Jumbo Hand Lenses

Magnetic Wands

A Typical Weekly Lesson Plan

Each week of *The DLM Early Childhood Express* is organized the same way to provide children with the structure and routines they crave. Each week begins with a weekly opener that introduces the focus question for the week and includes a review of the week's Learning Goals, the Materials and Resources needed for the week, a Daily Planner, and a plan for the Learning Centers children will use throughout the week.

Each day's lesson includes large-group Circle Time and small-group Center Time. Each day includes Literacy, Math, and Social and Emotional Development activities during Circle Time. On Day 1, children explore Science. On Days 2 and 4, they work on more in-depth math lessons. On Day 3, Social Studies is the focus. Fine Art or Music/Movement activities take place during Circle Time on Day 5.

You will find the **Program Materials** and **Other Materials** needed for each day on the Materials and Resources page.

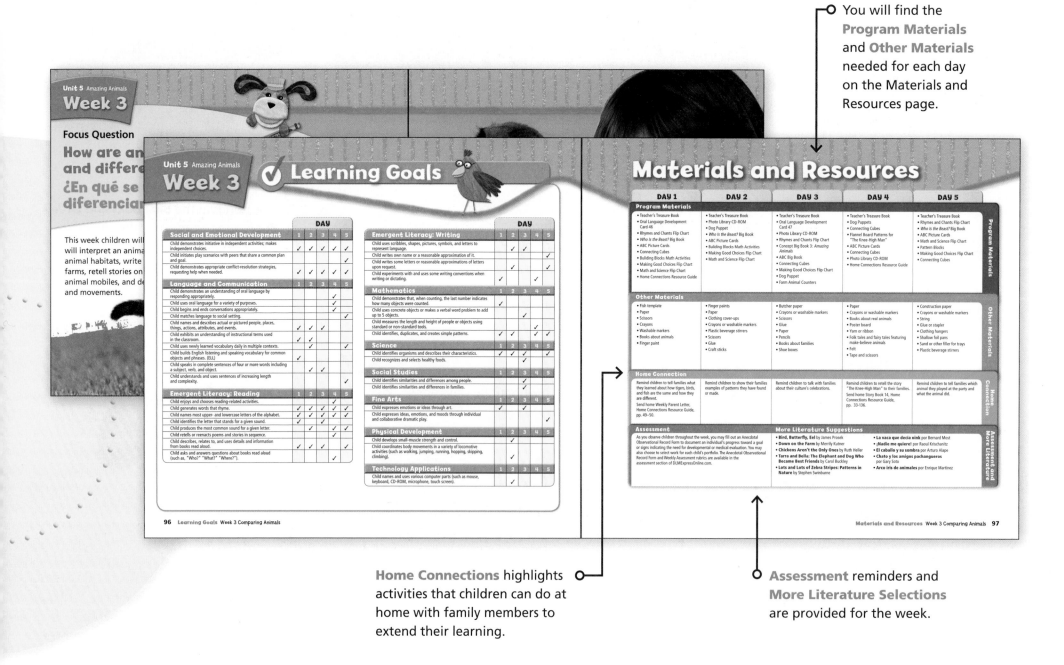

Home Connections highlights activities that children can do at home with family members to extend their learning.

Assessment reminders and **More Literature Selections** are provided for the week.

The **Daily Planner** provides a Week-at-a-Glance view of the daily structure and lesson topics for each week.

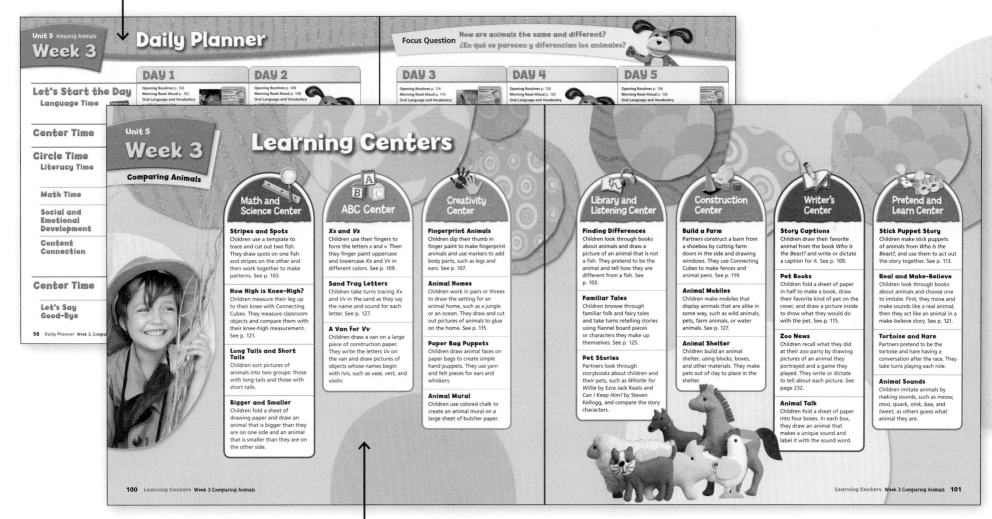

Learning Centers should be used throughout the week during Center Time. This page provides an overview of center activities to set up for children. Additional information about some center activities is provided in the daily lessons. The Learning Centers are intended to remain open for the entire week. These centers provide the opportunity for children to explore a wide range of curricular areas.

Lesson Overview

Our **Teacher's Editions** are organized by theme, week, and day. Each day's lesson is covered in six page spreads. The lessons integrate learning from the skill domain areas of: Social Emotional Development, Language and Communication, Emergent Literacy Reading and Writing, Mathematics, Science, Social Studies, Fine Arts, Physical Development, and Technology.

Each day begins with **Opening Routines** and a **Read Aloud** selection. This structured time helps children settle into their day.

The **Learning Goals** met by the lesson are listed on each page.

Observational Checks at point of use help to focus learning. These informal assessment questions help to ensure children are meeting lesson objectives.

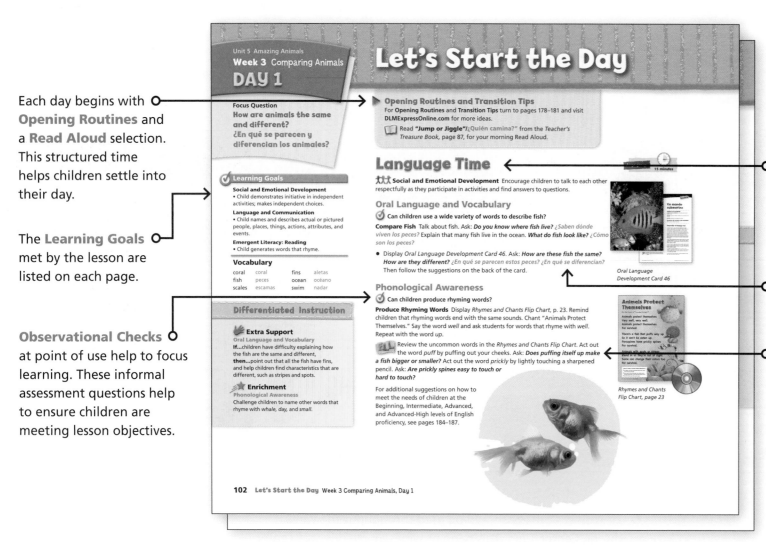

Unit 5 Amazing Animals
Week 3 Comparing Animals

DAY 1

Focus Question
How are animals the same and different?
¿En qué se parecen y diferencian los animales?

Let's Start the Day

▶ **Opening Routines and Transition Tips**
For **Opening Routines** and **Transition Tips** turn to pages 178–181 and visit DLMExpressOnline.com for more ideas.

Read **"Jump or Jiggle"**/¿Quién camina?" from the *Teacher's Treasure Book*, page 87, for your morning Read Aloud.

Language Time

15 minutes

👥 **Social and Emotional Development** Encourage children to talk to each other respectfully as they participate in activities and find answers to questions.

Oral Language and Vocabulary

✓ Can children use a wide variety of words to describe fish?

Compare Fish Talk about fish. Ask: *Do you know where fish live?* ¿Saben dónde viven los peces? Explain that many fish live in the ocean. *What do fish look like?* ¿Cómo son los peces?

● Display *Oral Language Development Card 46*. Ask: *How are these fish the same? How are they different?* ¿En qué se parecen estos peces? ¿En qué se diferencian? Then follow the suggestions on the back of the card.

Oral Language Development Card 46

Phonological Awareness

✓ Can children produce rhyming words?

Produce Rhyming Words Display *Rhymes and Chants Flip Chart*, p. 23. Remind children that rhyming words end with the same sounds. Chant "Animals Protect Themselves." Say the word *well* and ask students for words that rhyme with *well*. Repeat with the word *up*.

ELL Review the uncommon words in the *Rhymes and Chants Flip Chart*. Act out the word *puff* by puffing out your cheeks. Ask: *Does puffing itself up make a fish bigger or smaller?* Act out the word *prickly* by lightly touching a sharpened pencil. Ask: *Are prickly spines easy to touch or hard to touch?*

For additional suggestions on how to meet the needs of children at the Beginning, Intermediate, Advanced, and Advanced-High levels of English proficiency, see pages 184–187.

Rhymes and Chants Flip Chart, page 23

✓ Learning Goals

Social and Emotional Development
• Child demonstrates initiative in independent activities; makes independent choices.
Language and Communication
• Child names and describes actual or pictured people, places, things, actions, attributes, and events.
Emergent Literacy: Reading
• Child generates words that rhyme.

Vocabulary

coral	coral	fins	aletas
fish	peces	ocean	océano
scales	escamas	swim	nadar

Differentiated Instruction

✋ **Extra Support**
Oral Language and Vocabulary
If...children have difficulty explaining how the fish are the same and different, **then...**point out that all the fish have fins, and help children find characteristics that are different, such as stripes and spots.

⭐ **Enrichment**
Phonological Awareness
Challenge children to name other words that rhyme with *whale*, *day*, and *small*.

102 Let's Start the Day Week 3 Comparing Animals, Day 1

Language Time is the first large-group activity of the day. It includes Oral Language and Vocabulary Development as well as Phonological Awareness activities.

Instructional questions are provided in both **English and Spanish.**

Tips for working with **English Language Learners** are shown at point of use throughout the lessons. Teaching strategies are provided to help children of of all language backgrounds and abilities meet the lesson objectives.

Center Time provides additional information for teacher-guided small-group activities and suggestions for independent activities children will complete during weekly Center Rotation.

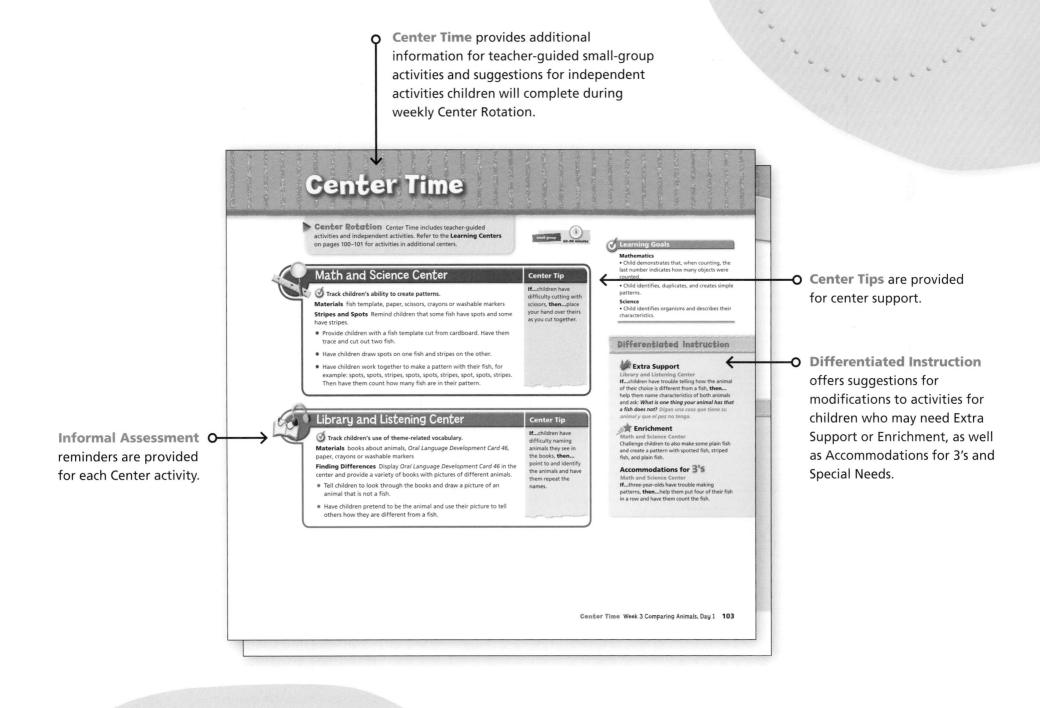

Center Time

▶ **Center Rotation** Center Time includes teacher-guided activities and independent activities. Refer to the **Learning Centers** on pages 100–101 for activities in additional centers.

small group | *60–90 minutes*

Math and Science Center

✓ Track children's ability to create patterns.

Materials fish template, paper, scissors, crayons or washable markers

Stripes and Spots Remind children that some fish have spots and some have stripes.

- Provide children with a fish template cut from cardboard. Have them trace and cut out two fish.
- Have children draw spots on one fish and stripes on the other.
- Have children work together to make a pattern with their fish, for example: spots, spots, stripes, spots, spots, stripes, spot, spots, stripes. Then have them count how many fish are in their pattern.

Center Tip
If...children have difficulty cutting with scissors, **then**...place your hand over theirs as you cut together.

Library and Listening Center

✓ Track children's use of theme-related vocabulary.

Materials books about animals, *Oral Language Development Card 46*, paper, crayons or washable markers

Finding Differences Display *Oral Language Development Card 46* in the center and provide a variety of books with pictures of different animals.

- Tell children to look through the books and draw a picture of an animal that is not a fish.
- Have children pretend to be the animal and use their picture to tell others how they are different from a fish.

Center Tip
If...children have difficulty naming animals they see in the books, **then**...point to and identify the animals and have them repeat the names.

✓ Learning Goals

Mathematics
- Child demonstrates that, when counting, the last number indicates how many objects were counted.
- Child identifies, duplicates, and creates simple patterns.

Science
- Child identifies organisms and describes their characteristics.

Differentiated Instruction

Extra Support
Library and Listening Center
If...children have trouble telling how the animal of their choice is different from a fish, **then**... help them name characteristics of both animals and ask: *What is one thing your animal has that a fish does not?* *Digan una cosa que tiene su animal y que el pez no tenga.*

Enrichment
Math and Science Center
Challenge children to also make some plain fish and create a pattern with spotted fish, striped fish, and plain fish.

Accommodations for 3's
Math and Science Center
If...three-year-olds have trouble making patterns, **then**...help them put four of their fish in a row and have them count the fish.

Center Time Week 3 Comparing Animals, Day 1   **103**

Center Tips are provided for center support.

Differentiated Instruction offers suggestions for modifications to activities for children who may need Extra Support or Enrichment, as well as Accommodations for 3's and Special Needs.

Informal Assessment reminders are provided for each Center activity.

Lesson Overview

Children have **Literacy Time** every day. During this time, children listen to and discuss a second Read Aloud from a nonfiction *Concept Big Book* or a *Big Book/Little Book* literature selection

Building Blocks online activities are provided each week during Math Time.

Children work in large groups on 15 minute math activities during daily **Math Time.**

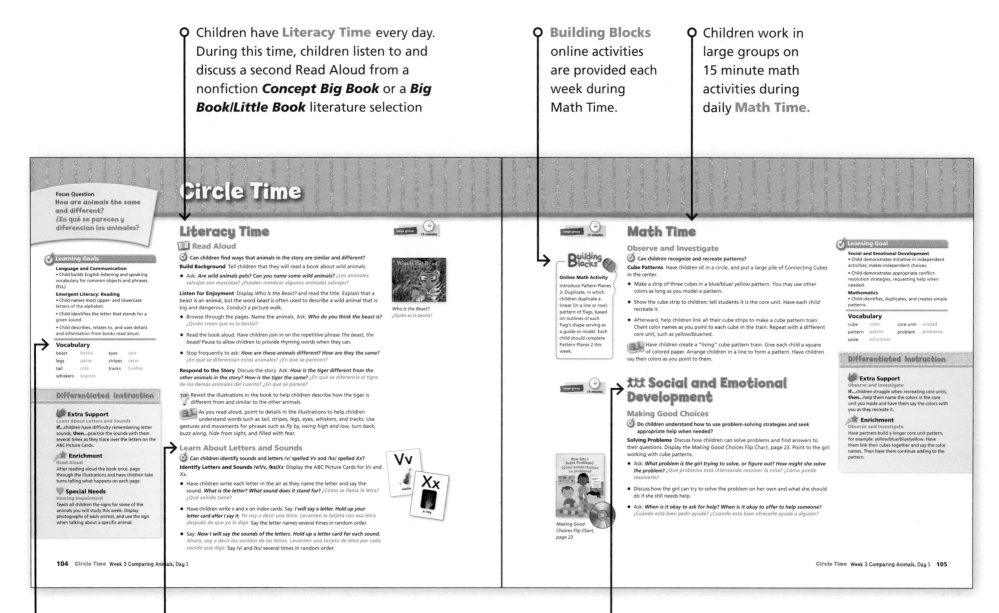

Focus Question
How are animals the same and different?
¿En qué se parecen y diferencian los animales?

Circle Time

Literacy Time

Read Aloud

✓ Can children find ways that animals in the story are similar and different?
Build Background Tell children that they will read a book about wild animals.

- Ask: *Are wild animals pets? Can you name some wild animals?* ¿Los animales salvajes son mascotas? ¿Pueden nombrar algunos animales salvajes?

Listen for Enjoyment Display *Who Is the Beast?* and read the title. Explain that a beast is an animal, but the word *beast* is often used to describe a wild animal that is big and dangerous. Conduct a picture walk.

- Browse through the pages. Name the animals. Ask: *Who do you think the beast is?* ¿Quién creen que es la bestia?
- Read the book aloud. Have children join in on the repetitive phrase *The beast, the beast!* Pause to allow children to provide rhyming words when they can.
- Stop frequently to ask: *How are these animals different? How are they the same?* ¿En qué se diferencian estos animales? ¿En qué se parecen?

Respond to the Story Discuss the story. Ask: *How is the tiger different from the other animals in the story? How is the tiger the same?* ¿En qué se diferencia el tigre de los demás animales del cuento? ¿En qué se parece?

TIP Revisit the illustrations in the book to help children describe how the tiger is different from and similar to the other animals.

ELL As you read aloud, point to details in the illustrations to help children understand words such as *tail, stripes, legs, eyes, whiskers,* and *tracks.* Use gestures and movements for phrases such as *fly by, swing high and low, turn back, buzz along, hide from sight,* and *filled with fear.*

Learn About Letters and Sounds

✓ Can children identify sounds and letters /v/ spelled *Vv* and /ks/ spelled *Xx*?
Identify Letters and Sounds /v/Vv, /ks/Xx Display the ABC Picture Cards for *Vv* and *Xx*.

- Have children write each letter in the air as they name the letter and say the sound. *What is the letter? What sound does it stand for?* ¿Cómo se llama la letra? ¿Qué sonido tiene?
- Have children write *v* and *x* on index cards. Say: *I will say a letter. Hold up your letter card after I say it.* Yo voy a decir una letra. Levanten la tarjeta con esa letra después de que yo la diga. Say the letter names several times in random order.
- Say: *Now I will say the sounds of the letters. Hold up a letter card for each sound.* Ahora, voy a decir los sonidos de las letras. Levanten una tarjeta de letra por cada sonido que diga. Say /v/ and /ks/ several times in random order.

large group 15 minutes

Who Is the Beast?
¿Quién es la bestia?

Vv
violin

Xx
x-ray

Learning Goals

Language and Communication
- Child builds English listening and speaking vocabulary for common objects and phrases. (ELL)

Emergent Literacy: Reading
- Child names most upper- and lowercase letters of the alphabet.
- Child identifies the letter that stands for a given sound.
- Child describes, relates to, and uses details and information from books read aloud.

Vocabulary

beast	bestia
legs	patas
tail	cola
whiskers	bigotes
eyes	ojos
stripes	rayas
tracks	huellas

Differentiated Instruction

Extra Support
Learn About Letters and Sounds
If...children have difficulty remembering letter sounds, *then*...practice the sounds with them several times as they trace over the letters on the ABC Picture Cards.

Enrichment
Read Aloud
After reading aloud the book once, page through the illustrations and have children take turns telling what happens on each page.

Special Needs
Hearing Impairment
Teach all children the signs for some of the animals you will study this week. Display photographs of each animal, and use the sign when talking about a specific animal.

Math Time

Observe and Investigate

✓ Can children recognize and recreate patterns?
Cube Patterns Have children sit in a circle, and put a large pile of Connecting Cubes in the center.

- Make a strip of three cubes in a blue/blue/ yellow pattern. You may use other colors as long as you model a pattern.
- Show the cube strip to children; tell students it is the core unit. Have each child recreate it.
- Afterward, help children link all their cube strips to make a cube pattern train. Chant color names as you point to each cube in the train. Repeat with a different core unit, such as yellow/blue/red.

ELL Have children create a "living" cube pattern train. Give each child a square of colored paper. Arrange children in a line to form a pattern. Have children say their colors as you point to them.

large group 15 minutes

Building Blocks

Online Math Activity
Introduce Pattern Planes 2: Duplicate, in which children duplicate a linear (in a line or row) pattern of flags, based on outlines of each flag's shape serving as a guide or model. Each child should complete Pattern Planes 2 this week.

🏃 Social and Emotional Development

Making Good Choices

✓ Do children understand how to use problem-solving strategies and seek appropriate help when needed?
Solving Problems Discuss how children can solve problems and find answers to their questions. Display the *Making Good Choices Flip Chart*, page 23. Point to the girl working with cube patterns.

- Ask: *What problem is the girl trying to solve, or figure out? How might she solve the problem?* ¿Qué problema está intentando resolver la niña? ¿Cómo puede resolverlo?
- Discuss how the girl can try to solve the problem on her own and what she should do if she still needs help.
- Ask: *When is it okay to ask for help? When is it okay to offer to help someone?* ¿Cuándo está bien pedir ayuda? ¿Cuándo está bien ofrecerle ayuda a alguien?

large group 15 minutes

Making Good Choices Flip Chart, page 23

Learning Goal

Social and Emotional Development
- Child demonstrates initiative in independent activities; makes independent choices.
- Child demonstrates appropriate conflict-resolution strategies, requesting help when needed.

Mathematics
- Child identifies, duplicates, and creates simple patterns.

Vocabulary

cube	cubo
pattern	patrón
solve	solucionar
core unit	unidad
problem	problema

Differentiated Instruction

Extra Support
Observe and Investigate
If...children struggle when recreating core units, *then*...help them name the colors in the core unit you made and have them say the colors with you as they recreate it.

Enrichment
Observe and Investigate
Have partners build a longer core unit pattern, for example: yellow/blue/blue/yellow. Have them link their cubes together and say the color names. Then have them continue adding to the pattern.

Vocabulary is provided in English and Spanish to help expand children's ability to use both languages.

Children learn about **Letters and Sounds** every day. The sound is introduced with the letter. Children also practice letter formation.

Social and Emotional Development concepts are addressed every day to help children better express their emotions and needs, and establish positive relationships.

Circle Time is devoted to longer activities focusing on different cross-curricular concepts each day. Day 1 is Science Time. Days 2 and 4 are Math Time. On Day 3, children have Social Studies Time. Fine arts are covered in Art Time or Music and Movement Time on Day 5.

An end-of-the-day **Writing** activity is provided each day.

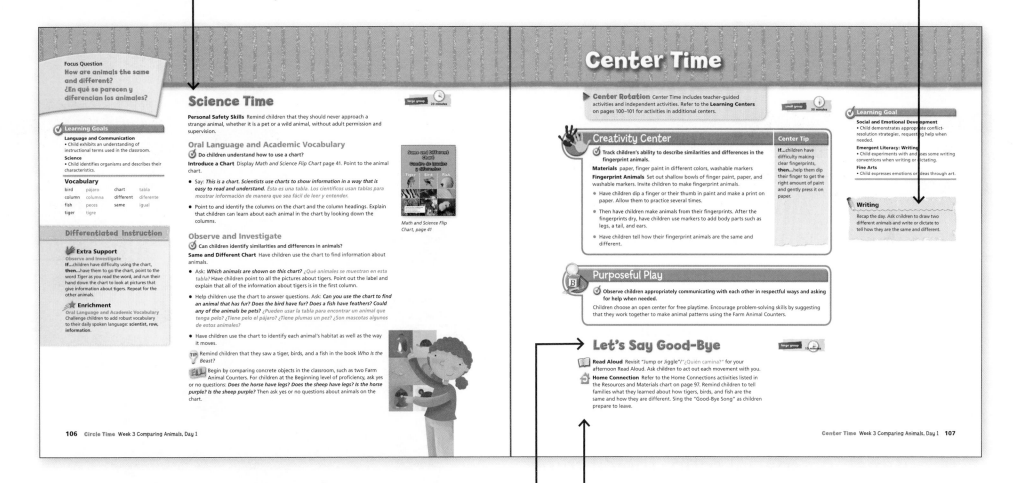

Focus Question
How are animals the same and different?
¿En qué se parecen y diferencian los animales?

✓ **Learning Goals**

Language and Communication
• Child exhibits an understanding of instructional terms used in the classroom.

Science
• Child identifies organisms and describes their characteristics.

Vocabulary

bird	pájaro	chart	tabla
column	columna	different	diferente
fish	peces	same	igual
tiger	tigre		

Differentiated Instruction

★ Extra Support
Observe and Investigate
If...children have difficulty using the chart, then...have them go the chart, point to the word *Tiger* as you read the word, and run their hand down the chart to look at pictures that give information about tigers. Repeat for the other animals.

★ Enrichment
Oral Language and Academic Vocabulary
Challenge children to add robust vocabulary to their daily spoken language: scientist, row, information.

Science Time

large group 20 minutes

Personal Safety Skills Remind children that they should never approach a strange animal, whether it is a pet or a wild animal, without adult permission and supervision.

Oral Language and Academic Vocabulary

✓ **Do children understand how to use a chart?**
Introduce a Chart Display *Math and Science Flip Chart* page 41. Point to the animal chart.

• Say: *This is a chart. Scientists use charts to show information in a way that is easy to read and understand. Ésta es una tabla. Los científicos usan tablas para mostrar información de manera que sea fácil de leer y entender.*

• Point to and identify the columns on the chart and the column headings. Explain that children can learn about each animal in the chart by looking down the columns.

Observe and Investigate

✓ **Can children identify similarities and differences in animals?**
Same and Different Chart Have children use the chart to find information about animals.

• Ask: *Which animals are shown on this chart? ¿Qué animales se muestran en esta tabla?* Have children point to all the pictures about tigers. Point out the label and explain that all of the information about tigers is in the first column.

• Help children use the chart to answer questions. Ask: *Can you use the chart to find an animal that has fur? Does the bird have fur? Does a fish have feathers? Could any of the animals be pets? ¿Pueden usar la tabla para encontrar un animal que tenga pelo? ¿Tiene pelo el pájaro? ¿Tiene plumas un pez? ¿Son mascotas algunos de estos animales?*

• Have children use the chart to identify each animal's habitat as well as the way it moves.

TIP Remind children that they saw a tiger, birds, and a fish in the book *Who Is the Beast?*

ELL Begin by comparing concrete objects in the classroom, such as two Farm Animal Counters. For children at the Beginning level of proficiency, ask yes or no questions: *Does the horse have legs? Does the sheep have legs? Is the horse purple? Is the sheep purple?* Then ask yes or no questions about animals on the chart.

Math and Science Flip Chart, page 41

106 Circle Time Week 3 Comparing Animals, Day 1

Center Time

▶ **Center Rotation** Center Time includes teacher-guided activities and independent activities. Refer to the **Learning Centers** on pages 100–101 for activities in additional centers.

small group 30 minutes

Creativity Center

✓ Track children's ability to describe similarities and differences in the fingerprint animals.

Materials paper, finger paint in different colors, washable markers
Fingerprint Animals Set out shallow bowls of finger paint, paper, and washable markers. Invite children to make fingerprint animals.

• Have children dip a finger or their thumb in paint and make a print on paper. Allow them to practice several times.

• Then have children make animals from their fingerprints. After the fingerprints dry, have children use markers to add body parts such as legs, a tail, and ears.

• Have children tell how their fingerprint animals are the same and different.

Center Tip
If...children have difficulty making clear fingerprints, then...help them dip their finger to get the right amount of paint and gently press it on paper.

Purposeful Play

✓ Observe children appropriately communicating with each other in respectful ways and asking for help when needed.

Children choose an open center for free playtime. Encourage problem-solving skills by suggesting that they work together to make animal patterns using the Farm Animal Counters.

Let's Say Good-Bye

large group 15 minutes

📖 **Read Aloud** Revisit "Jump or Jiggle"/"¿Quién camina?" for your afternoon Read Aloud. Ask children to act out each movement with you.

Home Connection Refer to the Home Connections activities listed in the Resources and Materials chart on page 97. Remind children to tell families what they learned about how tigers, birds, and fish are the same and how they are different. Sing the "Good-Bye Song" as children prepare to leave.

✓ **Learning Goal**

Social and Emotional Development
• Child demonstrates appropriate conflict-resolution strategies, requesting help when needed.

Emergent Literacy: Writing
• Child experiments with and uses some writing conventions when writing or dictating.

Fine Arts
• Child expresses emotions or ideas through art.

Writing
Recap the day. Ask children to draw two different animals and write or dictate to tell how they are the same and different.

Center Time Week 3 Comparing Animals, Day 1 **107**

Let's Say Good-Bye includes the closing routines for each day. The Read Aloud from the beginning of the day is revisited with a focus on skills practiced during the day.

Each day provides a **Home Connection.** At the start of each week, a letter is provided to inform families of the weekly focus and offer additional literature suggestions to extend the weekly theme focus.

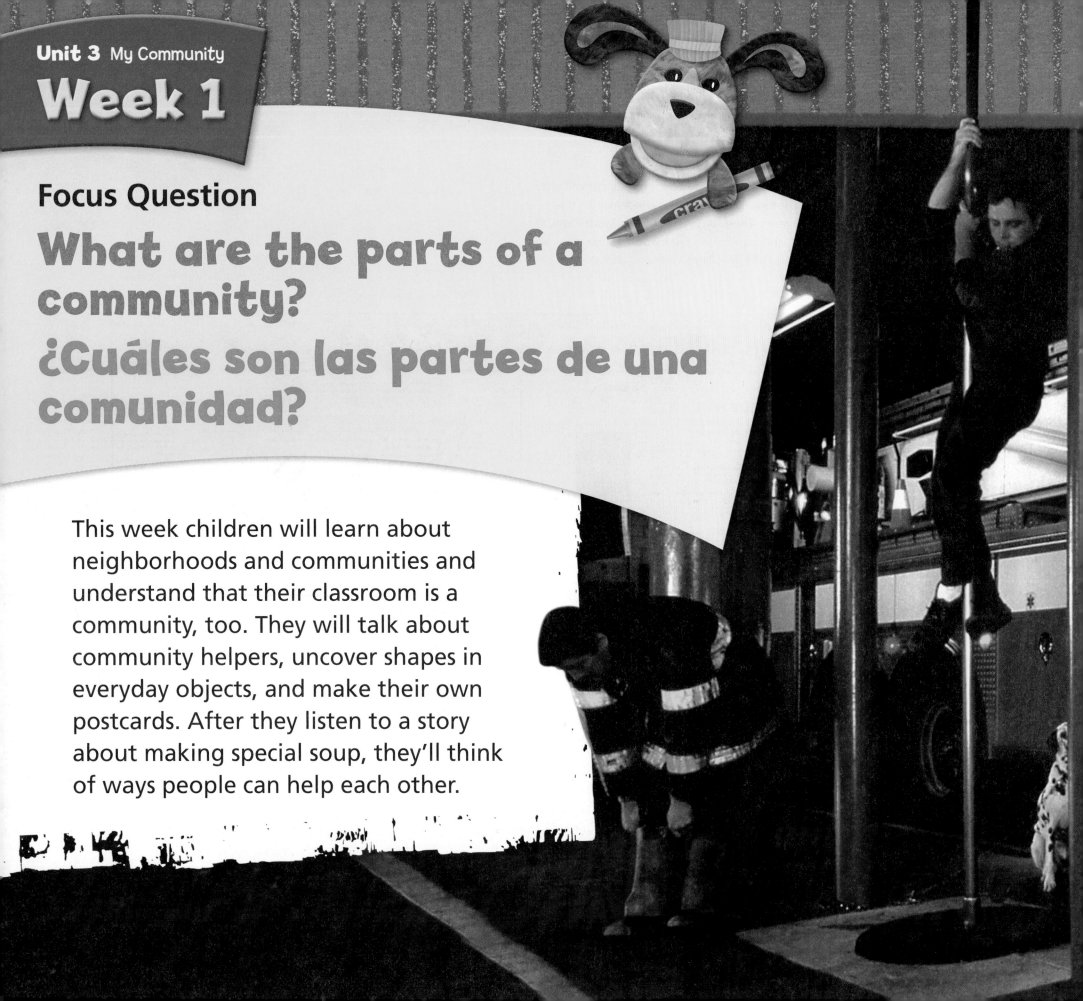

Week 1

Focus Question

What are the parts of a community?

¿Cuáles son las partes de una comunidad?

This week children will learn about neighborhoods and communities and understand that their classroom is a community, too. They will talk about community helpers, uncover shapes in everyday objects, and make their own postcards. After they listen to a story about making special soup, they'll think of ways people can help each other.

Learning Goals

Social and Emotional Development	1	2	3	4	5
Child uses classroom materials carefully.				✓	
Child maintains concentration/attention skills until a task is complete.				✓	
Child shows eagerness, curiosity, and confidence while learning new concepts and trying new things.			✓		✓
Child demonstrates positive social behaviors, as modeled by the teacher.			✓		✓
Child participates in a variety of individual, small- and large-group activities.	✓	✓	✓	✓	✓
Child initiates interactions with others in work and play situations.	✓	✓	✓	✓	
Child initiates play scenarios with peers that share a common plan and goal.	✓				
Child shows empathy and care for others.				✓	

Language and Communication	1	2	3	4	5
Child demonstrates an understanding of oral language by responding appropriately.	✓		✓	✓	✓
Child demonstrates some understanding of English spoken by teachers and peers. (ELL)	✓		✓		
Child uses oral language for a variety of purposes.			✓	✓	
Child begins and ends conversations appropriately.		✓		✓	✓
Child follows basic rules for conversations (taking turns, staying on topic, listening actively).			✓		
Child experiments with and produces a growing number of sounds in English words. (ELL)		✓			
Child names and describes actual or pictured people, places, things, actions, attributes, and events.	✓	✓			
Child builds English listening and speaking vocabulary for common objects and phrases. (ELL)	✓	✓	✓	✓	✓
Child speaks in complete sentences of four or more words including a subject, verb, and object.		✓			
Child tries to use newly learned vocabulary and grammar. (ELL)	✓		✓	✓	✓

Emergent Literacy: Reading	1	2	3	4	5
Child enjoys and chooses reading-related activities.			✓		
Child produces words with the same beginning sound.	✓	✓	✓	✓	✓
Child names most upper- and lowercase letters of the alphabet.		✓		✓	
Child produces the most common sound for a given letter.		✓			
Child describes, relates to, and uses details and information from books read aloud.		✓	✓	✓	✓
Child asks and answers questions about books read aloud (such as, "Who?" "What?" "Where?").	✓	✓	✓	✓	✓

Emergent Literacy: Writing	1	2	3	4	5
Child uses scribbles, shapes, pictures, symbols, and letters to represent language.	✓	✓	✓	✓	✓

Mathematics	1	2	3	4	5
Child recognizes, names, describes, matches, compares, sorts common two-dimensional shapes (such as circle, square, rectangle, triangle, rhombus).	✓	✓	✓	✓	✓

Science	1	2	3	4	5
Child follows basic health and safety rules.	✓				

Social Studies	1	2	3	4	5
Child understands basic human needs for food, clothing, shelter.			✓		
Child participates in voting for group decision-making.					✓
Child respects/appreciates the differing interests, skills, abilities, cultures, languages, and family structures of people.		✓			

Fine Arts	1	2	3	4	5
Child uses and experiments with a variety of art materials and tools in various art activities.					✓
Child expresses emotions or ideas through art.					✓
Child shares opinions about artwork and artistic experiences.					✓
Child participates in a variety of music activities (such as listening, singing, finger plays, musical games, performances).					✓

Materials and Resources

	DAY 1	DAY 2	DAY 3	DAY 4	DAY 5
Program Materials	• Teacher's Treasure Book • Oral Language Development Card 21 • Rhymes and Chants Flip Chart • Photo Library CD-ROM • Concept Big Book 2 • ABC Big Book • ABC Picture Cards • Alphabet Wall Cards • Online Building Blocks Math Activities • Making Good Choices Flip Chart • Math and Science Flip Chart • Shape Sets • Home Connections Resource Guide	• Teacher's Treasure Book • Concept Big Book 2 • Dog Puppet 1 and 2 • Photo Library CD-ROM • ABC Big Book • ABC Picture Cards • Alphabet Wall Cards • Online Building Blocks Math Activities • Numeral Cards • Making Good Choices Flip Chart • Math and Science Flip Chart • Shape Sets (different colors) • Home Connections Resource Guide	• Teacher's Treasure Book • Oral Language Development Card 22 • Rhymes and Chants Flip Chart • Photo Library CD-ROM • Flannel Board characters for "Keiko's Good Thinking" • ABC Big Book • ABC Picture Cards • Alphabet Wall Cards • Shape Sets • Making Good Choices Flip Chart • Dog Puppet 1 and 2 • Concept Big Book 2 • Home Connections Resource Guide	• Teacher's Treasure Book • ABC Big Book • ABC Picture Cards • Alphabet Wall Cards • Dog Puppet 1 and 2 • Making Good Choices Flip Chart • Math and Science Flip Chart • Home Connections Resource Guide	• Teacher's Treasure Book • Making Good Choices Flip Chart • Rhymes and Chants Flip Chart • Photo Library CD-ROM • Concept Big Book 2 • ABC Big Book • Shape Sets • Home Connections Resource Guide
Other Materials	• 3 shoeboxes • images of items that begin with the sounds /f/, /p/, /l/ • building blocks • toy people figures • musical triangle • picture books, magazines • paper, crayons	• pictures of items with initial sounds /t/, /e/, /g/ and /l/ • paint in tray • firefighter's hat • surgical mask • construction worker's hard hat • number cards 1–5	• large box, index cards • wooden cube • images of egg, elephant, gorilla, rabbit, turtle, tent • cartons, boxes, masking tape • toy people figures, toy cars, trucks	• sock puppets • recorded or print book about people helping in community, with pictures and appropriate player • onion, carrot, potato • boxes of various sizes, including one rectangular box with a square base, with mailing labels or stamps	• drawing paper, crayons • string, clothespins • images of items that begin w/ /f/, /p/, /l/ , and other sounds • boxes of various sizes, including one rectangular box with a square base • butcher paper • cardboard buildings, houses, trees • paper people figures
Home Connection	Invite children to show their families two different ways to be safe on the playground. Send home the following materials: Weekly Family Letter, Home Connections Resource Guide, pp. 29– 30, ABC Take-Home Book for *Tt,* (English) p. 26 or (Spanish) p. 57.	Encourage children to point out to family members different shapes they see in their home. ABC Take-Home Book for *Ee,* (English) p. 11 or (Spanish) p. 40.	Tell children to talk with their families about their own neighborhoods and neighbors. ABC Take-Home Book, Letter *Gg,* (English) p. 13 or (Spanish) p. 42.	ABC Take-Home Book, Letter *Rr,* (English) p. 24 or (Spanish) p. 55.	Encourage children to repeat the drawing activity at home with their families.

Assessment

As you observe children throughout the week, you may fill out an Anecdotal Observational Record Form to document an individual's progress toward a goal or signs indicating the need for developmental or medical evaluation. You may also choose to select work for each child's portfolio. The Anecdotal Observational Record Form and Weekly Assessment rubrics are available In the assessment section of DLMExpressOnline.com.

More Literature Suggestions

- **Bear About Town/Oso en la ciudad** by Stella Blackstone
- **Bats at the Library** by Brian Lies
- **Clang! Clang! Beep! Beep! Listen To the City** by Robert Burleigh
- **En el barrio** por Alma Flor Ada
- **Un paseo por el parque** por Ricardo Alcántara

Daily Planner

	DAY 1	**DAY 2**
Let's Start the Day **Language Time** `large group`	**Opening Routines** p. 26 **Morning Read Aloud** p. 26 **Oral Language and Vocabulary** p. 26 Neighborhoods **Phonological Awareness** p. 26 Identify Initial Sounds	**Opening Routines** p. 32 **Morning Read Aloud** p. 32 **Oral Language and Vocabulary** p. 32 Community Helpers **Phonological Awareness** p. 32 Review Initial Sounds
Center Time `small group`	**Focus On:** **ABC Center** p. 27 **Construction Center** p. 27	**Focus On:** **ABC Center** p. 33 **Pretend and Learn Center** p. 33
Circle Time **Literacy Time** `large group`	**Read Aloud** *In the Community/* *En la comunidad* p. 28 **Learn About Letters** **and Sounds: Learn** **About** *Tt* p. 28	**Read Aloud** *In the Community/* *En la comunidad* p. 34 **Learn About Letters and** **Sounds: Learn About** *Ee* p. 34
Math Time `large group`	**Three Straight Sides** p. 29 **Is It or Not?** p. 29	**Let's Jump!** p. 35
Social and **Emotional** **Development** `large group`	**How Can I Help in School?** p. 29	**Being Helpful** p. 35
Content **Connection** `large group`	**Science:** **Oral Language and Academic Vocabulary** p. 30 **Observe and Investigate** p. 30	**Math:** **Hidden Shapes** p. 36
Center Time `small group`	**Focus On:** **Math and Science Center** p. 31 **Purposeful Play** p. 31	**Focus On:** **Math and Science Center** p. 37 **Purposeful Play** p. 37
Let's Say **Good-Bye** `large group`	**Read Aloud** p. 31 **Writing** p. 31 **Home Connection** p. 31	**Read Aloud** p. 37 **Writing** p. 37 **Home Connection** p. 37

DAY 3

Opening Routines p. 38
Morning Read Aloud p. 38
Oral Language and Vocabulary
p. 38 Cities and Towns
Phonological Awareness
p. 38 Reviewing Initial Sounds

Focus On:
Writer's Center p. 39
Library and Listening Center p. 39

Read Aloud
"Keiko's Good Thinking"/
"¿Cuáles son las partes de una comunidad?" p. 40
Learn About Letters and Sounds:
Learn About *Gg* p. 40

Is It or Not? p. 41

Using Polite Words p. 41

Social Studies:
Oral Language and Academic Vocabulary
p. 42 Talking About a Neighborhood
Understand and Participate
p. 42 Building a Neighborhood

Focus On:
Pretend and Learn Center p. 43
Purposeful Play p. 43

Read Aloud p. 43
Writing p. 43
Home Connection p. 43

DAY 4

Opening Routines p. 44
Morning Read Aloud p. 44
Oral Language and Vocabulary
p. 44 Helping in the Neighborhood
Phonological Awareness p. 44
Review Initial Sounds

Focus On:
Pretend and Learn Center p. 45
Library and Listening Center p. 45

Read Aloud
"Stone Soup"/"La sopa de piedra" p. 46
Learn About Letters and Sounds:
Learn About *Rr* p. 46

Is It a Square or a Rectangle? p. 47

Taking Responsibility p. 47

Math:
Find That Shape! p. 48

Focus On:
Math and Science Center p. 49
Purposeful Play p. 49

Read Aloud p. 49
Writing p. 49
Home Connection p. 49

DAY 5

Opening Routines p. 50
Morning Read Aloud p. 50
Oral Language and Vocabulary
p. 50 Helping in the Classroom
Phonological Awareness
p. 50 Review Initial Sounds

Focus On:
Creativity Center p. 51
ABC Center p. 51

Read Aloud
In the Community/
En la comunidad p. 52
Review Letters and Sounds: Review Sounds of *Tt, Gg, Ee* and *Rr* p. 52

Is It a Square or a Rectangle? p. 53

Being Responsible in School p. 53

Art:
Oral Language and Academic Vocabulary
p. 54 Talking About Ideas for Art
Explore and Express
p. 54 Color Parts of a Town

Focus On:
Creativity Center p. 55
Purposeful Play p. 55

Read Aloud p. 55
Writing p. 55
Home Connection p. 55

Learning Centers

Math and Science Center

Investigate Good Habits
Children find pictures of good health and safety habits, p. 31.

Match Up!
Children match shapes, p. 37.

Boxes!
Children fit smaller boxes into one big one, p. 49.

Number Cheer
Tape a number from 1 to 5 on each child. Children form a circle and one child calls out a number. All children with that number go to the center of the circle, cheer, and then return to the circle.

Number Tree
Children trace numbers on construction paper, cut them out, and string them together in random order. Then drape the garland around a large plant or a branch stuck in a flowerpot. Occasionally point to a number on the "tree" and have them say it aloud.

ABC Center

Matching Initial Sounds
Children group words by initial sounds, p. 27.

Sorting Initial Sounds Drawings
Children match words to their initial sounds, p. 51.

Drawing Letters
Distribute paper cups, pencils, paper, and large index cards. Display the *ABC Picture Cards.* Children make letters by tracing lines and curves and using the *ABC Picture Cards* as a visual reference.

Which Letter?
Children work in pairs to form letters. One child draws the first stroke of a letter and says the sound of the letter he/she is thinking of. Partner adds another part and they continue until the letter is complete.

Creativity Center

Drawing Pictures
Children draw themselves helping in the classroom, p. 51.

Completing the Community
Children add people to a community they've created, p. 54.

Community Design
Children use small boxes and cups to lay out an imaginary community. They trace the objects on a large piece of paper to represent buildings, trees, houses, and so on. Encourage them to add people and animals.

Shelter and Food
Children work with clay to create a shelter and a healthful food item for a friend.

Different Hats
Children think about different hats or accessories community workers wear. Provide craft materials and have them make a hat or accessory one community worker might wear.

Library and Listening Center

Matching Initial Sounds
Children match initial sounds to the names of animals, p. 39.

Listening to a Story
Children listen to a story about a helpful character, p. 45.

Common Features
Children browse through books about different schools. They name common features among the pictures, and then they name common features among the pictures and their own school.

Sticky /r/ Pass
Children read *Rush Hour* with a partner and place a sticky note on the letter *R* when it appears. Then they listen to the story and make the /r/ sound whenever they come to a sticky note.

Communities
Children browse books about different neighborhoods and name things in the pictures that are like their neighborhood.

Construction Center

Build a Community
Children build a community out of blocks, p. 27.

Same Sound Buildings
Children build structures with materials that begin with the same sound (blocks/boxes; cubes/ cups).

Soup Pot
Children use various materials to build a soup pot. Have them put things in it to make their own "stone soup."

Neighborhood Building
Children work together to create a building or structure in their neighborhood. Allow children to use materials in other centers to add to their building, such as food from the Pretend and Learn Center for a bakery.

Writer's Center

Printing Letters
Children use sponges and paint to print letters, p. 33.

Mailing Letters
Children make postcards and put them in a mailbox, p. 39.

Thank You
Children make an appreciation card for a school worker. They write as much of the message as they can. Give them models of words to trace or copy, such as *Thank You*. As a class, distribute the notes.

Community Sign
Children make a sign that will help them and their classmates remember where to put specific classroom materials. Then post the signs around the class.

Pretend and Learn Center

Role Play Community Workers
Children pretend to be community workers, p. 33.

Role-Playing in the Neighborhood
Children use toys and people figures to role-play a neighborhood, p. 43.

Neighbors in Need
Children use puppets to role-play being helpful, p. 45.

Puppet Welcome
Have children use the puppets to act out welcoming a new family to the neighborhood.

Playground Safety
Children use stuffed animals to act out scenarios about how to play safely in the playground and classroom.

Let's Start the Day

Focus Question
What are the parts of a community?

¿Cuáles son las partes de una comunidad?

Learning Goals

Social and Emotional Development
• Child participates in a variety of individual, small- and large-group activities.

Language and Communication
• Child demonstrates an understanding of oral language by responding appropriately.

• Child tries to use newly learned vocabulary and grammar. (ELL)

Emergent Literacy: Reading
• Child produces words with the same beginning sound.

Vocabulary

apartment	departamento
community	comunidad
house	casa
neighborhood	vecindario
place	lugar
playground	patio de recreo

Differentiated Instruction

 Extra Support

Phonological Awareness
If...children have difficulty producing a word with the initial sound, **then...**say two words and have them identify the word that begins with the target sound.

Enrichment

Oral Language and Vocabulary
Challenge children to talk about other kinds of buildings in their community, such as stores, hospitals, schools, and police stations.

 Opening Routines and Transition Tips
For **Opening Routines** and **Transition Tips** turn to pages 178–181 and visit **DLMExpressOnline.com** for more ideas.

Read **"This Is the House That Jack Built"**/"Ésta es la casa que Juan construyó" from the *Teacher's Treasure Book*, page 277, for your morning Read Aloud.

large group   15 minutes

Language Time

Social and Emotional Development Encourage children to be helpful and assume their responsibilities in the classroom.

Oral Language and Vocabulary

☑ **Can children use an illustration to describe various components of a neighborhood?**

Neighborhoods Explain that a community is a place where people live and work. Point out that neighborhoods are part of communities. Say: *We all live in a neighborhood. Neighborhoods are parts of communities. Todos vivimos en un vecindario. Los vecindarios son partes de las comunidades.* Ask: *What buildings do you see in your neighborhood? What people do you see in your neighborhood? What do you like to do in your neighborhood? ¿Qué edificios ven en su vecindario? ¿Qué personas ven en su vecindario? ¿Qué les gusta hacer en su vecindario?*

• Display *Oral Language Development Card 21*. Talk about the setting of the picture. Ask: *What buildings do you see? What might the people do there? ¿Qué edificios ven? ¿Qué puede hacer allí la gente?* Then follow the suggestions on the back of the card.

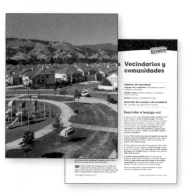

Oral Language Development Card 21

Phonological Awareness

☑ **Can children identify words that have the same initial sound?**

Identify Initial Sounds Display the *Rhymes and Chants Flip Chart*, page 13. Recite "Community Places," emphasizing the initial sounds of /f/, /p/, and /l/ in each stanza. Say the words *fire* and *fancy*, emphasizing the initial sound. Then ask children to think of a word that begins with the same sound. If applicable, bring attention to children's names that begin with that sound. Repeat the activity with *put/package* and *look/library*.

ELL Use the *Rhymes and Chants Flip Chart* to reinforce children's understanding of what happens in a fire station, a post office, and a library. Say the beginning of a sentence such as: *If I want to find a book...*Then help children complete the sentence, *I go to the library.*

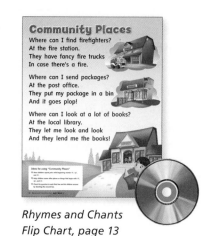

Rhymes and Chants Flip Chart, page 13

Center Time

▶ **Center Rotation** Center Time includes teacher-guided activities and independent activities. Refer to the **Learning Centers** on pages 24–25 for independent activity ideas.

 small group · 60–90 minutes

Learning Goals

Social and Emotional Development
• Child initiates play scenarios with peers that share a common plan and goal.

Language and Communication
• Child demonstrates an understanding of oral language by responding appropriately.

• Child demonstrates some understanding of English spoken by teachers and peers. (ELL)

Emergent Literacy: Reading
• Child produces words with the same beginning sound.

ABC Center

 Check to see that children have grouped pictures correctly.

Materials 3 shoeboxes, each with a picture of an item that begins with the sound of /f/, /p/, or /l/ from the *Photo Library CD-ROM*; 9 additional pictures of items that begin with the same sounds

Sorting by Sounds Point to each picture on the box, one at a time. Name the picture, emphasizing the initial sound.

● Have partners name the pictures in the box and sort them into the shoeboxes according to their initial consonant sounds.

● Have partners take turns naming the words in each box to see if they are sorted correctly.

Center Tip
If...children have difficulty sorting the pictures, **then**...demonstrate how they can emphasize the beginning sound of each word as they sort.

Differentiated Instruction

 Extra Support
ABC Center
If...children have difficulty sorting pictures according to three initial sounds, **then**...have them sort only two sounds at a time.

Enrichment
Construction Center
Challenge children to help each other use blocks to build a variety of public buildings and to create streets.

 Special Needs
Vision Loss
If...children have difficulty building a community, **then**...allow them additional time to become familiar with the materials.

Construction Center

✓ **Look for typical components of a neighborhood.**

✓ **Listen for the use of targeted oral vocabulary.**

✓ **Verify that children interact with peers during periods of pretend play.**

Materials building blocks, people figures

Build a Community Have partners or small groups of children use blocks to construct a variety of buildings found in a community. Ask them to identify the buildings.

● Tell children to add the people figures to their community and then have them pretend the figures are doing everyday activities such as working and playing.

● Ask questions such as: *Who works in the fire station? Why is someone going into the post office? ¿Quién trabaja en la estación de bomberos? ¿Por qué una persona está entrando al correo?*

Center Tip
If...children have difficulty beginning to construct a community, **then**...reread the "Community Places" verse on the *Rhymes and Chants Flip Chart* to remind them of buildings found in a community.

Focus Question

What are the parts of a community?

¿Cuáles son las partes de una comunidad?

Learning Goals

Language and Communication
• Child demonstrates an understanding of oral language by responding appropriately.

Emergent Literacy: Reading
• Child produces words with the same beginning sound.

• Child asks and answers questions about books read aloud (such as, "Who?" "What?" "Where?").

Vocabulary

community	comunidad
construction workers	trabajadores de la construcción
healthy neighborhood	vecindario saludable
neighbors	vecinos
sidewalks	aceras
trash	basura
street	calle

Differentiated Instruction

 Extra Support

Read Aloud
If...children are having a difficult time grasping the concept of a community,
then...help them relate the characteristics of a community to their own neighborhood.

 Enrichment

Learn About Letters and Sounds
Challenge children to look at picture books and name things that begin with the sound /t/.

 Special Needs

Cognitive Challenges
If...children have difficulty comprehending the book at one reading, **then...**read only a few pages at a time. Ask children what they remember about those pages before reading additional pages.

Literacy Time

large group · 15 minutes

📖 Read Aloud

✓ **Can children use illustrations to help them understand a story?**

Build Background Tell children that you will be reading a book about communities, or places where people live and work together.

● Explain that a neighborhood is a part of a community. Ask: *What can you tell me about your neighborhood?* *¿Qué pueden decirme de su vecindario?*

Listen for Enjoyment Display *Concept Big Book 2: In the Community* and read the title. Remind children that a community is a place where people live and work. Point out that the children all live in a community.

● Conduct a picture walk of the book.

● Ask questions such as: *What are these people doing? What building is this?* *¿Qué están haciendo estas personas? ¿Qué edificio es éste?*

● Read the book aloud.

Respond to the Story Discuss the story.

● Ask: *Is there a picture of something in the book that's in your community? Is there something in your community that does not appear in the book?* *¿Ven en el libro alguna imagen de algo que existe en su comunidad? ¿Hay algo en su comunidad que no aparezca en el libro?*

TIP Encourage children to raise their hands and ask questions if there is a word they hear that they don't understand.

ELL Help children with the multisyllabic words in the selection, such as *community, neighborhood, firefighter*, and *construction worker*. Have children repeat the words after you, as you clap out the syllables.

Learn About Letters and Sounds

✓ **Can children identify the letter *Tt* and the /t/ sound?**

Learn About *Tt* Display the *Tt* page of the *ABC Big Book* and point to the turtle. Ask: *What do you see?* Repeat *turtle*, emphasizing the initial /t/ sound. Continue with *television, toothbrush, train,* and *tent*. Then say the following words one at a time: *jellybeans, volcano, tent, after, train, hammer, turtle,* and *television*. Have children clap when they hear a word that begins with /t/.

● Say the /t/ sound and have children repeat it several times. Point to the upper case *T*, name it, and say its sound. Have children repeat several times. Explain that upper case *T* has the sound /t/ just as lower case *t* does. Slowly trace upper case *T*, demonstrating how it is formed. Using the *ABC Picture Card* for *Tt*, have volunteers repeat the process. Repeat the process with lower case *t*.

● Recite the alphabet together as you point to the *Alphabet Wall Cards*.

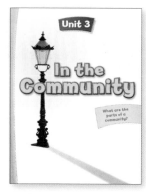

In the Community
En la comunidad

ABC Big Book

Math Time

large group 15 minutes

Observe and Investigate

✓ **Can children identify a triangle?**

Three Straight Sides Tell children they are going to sing a song about triangles. Ask children what they know about triangles.

● Show a triangle and sing the following to the tune of "Three Blind Mice." On the words "Three straight sides," tap on a side of the triangle. The Spanish version of this song is located in the *Teacher's Treasure Book,* page 54.

> Three straight sides, three straight sides,
>
> See how they meet, see how they meet,
>
> They follow the path that a triangle makes.
>
> Three straight sides and there's no mistakes.
>
> Three sides and three corners, that's all it takes.
>
> Three straight sides.

Is It or Not?

✓ **Can children name shapes?**

Invite children to play Is It or Not? Tell them to find the "fooler" shape.

● Show a musical triangle. Say: *This is not a true triangle. A true triangle has three straight connected sides. These sides do not connect. This is a fooler!* *Los triángulos de verdad tienen tres lados rectos conectados. Estos lados no están conectados. ¡Éste triángulo es engañoso!*

● Show true and untrue triangles. Point to the shapes and ask: *Is it a fooler? ¿Es ésta una figura engañosa?* Say: *Yell "Fooler!" if it is! ¡Engañosa!*

Building Blocks

Online Math Activity

Introduce Number Snapshots 2, in which children match a number to a different representation of that number. Each child should complete the activity this week.

large group 15 minutes

Making Good Choices Flip Chart, page 13

✦✦✦ Social and Emotional Development

Making Good Choices

✓ **Are children aware of their responsibilities in the classroom?**

How Can I Help in School? Discuss ways children can help their teacher and one another in the classroom. Display the *Making Good Choices Flip Chart,* page 13. Ask: *What are these children doing? Why are they putting the toys away? Who are they helping? ¿Qué hacen estos niños? ¿A quién están ayudando? ¿Por qué guardan los juguetes?*

● Point to the teacher and the children and discuss what they are doing.

✓ **Learning Goals**

Social and Emotional Development
● Child participates in a variety of individual, small- and large-group activities.

Language and Communication
● Child builds English listening and speaking vocabulary for common objects and phrases. (ELL)

Mathematics
● Child recognizes, names, describes, matches, compares, sorts common two-dimensional shapes (such as circle, square, rectangle, triangle, rhombus).

Vocabulary

chores	tareas	helpful	útil
not	no	triangle	triángulo
true	verdadero		

Differentiated Instruction

✋ **Extra Support**
Making Good Choices
If...children can't relate to the jobs pictured on the chart, **then...**discuss the daily chores that children are responsible for in your classroom.

⭐ **Enrichment**
Observe and Investigate
Challenge children with more difficult shapes, such as triangles that are oriented differently.

♥ **Special Needs**
Cognitive Challenges
If...the game is too difficult, **then...**discuss whether or not the shapes are true triangles.

Focus Question
What are the parts of a community?
¿Cuáles son las partes de una comunidad?

 Learning Goals

Social and Emotional Development
• Child participates in a variety of individual, small- and large-group activities.

Language and Communication
• Child names and describes actual or pictured people, places, things, actions, attributes, and events.

Science
• Child follows basic health and safety rules.

Vocabulary

habit	habito	helmet	casco
protection	protección	safety	seguro
take turns	turnarse	unsafe	inseguro

Differentiated Instruction

✋ **Extra Support**
Observe and Investigate
If...children have trouble identifying what is unsafe, **then...**describe an unsafe situation to explain how someone might get hurt.

⭐ **Enrichment**
Observe and Investigate
Challenge children to make a poster illustrating safe habits on the playground.

Accommodations for 3's
Oral Language and Academic Vocabulary
Ask children to explain why it's important to wear shoes while riding a bike.

Science Time

 large group · 20 minutes

Health Skills Model good habits of personal health by washing your hands before and after using the toilet.

Oral Language and Academic Vocabulary

✓ **Can children identify how to stay safe while riding their bikes?**
Point to the picture of the child in the *Math and Science Flip Chart,* page 21. Say: ***This child is being safe while having fun bike riding.*** *Esta niña se mantiene segura mientras se divierte andando en triciclo.*

● Have children point out the helmet. Ask why the child is wearing a helmet.

● Say: ***Wearing the correct gear is not the only way to stay safe while bike riding.*** *Usar el equipo adecuado no es la única manera de cuidarnos cuando andamos en bicicleta.* Discuss how to find safe places to ride and the importance of riding with an adult.

 Point to the helmet. Ask children to name it. Then ask them to tell why a helmet is important.

Math and Science Flip Chart, page 21

Observe and Investigate

✓ **Can children identify safe and unsafe habits on the playground?**
Take the children to the playground. Have two children use a piece of equipment, such as the slide. Ask: ***What do you need to remember to be safe while using a slide?*** *¿Qué deben recordar para usar el tobogán de manera segura?*

● Present an unsafe situation using the piece of equipment, such as sliding down right behind the person in front of you. Discuss why the situation is unsafe and how to make it safe.

● Say: ***If you take turns and wait until the person in front of you walks away from the slide before you go down, you are being safe.*** *Si se turnan y esperan hasta que la persona que está adelante se aleje del tobogán antes lanzarse, permanecerán seguros.*

● Have children use other playground equipment and point out safe and unsafe behaviors. Review the rules of keeping safe on the playground.

Center Time

small group 30 minutes

Math and Science Center

✓ **Observe children finding examples of personal safety habits.**

Materials picture books, magazines, paper, crayons

Investigate Good Habits Tell children that they will be investigators and look for examples of good habits of personal safety.

- Tell children to look through the books for characters or through the magazines for people who are being safe.

- Have the children draw an example of what they found. Encourage children to find different examples from what was already discussed in class.

Center Tip

If…children cannot draw an example, **then…**have them point to an example and tell you why the person or character is being safe.

Purposeful Play

✓ **Observe whether or not children make an effort to help clean up a play space after completing an activity.**

Children choose an open center for free playtime. Encourage children to be good friends by sharing toys as they play.

Learning Goals

Social and Emotional Development
- Child participates in a variety of individual, small- and large-group activities.
- Child initiates interactions with others in work and play situations.

Emergent Literacy: Writing
- Child uses scribbles, shapes, pictures, symbols, and letters to represent language.

Science
- Child follows basic health and safety rules.

Writing

Remind children that they learned about neighborhoods and communities. Ask: *What do you see in your neighborhood?* ¿Qué ven en su vecindario? Tell children to draw a picture of something they see every day in their own neighborhood. Write the word under each picture and have children trace the first letter of the word with different colored crayons. Display the work in the classroom.

Let's Say Good-Bye

large group 15 minutes

 Read Aloud Revisit "This Is the House That Jack Built"/"Ésta es la casa que Juan construyó" for your afternoon Read Aloud. Remind children to listen for the /f/ sound at the beginning of words in the story.

 Home Connection Refer to the Home Connections activities listed in the Resources and Materials chart on page 21. Remind children to tell their families about different parts of a community. Sing the "Good-Bye Song"/"Hora de ir a casa" as children prepare to leave.

Let's Start the Day

Focus Question

What are the parts of a community?

¿Cuáles son las partes de una comunidad?

 Learning Goals

Language and Communication
• Child begins and ends conversations appropriately.

• Child names and describes actual or pictured people, places, things, actions, attributes, and events.

• Child speaks in complete sentences of four or more words including a subject, verb, and object.

Emergent Literacy: Reading
• Child produces words with the same beginning sound.

Vocabulary

community helpers	trabajadores comunitarios
construction workers	trabajadores de la construcción
doctors	doctores
firefighters	bomberos
healthy	saludable

Differentiated Instruction

 Extra Support

Oral Language and Vocabulary
If...children have difficulty naming community helpers, **then...**point to a helper in an illustration, identify the helper, and ask childen to tell what that worker does.

 Enrichment

Phonological Awareness
Ask children to say a word that begins with the same sound as the word the puppet says.

▷ **Opening Routines and Transition Tips**
For **Opening Routines** and **Transition Tips** turn to pages 178–181 and visit **DLMExpressOnline.com** for more ideas.

 Read **"Counting My Blessings"/"Mis tesoros"** from the *Teacher's Treasure Book*, page 95, for your morning Read Aloud.

Language Time

large group / 15 minutes

Social and Emotional Development Ask children to think about their rules for listening to others, and to listen while others are speaking and to be quiet until it is their turn to talk.

Oral Language and Vocabulary

☑ **Can children name the roles of community workers?**

Community Helpers Talk about how it takes many kinds of workers to keep a community safe and clean. Ask: *What people in a community work to keep people safe? What people work to keep people healthy? What workers help keep the community clean? ¿Qué personas de la comunidad trabajan para mantener a la gente segura? ¿Qué personas trabajan para que otras personas estén saludables? ¿Qué trabajadores pueden ayudar a mantener limpia la comunidad?*

● Take a picture walk through pages 5–16 of *Concept Big Book 2: In the Community*. Ask children to name the various community helpers as you point to them. Guide children to use action words to describe what each worker does.

ELL Point to the doctor and say: *This is a doctor.* Have children repeat the sentence. Then ask: *Who is this?* Have children answer: *This is a doctor.* Repeat for other community workers.

Phonological Awareness

☑ **Can children recognize words with the same initial sounds?**

Review Initial Sounds Use the Dog Puppets to engage children in a game. Have one puppet say a word with the initial sound of /t/, /e/, /g/, or /r/. Then have the second puppet say a word. Instruct children to clap if the word begins with the target sound.

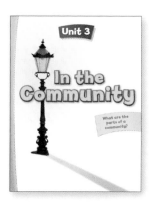

In the Community
En la comunidad

Center Time

▶ **Center Rotation** Center Time includes teacher-guided activities and independent activities. Refer to the **Learning Centers** on pages 24–25 for independent activity ideas.

small group 60–90 minutes

ABC Center

Center Tip

 Can children categorize words according to initial sounds?

Materials pictures of items with the intial sounds /t/, /e/, /g/, and /r/ from the *Photo Library CD-ROM*

Matching Initial Sounds Tell children they are going to play a game of matching.

● Look over all the pictures with the entire class. For each card, ask: *What is this? What is the first sound in that word?* ¿Qué es esto? ¿Cuál es el primer sonido que escuchan en esa palabra? If children have trouble naming the items, model the words for them.

● Challenge pairs of children to group the pictures according to their initial sounds. Have students say each word and then say the initial sound they have in common.

Center Tip

If…children have difficulty pronouncing the words properly, **then…**model the initial sound first, then say each word slowly and have children repeat it after you.

Pretend and Learn Center

Center Tip

 Can children identify community workers?

Materials firefighter's hat, doctor's mask, construction worker's hard hat, and so on

Role Play Community Workers Remind children of the community workers they learned about in the story. Display the props listed above and discuss what they are.

● Have children take turns choosing a prop to wear.

● While they are wearing the props, have each child pantomime the actions of the worker while others guess which worker he or she is.

Center Tip

If…children have difficulty pantomiming the actions of workers, **then…**model some actions that they can imitate.

✓ Learning Goals

Emergent Literacy: Reading
• Child produces words with the same beginning sound.
• Child produces the most common sound for a given letter.
• Child describes, relates to, and uses details and information from books read aloud.

Differentiated Instruction

🖐 Extra Support
Pretend and Learn Center
If…children have difficulty recalling what the community workers do, **then…**review the illustrations in *Concept Big Book 2: In the Community*, to see what the workers do.

⭐ Enrichment
ABC Center
Challenge children to say other words that share the same initial sounds.

Accommodations for 3's
ABC Center
If…children have difficulty grouping the words, **then…**help them say the words and separate the intial sounds.

Circle Time

Focus Question
What are the parts of a community?
¿Cuáles son las partes de una comunidad?

Learning Goals

Language and Communication
• Child experiments with and produces a growing number of sounds in English words. (ELL)

Emergent Literacy: Reading
• Child names most upper- and lowercase letters of the alphabet.

Social Studies
• Child respects/appreciates the differing interests, skills, abilities, cultures, languages, and family structures of people.

Vocabulary

construction worker	trabajadores de la construcción		
doctor	doctor	families	familias
firefighter	bombero	neighbors	vecinos
school	escuela	sidewalk	acera

Differentiated Instruction

✋ Extra Support
Learn About Letters and Sounds
If...children have difficulty saying the /e/ sound, **then**...model the shape your mouth forms when you make the sound.

⭐ Enrichment
Read Aloud
Challenge children to name pictured items that are not identified in the text, such as *grocery store, picnic, post office,* and *police officer.*

♥ Special Needs
Cognitive Challenges
If...children have difficulty absorbing the book as a whole, **then**...pause at the end of each page and ask them to name the things they know in the illustration.

Literacy Time

large group · 15 minutes

📖 Read Aloud

✓ **Can children describe buildings and workers in a community?**

Build Background Remind children that a community is a place where people live and work together. Display picture books of people from other cultures. Have children identify similarities among communities in their own culture and in other cultures.

● Ask: *What buildings might you see in any community? ¿Qué edificios pueden ver en cualquier comunidad?*

● Ask: *What workers keep a community safe and clean? ¿Qué trabajadores mantienen la comunidad segura y limpia?*

Listen for Understanding Display *Concept Big Book 2: In the Community.* Explain to children that you are going to reread the story as they match words and pictures.

● Read each page and then say a pictured word or words, such as *construction workers.* Have children point to the corresponding picture.

● Ask: *What does the picture show you about construction workers? ¿Qué muestra la ilustración sobre los trabajadores de la construcción?*

Respond to the Book Discuss the book. Help children recall the parts of the community. Ask: *Is there a park in this community? What is in the park? Are there construction workers? What are they building? ¿Hay un parque en esta comunidad? ¿Qué hay en el parque? ¿Hay trabajadores de la construcción en esta comunidad? ¿Qué están construyendo?*

💡 TIP Point out that the important words on the page are pictured in the illustrations. Explain that authors want to help their readers understand their stories.

Learn About Letters and Sounds

✓ **Can children identify the letter *Ee* and the sounds it makes?**

Learn About *Ee* Display the *Ee* page of the *ABC Big Book* and point to the egg. Ask: *What do you see? ¿Qué ven?* Repeat *egg,* emphasizing the inital /e/ sound. Continue with *eggplant.* Then say the following words one at a time: *empty, ask, egg, after, goat, elephant,* and *animal.* Have children clap when they hear a word that begins with /e/.

● Say the /e/ sound and have children repeat it several times. Then point to upper case *E,* name it, and say its short sound. Have children repeat several times. Explain that upper case *E* makes the sound /e/. Slowly trace the upper case *E,* demonstrating how it is formed. Using the *ABC Picture Card* for *Ee,* have volunteers repeat the process for upper case *E* and then lower case *e.*

● Conclude by reciting the alphabet together as you point to the corresponding *Alphabet Wall Cards.*

ELL Say the the word *community,* emphasizing how your voice goes higher on the second syllable. Have children say the word.

In the Community
En la comunidad

ABC Big Book

large group 15 minutes

Math Time

Observe and Investigate

Can children correctly identify a numeral they see?

Let's Jump! Lead children in a game of jumping to a count of numbers. Ask children if they can think of any animals they've seen in their community that jump.

- Show a Numeral Card (*Teacher's Treasure Book,* page 510) from 1 to 5. Have children say the numeral on the card.
- For the number 3, for example, say: ***Let's jump this many times!*** *¡Saltemos esta cantidad de veces!* as you hold up the card.
- Count the jumps in unison. Children may vary movements if they like.

ELL Before you begin the activity, provide support by modeling jumping as you say the word *jump*.

Building Blocks

Online Math Activity

Introduce Memory Geometry 1: Exact Matches from the *Building Blocks* software. This activity is based on the traditional Concentration game; children will match geometric shapes, clicking *Yes* or *No* to confim whether each pair is a match.

large group 15 minutes

Social and Emotional Development

Making Good Choices

Do children show a desire to help others in the classroom?

Being Helpful Use a puppet to review the content of the *Making Good Choices Flip Chart*, page 13.

- Have the puppet say: ***Tell me about this picture. What are the children doing? What is the teacher doing?*** *Cuéntenme qué ven en esta imagen. ¿Qué están haciendo los niños? ¿Qué está haciendo el maestro?*
- Have the puppet ask: ***How do you help in the classroom? How do you feel when you help?*** *¿Cómo ayudan en el salón de clases? ¿Cómo se sienten cuando ayudan?*
- Play "Everybody Needs Help Sometimes"/"Todos necesitan ayuda alguna vez" from the Making Good Choices Audio CD. Ask children what they think the song is telling them about why we should help others.

ELL Point to the fish and ask: ***What is this?*** Help children respond with a complete sentence: ***This is a fish.*** Repeat with other pictured items.

Making Good Choices Flip Chart, page 13

Learning Goals

Social and Emotional Development
- Child participates in a variety of individual, small- and large-group activities.

Language and Communication
- Child names and describes actual or pictured people, places, things, actions, attributes, and events.
- Child builds English listening and speaking vocabulary for common objects and phrases. (ELL)

Mathematics
- Child recognizes, names, describes, matches, compares, sorts common two-dimensional shapes (such as circle, square, rectangle, triangle, rhombus).

Vocabulary

animals	animales	community	comunidad
helpful	útil	job	trabajo
jump	saltar		

Differentiated Instruction

Extra Support

Observe and Investigate

If...children don't jump the correct number of times, **then...**use smaller numbers.

Enrichment

Observe and Investigate

Challenge children by using higher numbers during the jumping game.

Accommodations for 3's

Observe and Investigate

If...children need help knowing how many times to jump, **then...**use your fingers to show the number of times.

Focus Question
What are the parts of a community?
¿Cuáles son las partes de una comunidad?

Learning Goals

Mathematics
• Child recognizes, names, describes, matches, compares, sorts common two-dimensional shapes (such as circle, square, rectangle, triangle, rhombus).

Vocabulary

find	encontrar	hidden	escondido
hide	esconder	place	lugar
see	ver		

Differentiated Instruction

 Extra Support

Math Time

If...children have difficulty thinking of the shapes as "hidden," **then**...simply ask them where they have seen the shapes before.

Enrichment

Math Time

Encourage children to think of other shapes not shown on the *Math and Science Flip Chart*, and to think of where they might have seen them.

Accommodations for 3's

Math Time

If...children have trouble thinking of things with the target shape, **then**...provide examples.

Math Time

 large group   20 minutes

Hidden Shapes Invite children to play Hidden Shapes. Tell children some shapes have disappeared and are hiding themselves in the things we see every day. Tell them they are going to think of where they might have seen the shapes hiding.

● Display the *Math and Science Flip Chart,* page 22.

● Point to a shape. Ask: **What is this shape?** *¿Qué figura es ésta?* Help children identify the shape.

● Say (for example): **This is a rectangle. Where is a rectangle hiding? Think of the place where you sleep. Is a rectangle hiding there?** *¿Dónde se esconde un rectángulo? Piensen en el lugar donde duermen. ¿Hay un rectángulo escondido allí?* Repeat with the other shapes on the *Math and Science Flip Chart.*

● Make sure to suggest other items and places the child encounters every day.

Math and Science Flip Chart, page 22

Center Time

Center Rotation Center Time includes teacher-guided activities and independent activities. Refer to the **Learning Centers** on pages 24–25 for independent activity ideas.

 small group

Math and Science Center

☑ **Can children match shape sets?**

Materials Shape Sets

Match Up! Mix up the Shape Sets and spread them across a worktable for children. Tell children to find as many matching shapes as they can and to name the shapes.

- Give children plenty of time to find matches.

- Encourage children to work in pairs.

Center Tip

If...children have difficulty finding a partner, **then...**pair children together.

Purposeful Play

☑ **Do children follow rules in the classroom?**

Have children choose an open center for free playtime. Before playtime begins, ask children what rules they may need to follow when playing with their friends. Remind them of those rules as they play.

Learning Goals

Social and Emotional Development
- Child participates in a variety of individual, small- and large-group activities.
- Child initiates interactions with others in work and play situations.

Emergent Literacy: Writing
- Child uses scribbles, shapes, pictures, symbols, and letters to represent language.

Mathematics
- Child recognizes, names, describes, matches, compares, sorts common two-dimensional shapes (such as circle, square, rectangle, triangle, rhombus).

Writing

Remind children that community workers keep a community safe and clean. Provide clues that help children recall that doctors, firefighters, and construction workers are community helpers. Tell children to draw one of these workers. Label their pictures and have them copy the first letter of the word.

Let's Say Good-Bye

 large group 15 minutes

 Read Aloud Revisit "Counting My Blessings"/"Mis tesoros" for your afternoon Read Aloud. Remind children to look carefully at the pictures and to try to match pictures with words they hear.

 Home Connection Refer to the Home Connections activities listed in the Resources and Materials chart on page 21. Remind children to tell their families about different parts of a community. Sing the "Good-Bye Song"/ "Hora de ir a casa" as children prepare to leave.

Let's Start the Day

Focus Question
What are the parts of a community?
¿Cuáles son las partes de una comunidad?

Learning Goals

Social and Emotional Development
• Child participates in a variety of individual, small- and large-group activities.

Language and Communication
• Child follows basic rules for conversations (taking turns, staying on topic, listening actively).
• Child tries to use newly learned vocabulary and grammar. (ELL)

Emergent Literacy: Reading
• Child describes, relates to, and uses details and information from books read aloud.

Vocabulary

buildings	edificios	city	ciudad
park	parque	people	gente
town	ciudad		

Differentiated Instruction

 Extra Support
Phonological Awareness
If...children cannot identify words with the target sounds, **then...**have them listen to a few words and decide if they begin with the sound.

Enrichment
Phonological Awareness
After saying the sound /t/, /e/, /g/, or /r/, ask children to think of words that begin with that sound.

▶ Opening Routines and Transition Tips
For **Opening Routines** and **Transition Tips** turn to pages 178–181 and visit DLMExpressOnline.com for more ideas.

📖 Read **"Party at Daisy's"**/*"Fiesta en casa de Daisy"* from the *Teacher's Treasure Book,* page 180, for your morning Read Aloud.

Language Time

large group   15 minutes

👥 **Social and Emotional Development** Encourage children to follow the rule of raising their hands when they want to speak or answer a question.

Oral Language and Vocabulary

✓ **Can children name common components of a city or a town?**

Cities and Towns Explain that cities and towns are types of communities. Point out that cities are larger than towns. Say: **We live in (city or town name).** *Nosotros vivimos en (nombre de la ciudad o pueblo).* Ask: **Do you think (city or town name) is a city or a town? Why do you think that?** *¿Piensan que (nombre de la ciudad o pueblo) es una ciudad o un pueblo? ¿Por qué piensan eso?*

● Display *Oral Language Development Card 22.* Point out the various buildings. Then follow the suggestions on the back of the card.

Phonological Awareness

✓ **Can children identify words with the same initial sound?**

Reviewing Initial Sounds Display *Rhymes and Chants Flip Chart,* p. 13. Tell children to listen for the /f/ sound as you read the first line of the rhyme. Then repeat the sentence, instructing them to hop every time they hear a word that begins with the /f/ sound. Repeat with remaining lines and the initial sounds /p/ and /l/.

ELL Ask children questions about places they have been. For example, ask: **What type of buildings are there in (town or city where your school is)? Is there a park in (town or city where your school is)?** Help children answer in complete sentences. If appropriate, have English language learners describe the buildings of their town or city of birth.

Oral Language Development Card 22

Rhymes and Chants Flip Chart, page 13

Center Time

▶ **Center Rotation** Center Time includes teacher-guided activities and independent activities. Refer to the **Learning Centers** on pages 24–25 for independent activity ideas.

small group 60–90 minutes

Writer's Center

✓ **Look for examples of children helping one another and praise them when they do.**

Materials large box made to look like a mailbox, index cards or paper squares

Mailing Letters Remind children that the post office is a building in a neighborhood. Repeat the stanza of the *Rhymes and Chants Flip Chart,* page 13, about the post office.

● Have children make their own postcard by drawing a picture of something in their neighborhood on a card.

● Have them write their name on the opposite side of the card and put the card in the mailbox. At the end of the day, remove the "mail" and share the pictures that children have drawn.

Center Tip

If...children have difficulty writing their name, **then...**tell them to write only the first letter of their name.

Library and Listening Center

✓ **Model and look for examples of children saying "thank you" as they pass the cube to someone else.**

Materials a wooden cube with a picture of these items taped to each face: egg, elephant, gorilla, rabbit, turtle, tent

Matching Initial Sounds Teach children how to play a game. Begin by naming all the pictures on the cube.

● Have children take turns rolling the cube and naming the picture on the top of the cube.

● Tell players to emphasize the sound at the beginning of the word (egg, /e/), then say another word that begins with the same sound.

Center Tip

If...children have difficulty rolling the cube, **then...**have them turn the cube in their hands and place it in front of them.

✓ Learning Goals

Social and Emotional Development
• Child demonstrates positive social behaviors, as modeled by the teacher.

Language and Communication
• Child demonstrates some understanding of English spoken by teachers and peers. (ELL)

Emergent Literacy: Reading
• Child enjoys and chooses reading-related activities.

• Child produces words with the same beginning sound.

• Child describes, relates to, and uses details and information from books read aloud.

Differentiated Instruction

 Extra Support
Writer's Center
If...children have difficulty thinking of something to draw on their postcard, **then...** ask them to think about something or someone they can see from a window of their home.

 Enrichment
Writer's Center
Challenge children to label the pictures on their postcards.

Accommodations for 3's
Writer's Center
If...it is difficult for children to write the first letter of their name, **then...**write it for them and have them trace the letter several times with different colored crayons.

Focus Question
What are the parts of a community?
¿Cuáles son las partes de una comunidad?

Literacy Time

large group · 15 minutes

📖 Read Aloud

✓ **Do children understand how Keiko used pebbles to solve her problem?**

Build Background Tell children that you will be telling a story about three friends who play together in their neighborhood.

● Ask: *Who do you play with in your neighborhood? ¿Con quién juegan en su vecindario?*

● Ask: *What do you play in your neighborhood? ¿A qué juegan en su vecindario?*

Listen for Understanding Tell children that they are going to listen to a story called "Keiko's Good Thinking"/"Keiko resuelve un problema", *Teacher's Treasure Book*, page 169.

● Introduce some of the flannel board characters and other pieces, such as the three friends, the sandbox, and the paper sack.

● Explain that Keiko has a problem in the story. Tell them to listen carefully to find out how she solves her problem.

● Read the story aloud, using the flannel board characters to act out events.

Respond to the Story Discuss the story. Say: *The title of the story is "Keiko's Good Thinking." Why is that a good name for the story? El título del cuento es "Keiko resuelve un problema." ¿Por qué es éste un buen nombre para el cuento?*

ELL To support comprehension, use gestures and any necessary props to act out verbs such as *gather, race, count, stare,* and *thought.*

TIP Focus children's attention on the illustrations to help them understand unfamiliar vocabulary and story events.

Learn About Letters and Sounds

✓ **Can children identify the letter *Gg* and the sound /g/?**

Learn About Gg Display the *Gg* page of the *ABC Big Book* and point to the giraffe. Ask: *What do you see? ¿Qué ven?* Repeat *giraffe,* emphasizing the /g/ sound that begins it. Continue with *gingerbread man.* Then say the following words one at a time: *boat, general, tent, gentle, gym, sandbox,* and *pebble.* Have children clap when they hear a word that begins with the /g/ sound.

● Say the /g/ sound and have children repeat it several times. Then point to the upper case *G,* name it, and say its sound. Have children repeat several times. Explain that upper case *G* has the sound /g/. Slowly trace upper case *G,* demonstrating how it is formed. Using the *ABC Picture Card* for *Gg,* have volunteers repeat the process. Repeat the process with lower case *g.*

● Conclude by reciting the alphabet together with children as you point to the corresponding *Alphabet Wall Cards.*

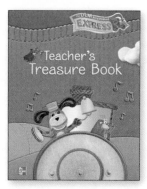

Teacher's Treasure Book, page 169

ABC Big Book

Gg
giraffe   girl

Alphabet Wall Cards

Learning Goals

Language and Communication
● Child demonstrates an understanding of oral language by responding appropriately.
● Child demonstrates some understanding of English spoken by teachers and peers. (ELL)

Emergent Literacy: Reading
● Child produces words with the same beginning sound.
● Child describes, relates to, and uses details and information from books read aloud.
● Child asks and answers questions about books read aloud (such as, "Who?" "What?" "Where?").

Vocabulary

bridges	puentes
bunch	desayuno
garages	garajes
gather	juntar
paper sack	bolsa de papel
pebbles	piedritas
sandbox	cajón de arena

Differentiated Instruction

✋ Extra Support
Read Aloud
If...children have difficulty following the story events, then...give them some toy cars, pebbles, and a paper bag and have them act out how Keiko solved her problem, using the props.

⭐ Enrichment
Read Aloud
Invite children to retell the story in their own words using the flannel board pieces.

Math Time

Online Math Activity

Continue to provide each child with a chance to complete Memory Geometry 1 and Number Snapshots 2.

Observe and Investigate

 Can children correctly identify shapes?

Is It or Not? Invite children to play the game *Is It or Not?* Tell them that they will have to find the "fooler" shape.

● Show or draw a box that looks like a rectangle but is not. For example, draw a shape that has a curved side, is not closed, or does not have right angles. Explain why it is not a true rectangle. Say: *This is not a true rectangle. A true rectangle has four straight sides that meet in corners like the corner of a piece of paper. This shape is a fooler! Éste no es un rectángulo verdadero. Un rectángulo verdadero tiene cuatro lados rectos que se encuentran en vértices como los de una hoja de papel. ¡Éste es un rectángulo engañoso!*

● Name and show a shape set of true rectangles and shapes that are not true rectangles.

● As you point to each shape, ask: *Is this a fooler? ¿Es esta figura engañosa?* Then say: *Yell "fooler!" if it is! "¡Engañosa!"*

ELL Provide visual support by placing different shapes on display and naming them. Emphasize how to say the name of each shape.

👥 Social and Emotional Development

Making Good Choices

 Do children know how to politely ask for and receive assistance?

Using Polite Words Assess what children remember from discussions by asking when people should say *please* and *thank you*. Role-play situations illustrated on the *Making Good Choices Flip Chart,* page 13.

● Point to the illustration on the chart. Say: *Let's pretend that Dog Puppet One and Dog Puppet Two are in this classroom. Hagamos de cuenta que Perro 1 y el Perro 2 están en el salón de clases.*

● Refer to the scenario on the chart and role-play scenes such as this one.

> Dog Puppet One: *I have snacks to pass out. Could you please help me? Tengo algunas cosas para convidar. ¿Me ayudas a repartirlas?*
> Dog Puppet Two: *Yes, I can help you. Sí, te ayudaré.*
> Dog Puppet One: *Thank you. Gracias.*

ELL Give children practice saying *please* and *thank you*. Have a child say: *Please give me a book.* Then have him or her say: *Thank you.*

Making Good Choices Flip Chart, page 13

Learning Goals

Social and Emotional Development
● Child participates in a variety of individual, small- and large-group activities.

Language and Communication
● Child uses oral language for a variety of purposes.

● Child builds English listening and speaking vocabulary for common objects and phrases. (ELL)

Mathematics
● Child recognizes, names, describes, matches, compares, sorts common two-dimensional shapes (such as circle, square, rectangle, triangle, rhombus).

Vocabulary

equal	igual	please	por favor
rectangle	rectángulo	sides	lados
thank you	gracias		

Differentiated Instruction

✋ **Extra Support**

Observe and Investigate
If...children have difficulty distinguishing between true rectangles and rectangles that are not true, **then...**review the attributes of a true rectangle.

⭐ **Enrichment**

Observe and Investigate
Challenge children with more difficult shapes, such as rectangles that are in different orientations.

Accommodations for 3's

Observe and Investigate
If...children have difficulty with the game Is It or Not?, **then...**go over each shape and tell why it is a true rectangle or not.

Focus Question

What are the parts of a community?

¿Cuáles son las partes de una comunidad?

Learning Goals

Social and Emotional Development
• Child maintains concentration/attention skills until a task is complete.
• Child participates in a variety of individual, small- and large-group activities.

Language and Communication
• Child demonstrates some understanding of English spoken by teachers and peers. (ELL)

Social Studies
• Child understands basic human needs for food, clothing, shelter.

Vocabulary

neighborhood	vecindario
neighbors	vecinos
parks	parques
school	escuelas
stores	tiendas
streets	calles

Differentiated Instruction

 Extra Support

Understand and Participate

If...children don't join in the activity, **then...**ask them questions such as: *Where can people shop for food? ¿Dónde puede la gente comprar comida?*

 Enrichment

Understand and Participate

Encourage children to draw features on the cardboard buildings, such as doors and windows.

 Special Needs

Behavioral Social/Emotional

If...building a whole neighborhood seems like an overwhelming task, **then...**help children build the neighborhood step-by-step, beginning with one house, then another, then a school, and so on.

Social Studies

large group ⏱ *20 minutes*

Language and Communication Skills Use words that describe parts of a community.

Oral Language and Academic Vocabulary

✓ **Can children use words that relate to neighbors in a neighborhood?**

Talking About a Neighborhood Display the illustrations on pages 6–15 of *Concept Big Book 2: In the Community.*

● Explain that these are pictures of a neighborhood where neighbors live, work, and play together.

● Guide children to use the Vocabulary words to answer questions such as: *Do these neighbors live in apartment buildings, houses, or housing developments? Why do people live in houses or other buildings? What buildings do they shop in? Are these nearby? Do they drive, walk, or take a bus to get there? Where might they play soccer or baseball? ¿Viven estos vecinos en departamentos, casas o condominios? ¿Por qué la gente vive en casas o en otros tipos de edificios? ¿Dónde hacen sus compras? ¿Viajan en autobús, caminan o conducen un carro? ¿Dónde juegan al fútbol o al béisbol?*

Understand and Participate

✓ **Can children contribute to constructing a neighborhood scene and remain focused on the activity?**

Building a Neighborhood Children will use different sizes of cartons and boxes to construct a neighborhood. Place a wide strip of tape on the floor to represent a main street of a town.

● Place a variety of cartons and boxes of different sizes in a group. Ask questions such as: *Which of these boxes could we use as a house in this neighborhood? Should we have more than one house? Which one should we use as a school? A store? ¿Cuál de estas cajas podríamos usar para hacer una casa en este vecindario? ¿Debería haber más de una casa? ¿Qué caja deberíamos usar para la escuela? ¿Y para una tienda?*

● As children choose boxes for houses and public buildings, help them place each box along the street. Discuss what people do in each kind of building.

ELL Ask children *yes/no* questions that will help them participate in the group activity, such as: *Is this a good box to use for a house? Do we need a bigger box for a school?*

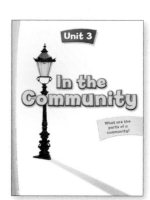

In the Community
En la comunidad

Center Time

▶ **Center Rotation** Center Time includes teacher-guided activities and independent activities. Refer to the **Learning Centers** on pages 24–25 for independent activity ideas.

small group · 30 minutes

Pretend and Learn Center

Center Tip

✓ Encourage children to use figures to show work and play in the neighborhood.

Materials people figures, small cars and trucks

Role-Playing in the Neighborhood Have children play with people and vehicles in the neighborhood they constructed.

- Have children show how neighbors play and work in the neighborhood.

- Have them discuss where cars and trucks are going in the neighborhood.

If...children move the cardboard buildings too much as they play, **then...**tape the buildings to the floor.

Purposeful Play

✓ Observe whether or not children use the words *please* and *thank you* as they play, and praise them for doing so.

Children choose an open center for free playtime. Encourage them to "play school," "play store," or "play house" so they can use the vocabulary words from the lesson.

Let's Say Good-Bye

large group · 15 minutes

 Read Aloud Revisit "Party at Daisy's"/"Fiesta en casa de Daisy" for your afternoon Read Aloud. Remind children to listen for words that describe things in a community.

 Home Connection Refer to the Home Connections activities listed in the Resources and Materials chart on page 21. Remind children to tell their families about different parts of a community. Sing the "Good-Bye Song"/ "Hora de ir a casa" as children prepare to leave.

 Learning Goals

Social and Emotional Development
- Child participates in a variety of individual, small- and large-group activities.
- Child initiates interactions with others in work and play situations.

Emergent Literacy: Writing
- Child uses scribbles, shapes, pictures, symbols, and letters to represent language.

Writing

Talk about the different kinds of buildings the class included in the neighborhood that they constructed. Tell children to draw a picture of a building in their community other than their own house. Label the building and have children copy the first two letters of the word you wrote.

Let's Start the Day

Focus Question
What are the parts of a community?
¿Cuáles son las partes de una comunidad?

✓ Learning Goals

Social and Emotional Development
• Child participates in a variety of individual, small- and large-group activities.

Language and Communication
• Child tries to use newly learned vocabulary and grammar. (ELL)

Emergent Literacy: Reading
• Child produces words with the same beginning sound.

Vocabulary

neighbors   vecinos   tale   cuento

Differentiated Instruction

 Extra Support
Oral Language and Vocabulary
If...children cannot think of ways that people in their neighborhood can help one another, **then...**refer them to their Helping Charts to review or add to their helping options.

 Enrichment
Phonological Awareness
Ask children to repeat the activity in a small group, using the /e/ sound.

♥ Special Needs
Cognitive Challenges
If...eight words are too difficult for children, **then...**draw only three or four petals on the flower so they can be successful.

▶ **Opening Routines and Transition Tips**
For **Opening Routines** and **Transition Tips** turn to pages 178–181 and visit **DLMExpressOnline.com** for more ideas.

📖 Read **"Roll On, Roll On"**/"Rueda, rueda" from the *Teacher's Treasure Book*, page 260, for your morning Read Aloud.

Language Time

 large group 15 minutes

👫 **Social and Emotional Development** Encourage children to build friendships and help one another.

Oral Language and Vocabulary

✓ **Can children suggest ways that neighbors help one another?**

Helping in the Neighborhood Remind children that a neighborhood is a community where people live, play, and work. Point out that a nice thing about living in a neighborhood is that neighbors often help each other.

● Ask: *What can people do to help a neighbor? ¿En qué puede ayudar una persona a un vecino?*

● Ask: *Have you ever helped a person who lives in your neighborhood? What did you do? How is that different from or the same as helping classmates? ¿Alguna vez han ayudado a un vecino? ¿Qué hicieron? ¿En qué se diferencia y en qué se parece ayudar a un vecino y ayudar compañero?*

Phonological Awareness

✓ **Can children identify words with the same initial sound?**

Review Initial Sounds Draw a flower with the outline of eight petals. Say the /t/ sound and ask children to take turns saying words that begin with that sound. Each time a child says an appropriate word, color in a petal using a different color. See if children can name enough words to color the entire flower. Repeat the activity with the /r/ sound and the soft sound of /g/.

 When you have completed the activity, help children name the colors of the petals.

Center Time

▶ **Center Rotation** Center Time includes teacher-guided activities and independent activitiaes. Refer to the **Learning Centers** on pages 24–25 for independent activity ideas.

 small group 60–90 minutes

Pretend and Learn Center

Center Tip

☑ **Notice ways the children think to help one another.**

Materials sock puppets

Neighbors in Need Remind children of all the ways that they thought of helping a neighbor.

- Have pairs of children use puppets to role-play a neighbor in need and a neighbor who helps.

- Remind children to have the puppets say *please* and *thank you*.

If...sock puppets are not readily available, **then...**use Dog Puppet One and Dog Puppet Two.

Library and Listening Center

Center Tip

☑ **Look for children who can focus their attention on the recording and not be distracted by other activities in the classroom.**

Materials recordable CD player, tape recorder, or other electronic audio device; recorded book in matching format about characters who help others in their community.

Listening to a Story Record a book about characters who help one another, such as *Horton Hatches the Egg,* by Dr. Seuss, or *Uncle Willie and the Soup Kitchen,* by DyAnne DiSalvo-Ryan.

- Have children listen to the recording.

- Have pairs of children discuss the story after they have listened to it.

If...you want to have children look at the book's illustrations as they listen to the story, **then...** include page-turning instructions in your recording.

Learning Goals

Social and Emotional Development
- Child uses classroom materials carefully.
- Child maintains concentration/attention skills until a task is complete.
- Child participates in a variety of individual, small- and large-group activities.
- Child shows empathy and care for others.

Language and Communication
- Child uses oral language for a variety of purposes.

Emergent Literacy: Reading
- Child describes, relates to, and uses details and information from books read aloud.

Differentiated Instruction

 Extra Support

Pretend and Learn Center
If...children need guidance, **then...**manipulate one of the puppets yourself and have the child respond to your questions or comments.

 Enrichment

Library and Listening Center
After children listen to the story, have them draw a picture of their favorite part of it. Challenge them to write a word or phrase that describes their picture.

Accommodations for 3's

Pretend and Learn Center
If...children find it difficult to use the hand puppets, **then...**make stick puppets for them to use instead.

Focus Question

What are the parts of a community?

¿Cuáles son las partes de una comunidad?

Learning Goals

Language and Communication
- Child demonstrates an understanding of oral language by responding appropriately.
- Child tries to use newly learned vocabulary and grammar. (ELL)

Emergent Literacy: Reading
- Child names most upper- and lowercase letters of the alphabet.
- Child asks and answers questions about books read aloud (such as, "Who?" "What?" "Where?").

Vocabulary

boil	hervir	carrots	zanahorias
onions	cebollas	potatoes	papas
solve	resolver	stone	piedra
tastiest	sabroso		

Differentiated Instruction

 Extra Support

Learn About Letters and Sounds
If...children have a difficult time remembering what sound they are to focus on, **then...**say the /r/ sound as you pantomime each action.

 Enrichment

Read Aloud
Invite children to draw pictures of other vegetables that could be added to stone soup.

 Special Needs

Speech and Language Delays
Pause often as you read, stopping to ask children questions about the story. If children can't answer correctly, reread the passage and ask the question again using simple sentence structures.

Literacy Time

 large group · 15 minutes

📖 Read Aloud

☑ **Can children identify the setting of the tale as a neighborhood?**

Build Background Tell children that you will be reading a story about neighbors who solve a problem by helping one another.

- Ask children to recall ways they thought neighbors could help one another.

Listen for Enjoyment Display the *Teacher's Treasure Book,* page 315, and read the title "Stone Soup"/"La sopa de piedra." Ask children if they think the title is a funny name and whether they have ever found stones in their soup.

- Ask: *What do you think these neighbors will do to help one another? ¿Qué crees que estos vecinos harán para ayudarse uno al otro?*

- Name the vegetables that neighbors put in the soup. Read the story aloud.

Respond to the Story Discuss the story. Help children recall the different vegetables that the neighbors added to the soup. Ask: *Why do you think the soup was tasty? ¿Por qué creen que la sopa era sabrosa?*

ELL Bring in an onion, a carrot, and a potato for children to touch and feel. Hand them to children as you say: *This is an onion (carrot, potato).* Have children repeat the sentences.

TIP To help children connect to the story, invite students to recall times that they shared food or something else with a neighbor.

Learn About Letters and Sounds

☑ **Can children identify the letter *Rr* and the sound /r/?**

Learn About *Rr* Display the *Rr* page of the *ABC Big Book* and point to the ring. Ask: *What do you see? ¿Qué ven?* Repeat *ring,* emphasizing the initial /r/ sound. Continue with *rabbit, rainbow, rake,* and *raccoon.* Then say the following words one at a time: *rainbow, ring, egg, raccoon, goat, elephant, monkey,* and *rake.* Have children clap when they hear a word that begins with /r/.

- Say the /r/ sound and have children repeat it several times. Then point to the upper case *R,* name it, and say its sound. Have children repeat several times. Explain that upper case *R* makes the sound /r/. Slowly trace upper case *R,* demonstrating how it is formed. Using the *ABC Picture Card* for *Rr,* have volunteers repeat the process. Repeat the process with lower case *r.*

- Conclude by reciting the alphabet together with children as you point to the corresponding *Alphabet Wall Cards.*

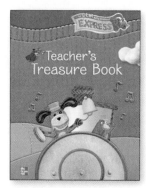

Teacher's Treasure Book, page 315

ABC Big Book

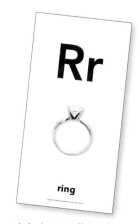

Rr

ring

Alphabet Wall Cards

large group 🕐 **15 minutes**

Online Math Activity

Children can complete Memory Geometry 1 and Number Snapshots 2 during computer time or Center Time.

large group 🕐 **15 minutes**

Making Good Choices Flip Chart, page 13

Math Time

Observe and Investigate

✓ **Can children identify rectangles?**

Is It a Square or a Rectangle? Invite children to explore boxes they see in daily life. Encourage children to bring in boxes from home the next time they come to class.

● Draw a large rectangle for the class to look at, and trace it, counting each side as you go.

● Show children a variety of boxes. Bring in "used" boxes that have mailing labels, stamps, or markings on them. Make sure you have an example of a rectangular box with a square base.

● On large paper, trace the base of the box. Ask: *Is this a square or a rectangle?* ¿*Es esto un cuadrado o un rectángulo?* Discuss why the shape is a square.

● Place the box on its side. Trace the shape onto paper. Ask: *Is this a rectangle or a square?* ¿*Es esto un rectángulo o un cuadrado?* Discuss why the shape is a rectangle.

● Have children repeat with other boxes.

ⅩⅩⅩ Social and Emotional Development

Making Good Choices

✓ **Do children assume responsibilities in the classroom?**

Taking Responsibility Use the two Dog Puppets to make a point about accepting responsibility and doing the right thing.

● Have Dog One say: *It's my turn to feed the fish today. I really want to go outside and play with my friends, so I don't think I'll feed them.* *Hoy es mi turno de alimentar al pez. Pero tengo muchas ganas de jugar con mis amigos afuera, así que no creo que los alimente.*

● Have Dog Two say: *That's not right! The fish need food. You need to do your job. You can play with your friends after you feed the fish.* *Eso no está bien. Los peces necesitan alimento. Debes hacer tu trabajo. Puedes jugar con tus amigos una vez que hayas alimentado a los peces.*

✓ **Learning Goals**

Social and Emotional Development
● Child participates in a variety of individual, small- and large-group activities.

Language and Communication
● Child begins and ends conversations appropriately.

Mathematics
● Child recognizes, names, describes, matches, compares, sorts common two-dimensional shapes (such as circle, square, rectangle, triangle, rhombus).

Vocabulary

box	caja	mail	correo
package	paquete	rectangle	rectángulo
send	enviar	square	cuadrado

Differentiated Instruction

✋ **Extra Support**

Observe and Investigate

If...children need help telling why a shape is a rectangle or square, **then**...review the attributes of each shape.

⭐ **Enrichment**

Observe and Investigate

Challenge children to draw a rectangle in the air and count each side as they draw it.

Accommodations for 3's

Observe and Investigate

If...children have trouble tracing boxes, **then**...have them match boxes to already-drawn shapes.

Focus Question
What are the parts of a community?
¿Cuáles son las partes de una comunidad?

Learning Goals

Language and Communication
• Child builds English listening and speaking vocabulary for common objects and phrases. (ELL)

Mathematics
• Child recognizes, names, describes, matches, compares, sorts common two-dimensional shapes (such as circle, square, rectangle, triangle, rhombus).

Vocabulary

find	encontrar	shape	figura
where	dónde		

Differentiated Instruction

 Extra Support

Math Time
If...children have difficulty finding shapes, **then...**simply ask them to describe the shapes.

 Enrichment

Math Time
Encourage children to think of other shapes not shown on the *Math and Science Flip Chart* and to think of where they might have seen them.

Accommodations for 3's

Math Time
If...children struggle with completing the task, **then...**walk with them and point out examples or pair them with another child.

Math Time

large group — 15 minutes

✓ **Can children identify matching shapes?**

Find That Shape! Invite children to play a game in which they look around the room for shapes.

● Display the *Math and Science Flip Chart,* page 22. Go over the names of the shapes with children.

● Ask children to choose a shape on the chart.

● Say: *Is there something in the classroom with that shape? Find that shape!* ¿Hay algo en el salón de clases que tenga esa forma? ¡Encuéntrenlo!

● Encourage children to walk around the classroom to find an item with the same shape.

● Repeat with the other shapes on the chart.

ELL Provide individual support by walking with children and asking yes/no questions about objects in the room, determining whether the shape is the same as the one on the chart.

Math and Science Flip Chart, page 22

Center Time

▶ **Center Rotation** Center Time includes teacher-guided activities and independent activities. Refer to the **Learning Centers** on pages 24–25 for independent activity ideas.

 small group 30 minutes

Learning Goals

Social and Emotional Development
• Child participates in a variety of individual, small- and large-group activities.
• Child initiates interactions with others in work and play situations.

Emergent Literacy: Writing
• Child uses scribbles, shapes, pictures, symbols, and letters to represent language.

Mathematics
• Child recognizes, names, describes, matches, compares, sorts common two-dimensional shapes (such as circle, square, rectangle, triangle, rhombus).

Math and Science Center

| | Center Tip |

✓ **Encourage children to fill and play with boxes.**

Materials used boxes gathered from the community

Boxes! Provide a set of boxes and child-friendly items to pack in the boxes. Tell children to pack the boxes any way they wish.

• Tape the boxes shut when children are finished "packing" them.

• Encourage children to tell how many items they packed in each box.

Center Tip

If...children have difficulty packing the boxes, **then...** encourage them to play with a partner.

Purposeful Play

✓ **Observe which children make friends easily and which ones need guidance.**

Children choose an open center for free playtime. Encourage children to work in small groups and to use props to act out the story "Stone Soup."

 Writing

Remind children that the neighbors in "Stone Soup" shared food to make a pot of soup. Ask children to draw a picture of a favorite food that they might share with a neighbor. Label each picture with dotted letters. Have children connect the dots to form the letters of their word.

Let's Say Good-Bye

large group 15 minutes

Read Aloud Revisit "Roll On, Roll On"/"Rueda, rueda" for your afternoon Read Aloud. Remind children to think what the story has to do with a neighborhood or community.

Home Connection Refer to the Home Connections activities listed in the Resources and Materials chart on page 21. Remind children to tell their families about different parts of a community. Sing the "Good-Bye Song"/"Hora de ir a casa" as children prepare to leave.

Let's Start the Day

Focus Question

What are the parts of a community?

¿Cuáles son las partes de una comunidad?

Learning Goals

Social and Emotional Development
• Child participates in a variety of individual, small- and large-group activities.

Language and Communication
• Child demonstrates an understanding of oral language by responding appropriately.
• Child tries to use newly learned vocabulary and grammar. (ELL)

Emergent Literacy: Reading
• Child produces words with the same beginning sound.

Fine Arts
• Child participates in a variety of music activities (such as listening, singing, finger plays, musical games, performances).

Vocabulary

cars	carros	fish	pez
paintbrush	pincel	toys	juguetes
trucks	camiones	watering	riego

Differentiated Instruction

 Extra Support
Phonological Awareness
If...children have difficulty thinking of words that begin with the initial target sounds, **then...** name two words and have children identify the word with the target sound.

Enrichment
Oral Language and Vocabulary
Challenge children to pretend being the teacher and "teach" a partner what is happening in the illustration.

Opening Routines and Transition Tips
For **Opening Routines** and **Transition Tips** turn to pages 178–181 and visit DLMExpressOnline.com for more ideas.

 Read **"Anansi and the Pot of Wisdom"/**"Anansi y la olla de la sabiduría" from the *Teacher's Treasure Book*, page 312, for your morning Read Aloud.

Language Time

large group   15 minutes

Social and Emotional Development Encourage children to be aware of opportunities to help you or their friends.

Oral Language and Vocabulary

✓ **Can children use nouns and verbs to describe the illustration on the *Making Good Choices Flip Chart*?**

Helping in the Classroom Ask children what they have been learning about ways they can help others in the classroom. Ask: **How do you help your friends in school? What is a way that you can help me?** *¿De qué manera pueden ayudar a sus amigos en la escuela? ¿De qué manera pueden ayudarme a mí?*

● Display the *Making Good Choices Flip Chart,* page 13. Guide children to name actions in the illustration and discuss the different ways that children are being helpful in the classroom.

ELL Point out that the word *water* can be used as both a noun and a verb. Say: **I water the flower with water.** Have children repeat the sentence. Then ask: **What do I give the flowers?** (water) **What can I do with water?** (water the plants)

Phonological Awareness

✓ **Can children produce words with matching initial sounds?**

Review Initial Sounds Display the *Rhymes and Chants Flip Chart* to revisit the initial sounds /f/, /p/, and /l/. Alternate with children speaking lines of the rhythmic chant: **Where can I find fire trucks? / At the fire station.** *Del cuartel sale el bombero / Muy veloz en la autobomba.* Ask children to name other words that begin with the sounds /f/, /p/, and /l/.

Making Good Choices Flip Chart, page 13

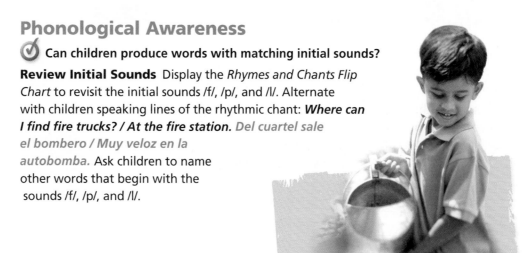
Rhymes and Chants Flip Chart, page 13

Center Time

▶ **Center Rotation** Center Time includes teacher-guided activities and independent activities. Refer to the **Learning Centers** on pages 24–25 for independent activity ideas.

 small group 60–90 minutes

 Learning Goals

Social and Emotional Development
• Child participates in a variety of individual, small- and large-group activities.

Emergent Literacy: Reading
• Child produces words with the same beginning sound.

Creativity Center

 Look for examples of children taking responsibility in the classroom.

Materials drawing paper, crayons

Drawing Pictures Show children the illustration on the *Making Good Choices Flip Chart,* page 13, and review the ways in which the children are being helpful in the classroom.

● Have children draw pictures of themselves being helpful in the classroom.

● Encourage children to draw pictures of helpful things they do that are not shown in the picture.

Differentiated Instruction

✋ Extra Support

Creativity Center
If...children have difficulty thinking of a time when they were helpful in the classroom, **then...**help brainstorm situations they can draw.

⭐ Enrichment

ABC Center
Encourage children to find and cut out pictures of objects from magazines or catalogs that begin with the initial target sounds. Have children hang the pictures on the appropriate lines.

💜 Special Needs

Behavioral Social/Emotional Problems
If...children are frustrated by too many choices, **then...**only hang two clotheslines and limit the number of pictures to hang.

ABC Center

Center Tip

 Look for children who handle the activity supplies responsibly. Praise them for their good work.

Materials string; clothespins; pictures of a fish, a pig, and a lion from the *ABC Big Book;* pictures of items that begin with /f/, /p/, and /l/ from the *Photo Library CD-ROM;* pictures of things that begin with other initial sounds from the *Photo Library CD-ROM*

Sorting Initial Sounds Drawings Attach three lengths of string to a wall, each about 3 feet long. Use a clothespin to attach the pictures of the fish, pig, and lion on each "clothesline." Place the other pictures near the clotheslines.

● Have children look at each picture and name it.

● Tell children to hang the pictures on the clothesline with the picture that begins with the same sound. Then have each child ask a classmate to check his or her work. Remove all the pictures except the target sound pictures when children are finished.

● Remind children to handle the pictures carefully so others can use them.

If...children have difficulty using the clothespins, **then...** tape the pictures to small wire hangers instead.

Circle Time

Focus Question
What are the parts of a community?
¿Cuáles son las partes de una comunidad?

Learning Goals

Language and Communication
• Child demonstrates an understanding of oral language by responding appropriately.
• Child tries to use newly learned vocabulary and grammar. (ELL)

Emergent Literacy: Reading
• Child produces words with the same beginning sound.
• Child describes, relates to, and uses details and information from books read aloud.
• Child asks and answers questions about books read aloud (such as, "Who?" "What?" "Where?").

Vocabulary

| healthy | saludables | neighbors | vecinos |
| sidewalk | acera | trash | basura |

Differentiated Instruction

👋 **Extra Support**
Review Letters and Sounds
If...children have difficulty identifying items that begin with the target sound, **then...**point to an object, name it, and ask whether or not it begins with the target sound.

⭐ **Enrichment**
Review Letters and Sounds
Invite children to find pictures of items from advertising flyers that begin with the sounds /t/ and /r/. Tell them to circle the items they find.

Accommodations for 3's
Read Aloud
If...children have difficulty thinking about how the community in the book is the same as their community, **then...**say things such as: *The neighborhood in the book has a fire station. Do we have a fire station in our community?*
El vecindario del libro tiene una estación de bomberos. ¿Hay una estación de bomberos en nuestra comunidad?

Literacy Time

large group — 15 minutes

📖 Read Aloud

✅ **Can children make connections between the book and their own community?**

Build Background Tell children that you will be reading *Concept Big Book 2: In the Community* to them again. Ask children to use their own words to explain what a community is.

● Ask: *What do you remember about this book? ¿Qué recuerdan de este libro?*

Listen for Understanding Display *Concept Big Book 2: In the Community* and read the title. Remind children that a community is a place where people live and work together.

● Read the book aloud.

● After reading, conduct a picture walk of the book and have children use the pictures to retell the story.

Respond and Connect Ask children to tell what part of the book they liked best. Make a chart to record or tally their answers. Ask: *What did you like about the buildings? What did you like about the community helpers? Was it learning about the ways people can help one another? How is the community in the book like our community? ¿Qué les gusta de los edificios? ¿Qué les gusta de los trabajadores comunitarios? ¿Qué aprendimos sobre los modos en que pueden ayudarse las personas? ¿En qué se parece nuestra comunidad a la comunidad del libro?*

ELL Play a game of *I Spy* with children as you look at the illustrations. Say: *I see a truck in this picture. Do you see it?* Help children find the item and have them say: *I see the truck.*

Review Letters and Sounds

✅ **Can children identify the initial sounds /t/, soft /g/, /ĕ/, and /r/?**

Review Sounds of *Tt, Gg, Ee,* and *Rr*.

● One at a time, display pictures from the *ABC Big Book* for each initial sound. Ask questions such as this: *What is this?* (a television) *What sound do you hear at the beginning of (television)? ¿Qué es esto? ¿Qué sonido escuchan al principio de esa palabra?*

● Ask children to look around the room and find something that begins with the same initial sound.

In the Community
En la comunidad

ABC Big Book

Online Math Activity

Continue to provide each child with a chance to complete Memory Geometry 1 and Number Snapshots 2.

Math Time

Observe and Investigate

✓ **Can children identify rectangles?**

Is It a Square or a Rectangle? Invite children to explore how boxes can be rectangles and squares.

- Draw a large rectangle for the class to see, and then trace it, counting each side as you go.

- Show children a variety of boxes. Make sure you have an example of a rectangular box with a square base.

- On a large sheet of paper, trace the base of the box. Ask: *Is this a square or a rectangle? ¿Es esto un cuadrado o un rectángulo?* Discuss the reason why the shape is a square.

- Place the box on its side. Trace the shape onto paper. Ask: *Is this a rectangle or a square? ¿Es esto un rectángulo o un cuadrado?* Discuss the reason why the shape is a rectangle.

- Have children trace their own boxes and discuss the shapes.

ELL Provide visual support by showing a square and rectangle from a shape set. As you say the name of each shape, trace its sides with your finger, and ask children to notice the lengths.

Making Good Choices Flip Chart, page 13

✕✕✕ Social and Emotional Development

Making Good Choices

✓ **Do children take responsibility for being helpful in the classroom?**

Being Responsible in School Display the *Making Good Choices Flip Chart* and discuss responsibilities shown on this chart and children's Helping Chart.

- Ask: *Is the teacher doing all the jobs in this classroom? Why not? ¿Hace el maestro todas las tareas del salón de clases? ¿Por qué no?*

- Point out and read aloud the list of the tasks being performed in the illustration. Say: *Let's make a list of jobs we can share in our classroom. Hagan una lista de las tareas que podemos compartir en nuestro salón de clases.* Record children's suggestions. You might want to develop a rotation chart that shows who is responsible for which classroom tasks each week.

ELL When you read the list of chores in the illustration, act out the chores with the students if students do not understand them.

Vocabulary

box	caja	jobs	tareas
match	coincidir	share	compartir
trace	trazar		

Differentiated Instruction

 Extra Support

Observe and Investigate

If...children need help telling why a shape is a rectangle or square, **then...**review the attributes of each shape.

Enrichment

Observe and Investigate

Challenge children to draw a rectangle in the air and count each side as they draw it.

 Special Needs

Cognitive Challenges

If...children have trouble tracing boxes, **then...**have them match boxes to already-drawn shapes.

Focus Question
What are the parts of a community?
¿Cuáles son las partes de una comunidad?

Learning Goals

Social and Emotional Development
• Child demonstrates positive social behaviors, as modeled by the teacher.

Language and Communication
• Child begins and ends conversations appropriately.

Social Studies
• Child participates in voting for group decision-making.

Fine Arts
• Child expresses emotions or ideas through art.

Vocabulary

community helpers	trabajadores comunitarios
fire station	estación de bomberos
homes	hogares
parks	parques
stores	tiendas

Differentiated Instruction

 **Extra Support**
Explore and Express
If…children can't make a decision about what to color, **then…**give them a choice, such as: **Which do you want to color—a big building or a house?** *¿Qué tienen ganas de colorear, un edificio grande o una casa?*

Enrichment
Explore and Express
Challenge children to draw additional features for the town, such as a lake, parking lots, and railroad tracks.

Accommodations for 3's
Explore and Express
If…children are reluctant to color on their own, **then…**pair them with another child and have the two work together.

Art Time

Oral Language and Vocabulary Model for students your thinking process as you decide what you are going to do by saying: **What part of our community should I draw?** *¿Qué parte de nuestra comunidad debo dibujar?* Then model how to state what you plan to create by saying: **I am going to draw a school for our town.** *Voy a dibujar la escuela de nuestro pueblo.*

Oral Language and Academic Vocabulary

✓ **Can children express opinions?**

Talking About Ideas for Art Tell children that the whole class is going to draw a town as a group. Ask: **What should we name our town?** *¿Cómo deberíamos llamar a nuestra ciudad?* Have children vote on a name and print the name on a long sheet of butcher paper.

● Talk about the parts of a community. Initiate a discussion by asking questions such as: **What buildings should be in our community? Should we have a park? What else do we want?** *¿Qué edificios debería haber en nuestra comunidad? ¿Deberíamos tener un parque? ¿Qué más les gustaría incluir?*

● Guide children to think about homes, public buildings, and community helpers.

Explore and Express

✓ **Can children compliment their classmates' artwork?**

Color Parts of a Town Have children choose the part of the community they want to color.

● Make available a variety of cardboard shapes of large buildings, smaller houses, trees, and so on, and have children choose one to color.

● Encourage children to say nice things about their classmates' artwork.

● When children have completed their artwork, work as a group to place the homes, public buildings, trees, and so on, on the butcher paper.

Center Time

▶ **Center Rotation** Center Time includes teacher-guided activities and independent activities. Refer to the **Learning Centers** on pages 24–25 for independent activity ideas.

  small group **30 minutes**

Creativity Center

 Encourage children to compliment each other's artwork.

Materials paper, people figures, crayons

Completing the Community Direct children's attention to the community that they made the previous day. Ask: **What things are in our community?** *¿Qué cosas tiene nuestra comunidad?* Then ask: **What are we missing in our community?** *¿Qué le falta a nuestra comunidad?*

- Give children paper figures of people and have them draw faces and clothing on them.

- Model how to give recognition without making valuative comments about artwork and encourage children to do the same.

- Work together to add the people to the community. Have children discuss how people in the community might help one another.

Center Tip

If...children have difficulty handling paper figures, **then** use cardboard or oaktag to make the figures.

Purposeful Play

✓ **Observe how children play in a group and share common materials.**

Children choose an open center for free playtime. Remind them that a playgroup is a small community.

Let's Say Good-Bye

 large group **15 minutes**

 Read Aloud Revisit "Anansi and the Pot of Wisdom"/"Anansi y la olla de la sabiduría" for your afternoon Read Aloud. Tell children to listen for words that begin with the /t/ sound.

 Home Connection Refer to the Home Connections activities listed in the Resources and Materials chart on page 21. Remind children to tell their families about different parts of a community. Sing the "Good-Bye Song"/ "Hora de ir a casa" as children prepare to leave.

✓ Learning Goals

Social and Emotional Development
- Child shows eagerness, curiosity, and confidence while learning new concepts and trying new things.

Language and Communication
- Child begins and ends conversations appropriately.

Emergent Literacy: Writing
- Child uses scribbles, shapes, pictures, symbols, and letters to represent language.

Fine Arts
- Child shares opinions about artwork and artistic experiences.

Writing

Have children talk about ways that people in a neighborhood can help one another. Record their answers. Have children take turns circling the letters *t*, *e*, *g*, and *r* in the recorded answers. Then have each child draw the letters in the air or on an interactive whiteboard.

Focus Question

How does a community help me?

¿Cómo me ayuda una comunidad?

This week children will learn about how people in communities help each other. They will begin to understand location and learn about where they live and go to school. To celebrate the fun of parades, they will draw pictures and make marching figures.

Social and Emotional Development	1	2	3	4	5
Child is aware of self in terms of abilities, characteristics and preferences, and respects personal boundaries.					✓
Child uses classroom materials carefully.				✓	
Child maintains concentration/attention skills until a task is complete.				✓	
Child shows eagerness, curiosity, and confidence while learning new concepts and trying new things.			✓	✓	✓
Child participates in a variety of individual, small- and large-group activities.	✓			✓	✓
Child initiates interactions with others in work and play situations.		✓	✓	✓	
Child shows empathy and care for others.	✓	✓	✓	✓	✓

Language and Communication	1	2	3	4	5
Child demonstrates an understanding of oral language by responding appropriately.	✓		✓	✓	
Child uses oral language for a variety of purposes.			✓	✓	
Child begins and ends conversations appropriately.	✓		✓	✓	✓
Child names and describes actual or pictured people, places, things, actions, attributes, and events.		✓	✓		✓
Child exhibits an understanding of instructional terms used in the classroom.				✓	
Child uses newly learned vocabulary daily in multiple contexts.					✓

Emergent Literacy: Reading	1	2	3	4	5
Child independently engages in pre-reading behaviors and activities (such as, pretending to read, turning one page at a time).		✓			✓
Child produces words with the same beginning sound.	✓	✓	✓	✓	✓
Child names most upper- and lowercase letters of the alphabet.	✓	✓	✓	✓	✓
Child identifies the letter that stands for a given sound.	✓	✓	✓	✓	✓
Child asks and answers questions about books read aloud (such as, "Who?" "What?" "Where?").			✓		✓

Emergent Literacy: Writing	1	2	3	4	5
Child uses scribbles, shapes, pictures, symbols, and letters to represent language.	✓	✓	✓	✓	
Child writes own name or a reasonable approximation of it.					✓
Child writes some letters or reasonable approximations of letters upon request.					✓

Mathematics	1	2	3	4	5
Child counts 1–10 concrete objects correctly.	✓	✓	✓	✓	✓
Child demonstrates that, when counting, the last number indicates how many objects were counted.				✓	
Child recognizes and names numerals 0 through 9.	✓	✓	✓	✓	✓
Child compares the length, height, weight, volume (capacity), area of people or objects.	✓				

Science	1	2	3	4	5
Child observes, identifies, explores, describes, and compares earth materials (such as rocks, soil, sand, water) and their uses.	✓				

Social Studies	1	2	3	4	5
Child identifies common areas and features of home, school, and community.			✓		

Fine Arts	1	2	3	4	5
Child expresses thoughts, feelings, and energy through music and creative movement.					✓

Materials and Resources

DAY 1	DAY 2	DAY 3	DAY 4	DAY 5

Program Materials

DAY 1	DAY 2	DAY 3	DAY 4	DAY 5
• Teacher's Treasure Book • Oral Language Development Card 23 • Rhymes and Chants Flip Chart • Photo Library CD-ROM • *Rush Hour* Big Book • ABC Picture Cards • Counters • Math and Science Flip Chart • Numeral Cards • Online Building Blocks Math Activities • Making Good Choices Flip Chart • Sequence Cards set: "Building a Home" • Jumbo Hand Lens • Primary Balance Scale • Connecting Cubes • Home Connections Resource Guide	• Teacher's Treasure Book • *Rush Hour* Big Book • Listening Library CD • Dog Puppet 1 and 2 • Concept Big Book 2 • ABC Picture Cards • Online Building Blocks Math Activities • Making Good Choices Flip Chart • Math and Science Flip Chart • Two-Color Counters • Home Connections Resource Guide	• Teacher's Treasure Book • Oral Language Development Card 24 • Rhymes and Chants Flip Chart • Concept Big Book 2 • Photo Library CD-ROM • Numeral Cards • Making Good Choices Flip Chart • Dog Puppet 1 and 2 • Home Connections Resource Guide	• Teacher's Treasure Book • Flannel Board Characters for "The Ram in the Chile Patch" • ABC Big Book • Math and Science Flip Chart • Dog Puppet 1 and 2 • Farm Animal Counters • Numeral Cards • Two-Color Counters • Home Connections Resource Guide	• Teacher's Treasure Book • Rhymes and Chants Flip Chart • Photo Library CD-ROM • *Rush Hour* Big Book • Two-Color Counters • Making Good Choices Flip Chart • Oral Language Development Card 24 • Home Connections Resource Guide

Other Materials

DAY 1	DAY 2	DAY 3	DAY 4	DAY 5
• 3 shoeboxes • several images of items that begin with the sounds /l/, /t/, /s/ • elastic bandages, wash cloth • toy cars, trucks, boats, trains, planes • rocks, soil sand • drawing paper, crayons	• toy cars • homemade game board with path of 6 rocks across stream • cardboard turtles with T on shells • CD Player	• cardboard outlines of people (6"–8") • clay • cardboard outline of tree with 3 branches • paper leaves, crayons • 1 image each of sock, ladder, tent • tape, scissors • ping pong balls • cardboard outlines of buildings in community; newsprint	• drawing paper • crayons • audio recorder • book about make-believe animals • Numeral Train gameboards • number cubes	• toy telephones • cardboard dominoes with images of words beginning with /t/, /l/, /s/ sounds • masking tape • images of items beginning with /t/, /ē/, /ĕ/ sounds • marching music, empty coffee cans, cardboard tubes • paper, crayons • books and photos of parades

Home Connection

DAY 1	DAY 2	DAY 3	DAY 4	DAY 5
Invite children to tell their families what they learned about earth materials. Send home the following materials: Weekly Family Letter, Home Connections Resource Guide, pp. 31–32	Encourage children to count things around their house with their families, such as chairs and tables.	Have children tell their families what they learned about different buildings in the community.	Encourage children to tell their families what they learned about playing with children who are different than they are. Storybook 7, Home Connections Resource Guide, pp. 105–108	Tell children to show their families how they learned to keep the beat to marching music.

Assessment

As you observe children throughout the week, you may fill out an Anecdotal Observational Record Form to document an individual's progress toward a goal or signs indicating the need for developmental or medical evaluation. You may also choose to select work for each child's portfolio. The Anecdotal Observational Record Form and Weekly Assessment rubrics are available in the assessment section of DLMExpressOnline.com.

More Literature Suggestions

• **Whose Tools Are These?** by Sharon Katz Cooper
• **Lola at the Library/Lola en la biblioteca** by Anna McQuinn
• **Fireman Small** by Wong Herbert Yee
• **Nuestro autobús** por Suzanne Bloom
• **Quiero ser camionero** por Dan Liebman

Daily Planner

	DAY 1	DAY 2
Let's Start the Day **Language Time** `large group`	**Opening Routines** p. 64 **Morning Read Aloud** p. 64 **Oral Language and Vocabulary** p. 64 Nurse **Phonological Awareness** p. 64 Matching Initial Sounds	**Opening Routines** p. 70 **Morning Read Aloud** p. 70 **Oral Language and Vocabulary** p. 70 Action Words **Phonological Awareness** p. 70 Review Initial Sounds
Center Time `small group`	**Focus On:** **ABC Center** p. 65 **Pretend and Learn Center** p. 65	**Focus On:** **Creativity Center** p. 71 **Library and Listening Center** p. 71
Circle Time **Literacy Time** `large group`	**Read Aloud** *Rush Hour*/*Hora pico* p. 66 **Learn About Letters and Sounds:** **Review Letters** *Tt* and *Ee* p. 66	**Read Aloud** *Rush Hour*/*Hora pico* p. 72 **Learn About Letters and Sounds: Review the Letters** *Tt* and *Ee* p. 72
Math Time `large group`	**Numeral 6** p. 67 **How Many Now?** p. 67	**Sing "Little Bird"** p. 73
Social and Emotional Development `large group`	**We All Need to Help Each Other!** p. 67	**Being Helpful** p. 73
Content Connection `large group`	**Science:** **Oral Language and Academic Vocabulary** p. 68 **Observe and Investigate** p. 68	**Math:** **My Community** p. 74
Center Time `small group`	**Focus On:** **Math and Science Center** p. 69 **Purposeful Play** p. 69	**Focus On:** **Math and Science Center** p. 75 **Purposeful Play** p. 75
Let's Say Good-Bye `large group`	**Read Aloud** p. 69 **Writing** p. 69 **Home Connection** p. 69	**Read Aloud** p. 75 **Writing** p. 75 **Home Connection** p. 75

Focus Question
How does a community help me?
¿Cómo me ayuda una comunidad?

DAY 3

Opening Routines p. 76
Morning Read Aloud p. 76
Oral Language and Vocabulary
p. 76 Parades
Phonological Awareness
p. 76 Recognizing Same Initial Sounds

Focus On:
Construction Center p. 77
ABC Center p. 77

Read Aloud *In the Community/En la comunidad* p. 78
Learn About Letters and Sounds:
Review the Letters *Tt* and *Ee* p. 78

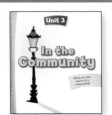

Let's Jump! p. 79

Caring for Others p. 79

Social Studies:
Oral Language and Academic Vocabulary
p. 80 Buildings in the Community
Understand and Participate
p. 80 Filling Community Buildings

Focus On:
Construction Center p. 81
Purposeful Play p. 81

Read Aloud p. 81
Writing p. 81
Home Connection p. 81

DAY 4

Opening Routines p. 82
Morning Read Aloud p. 82
Oral Language and Vocabulary
p. 82 Animals that Help
Phonological Awareness
p. 82 Review Initial Sounds

Focus On:
Writer's Center p. 83
Library and Listening Center p. 83

Read Aloud "The Ram in the Chile Patch"/"El carnero en el sembrado de chiles" p. 84
Learn About Letters and Sounds: Review the Letter *Ee* p. 84

Numeral 8 p. 85
Sing "Little Bird" p. 85

Being Empathetic p. 85

Math:
Numeral Train Choice p. 86

Focus On:
Math and Science Center p. 87
Purposeful Play p. 87

Read Aloud p. 87
Writing p. 87
Home Connection p. 87

DAY 5

Opening Routines p. 88
Morning Read Aloud p. 88
Oral Language and Vocabulary
p. 88 Help in the Community
Phonological Awareness
p. 88 Review Initial Sounds

Focus On:
Pretend and Learn Center p. 89
Creativity Center p. 89

Read Aloud *Rush Hour/Hora pico* p. 90
Learn About Letters and Sounds:
Review Letters *Tt* and *Ee* p. 90

How Many Now? p. 91

Being Responsible in School p. 91

Music and Movement:
Oral Language and Academic Vocabulary
p. 92 Talk About Parades
Explore and Express
p. 92 March in a Band

Focus On:
Writer's Center p. 93
Purposeful Play p. 93

Read Aloud p. 93
Writing p. 93
Home Connection p. 93

Learning Centers

Math and Science Center

Weighing Rocks
Children use a scale to weigh objects, p. 69.

Places
Children count objects they see in scenes, p. 75.

Match the Card
Children match counters and numeral cards, p. 87.

Mailing Letters
Supply old pieces of mail and a "mail" box. Children pull a Numeral Card (1–8) from a pile and "mail" that many letters into the mail slot.

Number Tree 2
Children use the Number Tree to identify numbers and find them on the tree. One child draws a Numeral Card from a pile and holds it up as a partner identifies it and finds it on the tree.

ABC Center

Sorting Sounds
Children sort photos based on initial sounds, p. 65.

Matching Initial Sounds
Children use a story to match initial sounds, p. 77.

Pick a Letter
Put letter cutouts or magnetic letters in a paper bag. Have each child draw out a letter, say the letter sound, and say two words that start with that sound. Then have them pass the bag to another child.

Start the Same
Children pull cards with an image of a child doing an activity, such as swimming or jumping, from a box. Then they say two names that begin with the same sound as the activity. For example, they could say: *Sam and Sally swim* or *Jen and Jamal jump.*

Creativity Center

Producing /t/ Words
Children play a turtle game, p. 71.

Playing with Dominoes
Children play letter dominoes, p. 89.

Workers' Tools
Children make tools out of various art supplies, such as cardboard tubes, flexible tubing, cardboard, and so on. Then they take turns holding their tool while others identify the worker who uses the tool.

Big Picture
Enlarge a photo of a community scene and cut it into squares. Children take one square and use art materials to transfer what they see in the photo onto a large square of paper. Assemble the original image and the children's larger image and compare the two.

Library and Listening Center

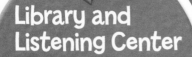

Act Out a Book
Children act out a book that's full of movement, p. 71.

Listening to a Story
Children listen to a story about imaginary animals, p. 83.

Soup Ingredients
Children listen to "Stone Soup" on CD and then compare the things that go in to the stone soup with soup that they eat.

Be Safe
Children look through books and identify pictures that show children being safe and acting in a safe way.

Construction Center

Building a Parade
Children make figures to use in a parade, p. 77.

Role-Playing in the Community
Children design a structure to honor community helpers. Then they build a miniature structure out of modeling clay or a large structure out of building materials, p. 81.

Shape Buildings
Children choose a shape and use only that shape to build something in their school community.

Building Roads
Children build a road out of materials in the center. They use a box as their house and build a road from their "house" to their friend's "house," the "school," the "library," and so on.

Writer's Center

Make-Believe Animals
Children draw pictures of imaginary animals, p. 83.

My Parade
Children draw a pictures of themselves in a parade, p. 93.

Left to Right
Supply sheets of paper, folded in the middle with a yellow star on the left side. Children draw a picture of community worker's tool under the star and a community worker on the right side. Then they write a label from left (the tool) to right (the worker).

Natural Letters
Provide small nature items, such as pine needles, leaves, and so on. Children write their name on a card, with assistance if needed. Then they build "nature letters" by gluing items on top of the letters.

Pretend and Learn Center

Role-Play a Nurse
Children pretend to be nurse and patient, p. 65.

Calling Community Helpers
Children pretend to phone community helpers, p. 89.

Moving
Each child in a small group tells about one person they know who works in a community, such as a baker, car mechanic, teacher, and so on. Then they work together to act out one community where all these helpers work together.

Helping Out
Provide props for role-playing raking leaves or shoveling snow. Children act out helping another person in their neighborhood community.

DAY 1

Let's Start the Day

Focus Question

How does a community help me?

¿Cómo me ayuda una comunidad?

 Learning Goals

Social and Emotional Development
• Child shows empathy and care for others.

Language and Communication
• Child demonstrates an understanding of oral language by responding appropriately.

Vocabulary

bed	cama	healthy	saludable
helps	ayudar	nurse	enfermera
office	oficina		

Differentiated Instruction

 Extra Support
Phonological Awareness
If...children can't identify words in the sentence with the same initial sound, **then...** narrow their choice to two words.

Enrichment
Oral Language and Vocabulary
Challenge children to talk about other kinds of helpers at school, such as crossing guards.

Accommodations for 3's
Phonological Awareness
If...children can't identify words with the same initial sound, **then...**have children repeat the initial sounds of *letter, teachers,* and *school.*

Opening Routines and Transition Tips

For **Opening Routines** and **Transition Tips** turn to pages 178–181 and visit DLMExpressOnline.com for more ideas.

Read **"Frog Went a-Courtin"/"El sapo fue a cortejar"** from the *Teacher's Treasure Book,* page 213, for your morning Read Aloud.

Language Time

large group — 15 minutes

Social and Emotional Development Encourage children to be aware of their classmates' feelings.

Oral Language and Vocabulary

✓ **Can children use words to talk about people who help them in school?**

✓ **Can children think of times when they made a classmate feel better?**

Nurse Begin a discussion about a nurse. Explain that some schools have a nurse in the building to take care of children who don't feel well. Ask: *Who has been to see a nurse? How did she help you? Did she make you feel better? Have you ever helped a classmate feel better?* ¿Quiénes han necesitado de los servicios de la enfermera de la escuela? ¿De qué manera los ayudó? ¿Los hizo sentir mejor? ¿Alguna vez han ayudado a un amigo a sentirse mejor?

● Display *Oral Language Card 23.* Point out the nurse and ask what she's doing. Then follow the suggestions on the back of the card.

Oral Language Development Card 23

Phonological Awareness

✓ **Can children identify words with the same initial sound?**

Matching Initial Sounds Display the *Rhymes and Chants Flip Chart,* page 14. Recite "Community Workers." Then say: *Listen for a word that begins with the /l/ sound in this sentence: Who can bring us cards and letters? What word starts with the /l/ sound?* ¿Qué palabra empieza con el sonido /l/? Then read the last line of the second stanza. Read: **Lifeguards help us in water and sun!** and ask: *Do you hear a word that matches the beginning /l/ sound in letter? Yes! Lifeguards matches the beginning /l/ sound in letter.* ¿Escucharon alguna palabra que empiece con /l/, como letter? ¡Sí! Lifeguards también empieza con /l/. Repeat the process with the sound /t/, using the words *take* and *trash.*

ELL Point to each helper in the illustration and follow this routine. Say: *This is a mail carrier.* Have children repeat the sentence. Ask: *Who is this?* After they respond, say: *Yes, this is a mail carrier. He helps bring you letters.*

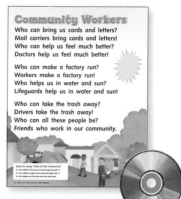

Rhymes and Chants Flip Chart, page 14

Center Time

▶ **Center Rotation** Center Time includes teacher-guided activities and independent activities. Refer to the **Learning Centers** on pages 62–63 for independent activity ideas.

small group 60–90 minutes

Learning Goals

Social and Emotional Development
• Child shows empathy and care for others.

Language and Communication
• Child begins and ends conversations appropriately.

Emergent Literacy: Reading
• Child produces words with the same beginning sound.

ABC Center

 Encourage partners to help one another with the activity.

 Check that children can match pictures according to initial sounds.

Materials 3 shoeboxes with a "mail slot" cut into the top; at least 12 pictures of items with intial sounds of /l/, /t/, and /s/ from the *Photo Library CD-ROM*

Sorting Sounds Paste two pictures with the same initial sound to each "mailbox." Label them with the appropriate initial sound. Ask: **What community worker helps people by delivering letters that are mailed to them?** *¿Qué personas que trabajan en la comunidad ayudan a las personas a enviar cartas por correo?* One at a time, point to each picture on a "mailbox." Name the object in the picture, emphasizing the initial sound.

● Have partners work together to name the additional objects, emphasizing initial sounds.

● Have partners take turns matching each picture to its corresponding mailbox and "mailing" it.

Center Tip

If...children have trouble matching items to boxes, **then...**help them name each of the items pictured.

Differentiated Instruction

✋ **Extra Support**
ABC Center
If...children have difficulty sorting pictures according to three initial sounds, **then...**have them sort only two sounds at a time.

⭐ **Enrichment**
ABC Center
Invite children to look in advertising flyers or magazines to find additional examples of words that begin with the target sounds. Help them cut out these examples and add them to the collection.

💜 **Special Needs**
Cognitive Challenges
If...children have difficulty role-playing both the nurse and the patient, **then...**play the role of the patient yourself and have the child play the part of the nurse.

Pretend and Learn Center

 Listen for conversation that indicates that children understand what nurses do.

Materials elastic bandages, washcloth

Role-Play a Nurse Relate what a nurse does with children by having them discuss their personal experiences. Set up a nurse's office in the center. Have children take turns pretending to be either the nurse or a child in need of help.

● Have sick or injured children tell the nurse why they need help.

● Have the nurse use some supplies to fix the problems. Model how the nurse might use words and actions that show she is caring and empathetic.

Center Tip

If...children have difficulty acting out these roles, **then...**show them Oral Language Development Card 23 again and discuss what they see in the picture.

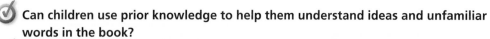

Circle Time

Focus Question

How does a community help me?

¿Cómo me ayuda una comunidad?

✓ Learning Goals

Language and Communication
• Child demonstrates an understanding of oral language by responding appropriately.

Emergent Literacy: Reading
• Child names most upper- and lowercase letters of the alphabet.
• Child identifies the letter that stands for a given sound.

Vocabulary

community	comunidad	rush hour	hora pico
rushing	apurarse	subways	metro
taxis	taxis	trains	trenes
trolleys	tranvías	tunnels	túneles
whizzing	zumbido		

Differentiated Instruction

 Extra Support

Learn About Letters and Sounds
If...children have a difficult time following the routine, **then**...guide them through each of the steps by asking questions such as: **What letter did you find? What is the sound of that letter? Can you think of a word that begins with that sound?** *¿Qué letra encontraron? ¿Cuál es el sonido de esa letra? ¿Se les ocurre alguna palabra que comience con ese sonido?*

⭐ **Enrichment**

Read Aloud
Challenge children to draw pictures of how they get to school—on foot, by car, or by bus. Help them label their pictures.

♥ **Special Needs**

Cognitive Challenges
Read the book in two parts—the morning rush hour and the evening rush hour. Briefly review the first half of the book before beginning the second half, asking children to tell what they remember about the morning rush hour.

Literacy Time

 large group | 15 minutes

📖 Read Aloud

✓ Can children use prior knowledge to help them understand ideas and unfamiliar words in the book?

✓ Do children ask questions if they don't understand words or ideas?

Build Background Tell children that you will be reading a book about rush hour in a community. Explain that rush hour is the time of day when many people go to work and school in the morning and come home from work and school in the late afternoon or evening.

● Ask: **Do most people go to work and school in the morning or in the evening?** *¿La mayoría de las personas va al trabajo de mañana o de noche?*

Listen for Enjoyment Display *Rush Hour* and read the title aloud. Explain that *rush* is another word for *hurry* and many people hurry to and from work or school in the morning and evening, so those times are called *rush hour*.

● Conduct a picture walk of the book. Have children name the different vehicles. Ask: **Why are the streets crowded during rush hour?** *¿Por qué las calles están repletas a la hora pico?*

● Read the book aloud. Pause often and encourage children to tell something they know about from what was read. (For example, a child might say, *My daddy rides a bus to work.*)

Respond to the Story Discuss the story. Review the illustrations and guide children to think about the community helpers who help people get to work and school. Ask: **What community helpers help you get to school safely?** *¿Qué personas que trabajan en la comunidad los ayudan a llegar a la escuela de manera segura?* (bus drivers, crossing guards)

💡 **TIP** Make sure children know that they should raise their hands if they want to contribute to the discussion.

ELL Use toy cars, trucks, boats, trains, and airplanes to help you tell the story. When you read the name of one of these vehicles in the book, hold up the appropriate toy and ask children to name it.

Learn About Letters and Sounds

✓ Can children recognize letters *Tt* and *Ee* and identify the focal sounds associated with them?

Review Letters *Tt* and *Ee* Display the *ABC Picture Card* for *Tt* and review that it stands for the sound /t/. Say: **/t/ /t/ two; /t/ /t/ toad.** Then display the letter *Ee* and review that it stands for the sound /ē/, as in *eagle*, and the sound /ĕ/, as in *egg*.

Rush Hour
Hora pico

ABC Picture Card

large group 15 minutes

Building Blocks

Online Math Activity

Introduce Party Time 2: Count Placemats. Have children help you solve a few problems. Have each child complete Party Time 2 this week.

Math and Science Flip Chart, page 24

large group 15 minutes

Making Good Choices Flip Chart, page 14

Math Time

Observe and Investigate

✓ **Can children recognize the numeral 6?**

Numeral 6 Explore the numeral 6 with children. Display the *Math and Science Flip Chart,* page 24. Ask: ***Where is the numeral 6? What are there six of on the chart?*** *¿Dónde está el número seis? ¿Dónde está el número seis en la tabla?* Say: ***This is how we make a 6.*** *Así hacemos un 6.* Practice drawing the number 6 in the air.

How Many Now? Have children play a game matching Numeral Cards (*Teacher's Treasure Book,* page 510) and counters.

✓ **Can children count items accurately?**

- Show children a number of counters. Say: ***How many counters are there?*** *¿Cuántas fichas hay?* Once children say the correct number, show the corresponding Numeral Card.

- Add one counter. Say: ***How many counters are there now?*** *¿Cuántas fichas hay ahora?* Check the answer by counting the counters together. Show the matching card.

- Repeat the process, adding and removing different numbers of counters.

✖✖✖ Social and Emotional Development

Making Good Choices

✓ **Are children aware of classmates' feelings and want to comfort them?**

✓ **Do children voluntarily help in the classroom?**

We All Need to Help Each Other! Discuss the importance of being aware of other people's feelings and ways to help others. Display the *Making Good Choices Flip Chart,* page 14.

- Ask: ***Why is the girl on the floor crying?*** *¿Por qué está llorando la niña que está en el piso?* Help children see that someone ripped a picture the girl drew.

- Ask: ***What are the other children doing? How do you think that makes her feel? Would you like to have a classmate like that?*** *¿Qué hacen los otros niños? ¿Creen que eso la hace sentir mejor? ¿Les gustaría tener amigos así?*

- Ask how other children in the illustration are being helpful.

ELL Point to items in the picture and name them. Have children repeat the words. If there are similar objects in your classroom, point to them and ask children to name them.

Learning Goals

Social and Emotional Development
- Child participates in a variety of individual, small- and large-group activities.
- Child shows empathy and care for others.

Mathematics
- Child counts 1–10 concrete objects correctly.
- Child recognizes and names numerals 0 through 9.

Vocabulary

caring	comprensivo	count	contar
feelings	sentimientos	helpful	servicial
how many	cuántos	six	seis
upset	molestar		

Differentiated Instruction

✋ **Extra Support**

Observe and Investigate

If...children have trouble adding or subtracting totals of counters, **then...**count slowly with them.

⭐ **Enrichment**

Observe and Investigate

Challenge children with higher numbers of counters, up to 10.

Accommodations for 3's

Observe and Investigate

If...children have difficulty drawing a 6 in the air, **then...**have them trace a 6 on their desk.

Differentiated Instruction

✋ **Extra Support**

Oral Language and Academic Vocabulary
If...children have difficulty seeing details on the *Math and Science Flip Chart*, **then...**demonstrate how to focus the hand lens on the details.

⭐ **Enrichment**

Oral Language and Academic Vocabulary
Explain to children that the words *earth materials* refer to natural things that are found in the earth or the ground. Examples of earth materials are rocks, sand, and soil.

💜 **Special Needs**

Vision Loss
If...children have difficulty comparing the earth materials, **then...**have them use descriptive words that refer to the sense of touch, such as *soft, hard, smooth, rough, heavy,* and *light.*

Science Time

  large group 20 minutes

Personal Safety Skills As children are using their hands to observe the earth materials, explain why they should avoid touching their face, their eyes, or other students. Have them wash their hands immediately after the activity.

Oral Language and Academic Vocabulary

✓ **Can children identify uses of earth materials?**

Point to the people working in the *Math and Science Flip Chart*, page 23. Say: ***These people are building a wall, making a garden, and building a house.*** *Estas personas están construyendo una pared, haciendo un jardín y construyendo una casa.*

Point to the different earth materials and have children identify them as rock, soil, or sand. Say: ***Plants need healthy soil to grow.*** *Las plantas necesitan un suelo saludable para crecer.*

• Guide children to see that earth materials are used to make bricks, concrete, and other building materials for houses and other constructions.

ELL Tell children that the word *build* is an action word that means *make.* Say: ***People build houses.*** Point to the landscaper building a wall. Say: ***This man is building a wall.***

Use the Sequence Cards set "Building a Home" as a visual reference.

Observe and Investigate

✓ **Can children identify differences among earth materials?**

Display rocks, soil, and sand. Tell children that the materials can all be found in the earth. Discuss where children might find each material around the school or in the community.

• Hold up a Jumbo Hand Lens and tell children that a hand lens can be used to see small details of objects. Allow children to use hand lenses to examine the different earth materials.

• Encourage children to touch the earth materials and compare how they feel as well as how they look. Discuss the differences among the earth materials.

💡 **TIP** Tell children they will have another chance to use the materials in the Math and Science Center.

Math and Science Flip Chart, page 23

Center Time

  small group · 30 minutes

▶ **Center Rotation** Center Time includes teacher-guided activities and independent activities. Refer to the **Learning Centers** on pages 62–63 for independent activity ideas.

Math and Science Center

☑ **Can children identify heavier and lighter rocks?**

Materials a variety of rocks, Primary Balance Scale, Connecting Cubes, drawing paper, crayons

Weighing Rocks Demonstrate how to put a rock on one side of the balance and add Connecting Cubes to the other side until the balance is level. Say: ***When the two sides of the balance are at the same level, the Connecting Cubes are as heavy as the rock.*** *Cuando ambos lados de la balanza están equilibrados, quiere decir que cubos conectables pesan lo mismo que las rocas.*

- Have children work in pairs or small groups to balance three rocks of different weights. Have children compare the number of Connecting Cubes needed to balance each rock.

- Have children divide a sheet of drawing paper into three columns and draw a rock in each column. Have children label each column with a representation of the number of Connecting Cubes used to balance each rock, using either a number or a drawing.

Center Tip

If...children have difficulty counting the Connecting Cubes, **then...** encourage them to find a different way to compare the amount.

☑ Learning Goals

Emergent Literacy: Writing
- Child uses scribbles, shapes, pictures, symbols, and letters to represent language.

Mathematics
- Child compares the length, height, weight, volume (capacity), area of people or objects.

Science
- Child observes, identifies, explores, describes, and compares earth materials (such as rocks, soil, sand, water) and their uses.

Writing

Remind children of the role-play activity they did when they pretended to be the nurse or the child who was not feeling well. Tell children to draw a picture of something a nurse might do to help children in their school. Write the word *nurse* and have children copy the letters to the best of their ability.

Purposeful Play

☑ **Observe children playing safely outdoors and handling earth materials appropriately.**

Challenge children to identify rocks, soil, sand, and other earth materials outdoors, and to use them to build with.

Let's Say Good-Bye

 large group · 15 minutes

 Read Aloud Revisit "Frog Went a-Courtin"/"El sapo fue a cortejar" for your afternoon Read Aloud. Remind children to listen for the /t/ sound at the beginning of words in the story.

 Home Connection Refer to the Home Connections activities listed in the Resources and Materials chart on page 59. Remind children to tell their families about how the community helps them. Sing the "Good-Bye Song"/ "Hora de ir a casa" as children prepare to leave.

Let's Start the Day

Focus Question

How does a community help me?

¿Cómo me ayuda una comunidad?

> **Opening Routines and Transition Tips**
> For **Opening Routines** and **Transition Tips** turn to pages 178–181 and visit DLMExpressOnline.com for more ideas.
>
> Read **"Helpful Friends"/**"Amigos útiles"** from the *Teacher's Treasure Book,* page 168, for your morning Read Aloud.

Language Time

 large group 🕐 **15 minutes**

Social and Emotional Development Ask children what their rules are for listening and speaking.

Oral Language and Vocabulary

 Can children use and understand action words that describe what people and vehicles do?

Action Words Talk about action words. Say: ***Let me see you jump. Now let me see you wave.*** *Muéstrenme cómo saltan. Ahora muéstrenme cómo saludan.* Point out that you used two different action words to tell children how to move.

- Say words from *Rush Hour* that name actions that people do, such as: *yawn, splash* (water), *brush* (teeth), and *comb* (hair). Repeat the words and have children act out the words.

- Say other verbs from the story that name actions that cars do, such as: *back up, whiz, and zip.* Repeat the words and have children act them out, pretending to be cars.

ELL Use toy cars to demonstrate the actions of *backing up, zipping,* and *whizzing.* Tell children to move the cars the same way as they *zip, zip, zip* and *whiz, whiz, whiz.*

Rush Hour
Hora pico

Phonological Awareness

 Can children recognize words with the same initial sounds?

Review Initial Sounds Use the Dog Puppets to play a game. Have Dog Puppet 1 say a word with the initial sound /t/, such as *turtle.* Then have Dog Puppet 2 ask: **Which word begins with the same sound—table or chair?** *¿Qué palabra comienza con el mismo sonido:* table *o* chair? Repeat the activity with words that begin with the sounds /ē/ and /ĕ/.

Learning Goals

Language and Communication
• Child names and describes actual or pictured people, places, things, actions, attributes, and events.

Vocabulary

jiggling	brincar
jumping	saltar
whizzing	zigzaguear
zipping	zumbar

Differentiated Instruction

✋ **Extra Support**

Phonological Awareness
If...children find it difficult to identify the word with the same initial sound, **then...**have them listen to a word the puppet says and then repeat the initial sound.

⭐ **Enrichment**

Phonological Awareness
Challenge children to say another word that begins with the same sound as the word Dog 1 says.

♥ **Special Needs**

Cognitive Challenges
If...there are too many unfamiliar words on a page, **then...**paraphrase the text so children can understand the main idea of the story.

Center Time

▶ **Center Rotation** Center Time includes teacher-guided activities and independent activities. Refer to the **Learning Centers** on pages 62–63 for independent activity ideas.

small group 60–90 minutes

Learning Goals

Social and Emotional Development
• Child shows empathy and care for others.

Language and Communication
• Child names and describes actual or pictured people, places, things, actions, attributes, and events.

Emergent Literacy: Reading
• Child produces words with the same beginning sound.

Creativity Center | Center Tip

☑ **Look for examples of how children help each other.**

Materials small cardboard turtles with the letter *T* printed on their shells, homemade game board with path of six rocks across a stream

Producing /t/ Words Have partners play *Turtle Time*. Give each child a turtle. Have children place the turtles on the edge of the stream.

● Have players take turns saying words that begin with the /t/ sound, such as *turtle* and *time*.

● When a player says a /t/ word, he or she moves his or her turtle to a rock in the stream. Players see if they can think of enough words to move their turtles to the other side of the stream. Encourage players to help one another think of words.

Center Tip

If...children have difficulty thinking of words that begin with /t/, **then...**let them use a picture dictionary.

Library and Listening Center | Center Tip

☑ **Look to see and acknowledge those children who can focus their attention on the recording and not be distracted by other activities in the classroom.**

☑ **Do children understand how words name different actions?**

Materials *Rush Hour* Big Book and *Listening Library* CD, CD player

Act Out a Book

● As children listen to the story, have them act out each action word as it is introduced.

● After they listen to the story, ask children to draw a picture of themselves acting out one of the action words from the story.

Center Tip

If...children have trouble recognizing action words, **then...** occasionally pause the CD player after an action word and have them act it out.

Differentiated Instruction

 Extra Support

Library and Listening Center
If...a child needs help understanding the story vocabulary, **then...**pair him or her with a child who has mastered the vocabulary, and have them listen and act out the verbs together.

 Enrichment

Creativity Center
Challenge children to use the game to produce words with other initial sounds, such as /s/ and /l/. Make snake and ladybug game pieces for them to use.

Accommodations for 3's

Creativity Center
If...it is too difficult for children to think of six words, **then...**modify the game board to show only three or four rocks.

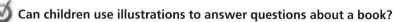

Focus Question

How does a community help me?

¿Cómo me ayuda una comunidad?

Emergent Literacy: Reading

• Child independently engages in pre-reading behaviors and activities (such as, pretending to read, turning one page at a time).

• Child names most upper- and lowercase letters of the alphabet.

• Child identifies the letter that stands for a given sound.

Vocabulary

ferry	barco
taxi	taxi
rush hour	hora pico

 Extra Support

Learn About Letters and Sounds

If...children have difficulty with the game, **then...**include additional guidance by saying: Taxi *begins with /t/. If you have the letter* T, *step forward.*

 Enrichment

Learn About Letters and Sounds

Challenge children to suggest words that could be used in the game. List the words, then repeat the game using their suggestions.

Accommodations for 3's

Read Aloud

Focus children's attention on the cover illustration. Ask children to name the vehicles they see.

Literacy Time

 large group · 15 minutes

📖 Read Aloud

✔ **Can children use illustrations to answer questions about a book?**

✔ **Do children know to read from top to bottom of a page and from front to back of a book?**

Build Background Display the cover of *Rush Hour* and tell children that you will be reading the book again. Remind them that *rush hour* refers to the busy times of day when people go to and come home from work and school.

● Ask: *How do people travel during rush hour? What do they ride in? ¿Cómo viaja la gente durante la hora pico? ¿Qué vehículos usan?*

● Ask: *Whizzing was one action word used to tell how cars move. What was another action word? Zigzaguear es una palabra de acción que usamos para describir cómo se mueven los automóviles. ¿Cuál era otra de las palabras de acción?*

Listen for Understanding Hold up the book. Ask a child to open the book and show you where you should begin to read.

● Ask these kinds of questions: *What do people do when they get up in the morning? What does this picture teach you about ferries? ¿Qué hacen las personas cuando se levantan a la mañana? ¿Qué les enseña esta fotografía sobre los barcos?*

Respond to the Story Discuss the book. Help children recall different vehicles that people use during rush hour and record their answers on a list. Read each vehicle on the list and ask: *Who has ridden in a (car, bus, subway, ferry, taxi)? ¿Quién está viajando en (carro, autobús, metro, barco, taxi)?*

💡 **TIP** Assure children that not all of them will have ridden in all the vehicles listed.

ELL Point to common items in the illustrations such as the bed, clock, coat and baby. Ask: *What is this? This is a (bed).* Have children repeat.

Learn About Letters and Sounds

✔ **Can children identify the letters Tt and Ee and the sounds /t/ and /ē/?**

Review the Letters Tt and Ee Use the *ABC Picture Cards* to review the sounds /t/ and /ē/.

● Give half of the children in the class a card with the letter *Tt* printed on it and give the other children a card with the letter *Ee* on it. Make sure each child knows what letter he or she has and what sound that letter makes.

● Explain that you are going to say words. Some will begin with /t/ and some will begin with /ē/. Tell children to hold up their letter and take one step forward when they hear a word that begins with the sound of the letter on their card.

Rush Hour
Hora pico

ABC Picture Cards

Math Time

Observe and Investigate

Sing "Little Bird" Invite children to sing a song about seven little birds. Demonstrate the finger play as you sing the song.

> One little bird with lovely feathers blue *(Show first finger.)*
> Sat beside another one, then there were two. *(Show second finger.)*
> Two little birds singing in the tree, another came to join them,
> Then there were three. *(Show third finger.)*
> Three little birds wishing there were more, along came another bird,
> Then there were four. *(Show fourth finger.)*
> Four little birds glad to be alive, found a lonely friend,
> Then there were five. *(Show fifth finger.)*
> Five little birds picking up sticks, along came a helper,
> Then there were six. *(Show fingers on one hand and a finger on the other.)*
> Six little birds with one named Kevin, another bird joined them,
> Then there were seven. *(Show one hand and two fingers on the other.)*
> Seven little birds just as happy as can be,
> Seven little birds singing songs for you and me.

🏃 Social and Emotional Development

Making Good Choices

✓ **Can children recognize empathy in others?**

Being Helpful Use Dog Puppet 1 to review the content of the *Making Good Choices Flip Chart*, page 14. First, say: **Children, tell (Dog Puppet's name) what's happening in this classroom.** *Niños, díganle a (nombre del títere) qué está sucediendo en este salón de clases.* Invite children to tell the puppet about what they observe.

- Say to the puppet: **This looks like a very nice classroom!** *¡Este salón de clases es muy bonito!* Then have the puppet respond: **What's so nice about it? Is it the toys in the classroom?** *¿Qué es lo que tiene de bonito? ¿Son los juguetes?*

- Say: **No, it's the children! They are being so nice and helpful! Look at the two girls. One seems very sad and another child is trying to make her feel better.** *¡No! ¡Son los niños! ¡Se están portando bien y están ayudando! Miren a las dos niñas que están en el piso. Una parece muy triste, y su amiga intenta que se sienta mejor.* Have the children identify other ways to be nice and helpful.

 Point to the crying girl and talk about why people cry. Ask questions such as: **When do you cry? When you cry, how are you feeling? Have you ever seen anyone cry when he or she was happy?**

Building Blocks

Online Math Activity

Introduce Memory Number 1: Counting Cards, in which children match cards with both numerals and dots. Each child should complete the activity this week.

Making Good Choices Flip Chart, page 14

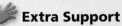 **Learning Goals**

Social and Emotional Development
- Child shows empathy and care for others.

Mathematics
- Child counts 1–10 concrete objects correctly.

Vocabulary

bird	pájaro	helpful	útil
job	trabajo	little	pequeño
seven	siete		

 Differentiated Instruction

✋ Extra Support
Social and Emotional Development
If...children have difficulty responding to the puppet, **then...**point to the flip chart to prompt them about what to tell the puppet.

🌟 Enrichment
Observe and Investigate
Challenge children to tell how many little birds would be in the tree if two more joined them.

💙 Special Needs
Delayed Motor Development
If...children have difficulty holding up their fingers to show the number, **then...**provide individual support.

Mathematics

• Child recognizes and names numerals 0 through 9.

Vocabulary

crossing guard	inspector de tránsito
house	casa
post office	oficina de correos
school	escuela
store	tienda

Differentiated Instruction

 Extra Support

Math Time

If...children have difficulty counting the images on the chart, **then...**point clearly to the numeral on the chart.

 Enrichment

Math Time

Ask children to tell about other places they like to go in their community.

Accommodations for 3's

Math Time

If...children have difficulty identifying the places on the chart, **then...**help them by telling them what people typically do in those places.

Math Time

large group · 20 minutes

 Can children recognize numbers on the chart?

My Community Invite children to talk about their community. Ask them about the places they often go in their community.

● Display the *Math and Science Flip Chart,* page 24. Ask: *Which of these do you recognize? ¿Reconocen algo?* Allow children time to discuss the people and places pictured: crossing guard, house, post office, store, and school.

● Ask: *How many post offices are there? ¿Cuántas oficinas de correos hay allí?* Allow children time to count the post offices. Point to the numeral 8 on the chart and ask: I**s *this the correct number? Look carefully, in case I make a mistake.*** (yes) *¿Es el número correcto? Miren atentamente, por si cometo un error.*

● Then ask: *How many schools are on the chart? ¿Cuántas escuelas hay en el rotafolio?* Allow children time to count the schools. Point to the numeral 7 on the chart and ask: I**s *this the correct number? Look carefully, in case I make a mistake.*** (no) *¿Es el número correcto? Miren atentamente, por si cometo un error.*

● Repeat with the other images on the chart.

ELL Explain to children that a post office is a place where people go to send letters and packages. Tell them that a crossing guard is a person who stops cars and helps children cross the street. Help them with other unknown vocabulary.

Math and Science Flip Chart, page 24

Center Time

▶ **Center Rotation** Center Time includes teacher-guided activities and independent activities. Refer to the **Learning Centers** on pages 62–63 for independent activity ideas.

small group   30 minutes

Math and Science Center

☑ Encourage children to use counters on each scene to count the items in the scene.

Materials Two-Color Counters, *Rush Hour* Big Book

Places Provide several counters for children. Tell children to turn to a page and count the number of things they see, such as cars or buses.

● Say: **Look at this place. How many (items) do you see in this place?**
Observen este lugar. ¿Cuántas cosas ven en estos lugares?

● Instruct children to place the counters over the scenes to represent the number of items counted.

Center Tip

If...children have difficulty counting items in the scenes, **then...**have them choose an item and count the items with them.

✓ Learning Goals

Social and Emotional Development
• Child initiates interactions with others in work and play situations.
• Child shows empathy and care for others.

Emergent Literacy: Writing
• Child uses scribbles, shapes, pictures, symbols, and letters to represent language.

Mathematics
• Child counts 1–10 concrete objects correctly.

Purposeful Play

☑ Do children show empathy towards others?

☑ Do children welcome others to join an activity?

Children choose an open center for free playtime. Encourage children to tell stories about their scenes. Suggest that as they play and talk, they should make sure that they don't hurt anyone's feelings. Encourage them to treat their classmates the way they like to be treated.

✏ Writing

Help children come up with a list of the different kinds of vehicles that people use during rush hour. Then have children draw one of the vehicles. Have them write the name of the vehicle by copying any letters they know. Ask children to come up with a sound that the vehicle makes. Encourage them to write letters that create that sound. Display finished work in the room.

Let's Say Good-Bye

large group   15 minutes

 Read Aloud Revisit "Helpful Friends"/"Amigos útiles" for your afternoon Read Aloud. Have children tell you where to start the story and what to do at the end of each page.

 Home Connection Refer to the Home Connections activities listed in the Resources and Materials chart on page 59. Remind children to tell their families how the community helps them. Sing the "Good-Bye Song"/"Hora de ir a casa" as children prepare to leave.

Let's Start the Day

Focus Question

How does a community help me?

¿Cómo me ayuda una comunidad?

✓ Learning Goals

Language and Communication
• Child demonstrates an understanding of oral language by responding appropriately.
• Child uses oral language for a variety of purposes.

Emergent Literacy: Reading
• Child produces words with the same beginning sound.

Vocabulary

balloon	globo	celebrate	celebrar
flag	bandera	march	marchar
parade	desfile	proud	orgulloso
uniform	uniforme		

Differentiated Instruction

✋ Extra Support

Phonological Awareness
If...children have difficulty identifying words with the same initial sound, **then...**have them listen to one word at a time and decide if it begins with the target sound.

⭐ Enrichment

Oral Language and Vocabulary
Challenge children to use the word *and* to tell about two things they see in the illustration.

Accommodations for 3's

Oral Language and Vocabulary
If...children have difficulty drawing people, **then...**tell them to draw the balloons or flags at a parade.

 Opening Routines and Transition Tips
For **Opening Routines** and **Transition Tips** turn to pages 178–181 and visit DLMExpressOnline.com for more ideas.

Read **"Why Goldfinches Are Yellow Like the Sun"/"Por qué los jilgueros son amarillos como el sol"** from the *Teacher's Treasure Book*, page 310, for your morning Read Aloud.

Language Time

 large group   15 minutes

👥 **Social and Emotional Development** Ask children to tell what the rule is when they want to answer a question.

Oral Language and Vocabulary

✓ Can children tell why communities have parades?

✓ Can children answer questions about parades?

Parades Begin a discussion about parades. Ask: *Who has seen a parade? What kinds of things did you see in the parade? Was there music in the parade? ¿Quién vio un desfile? ¿Qué cosas vieron en el desfile? ¿Había música en el desfile?*

● Display *Oral Language Development Card 24.* Point out the parade participants and the Fourth of July decorations. Then follow the suggestions on the back of the card.

ELL Use the image on *Oral Language Card 24* to reinforce the vocabulary words such as *parade, flag,* and *uniform.* Have children repeat the words. Ask: *Where is the flag?*

Phonological Awareness

✓ Can children match words that have the same initial sound?

Recognizing Same Initial Sounds Read aloud *Rhymes and Chants Flip Chart,* page 14. Say: **Letters** *and* **lifeguards** *are words in this rhyme.* **Letters** *and* **lifeguards** *begin with the /l/ sound. Which word also begins with the /l/ sound—***doctor** *or* **learn?** **Lion** *or* **tiger?** **Apple** *or* **lemon?** *¿Qué otra palabra comienza con el sonido /l/? ¿Doctor o learn? ¿Lion o tiger? ¿Apple o lemon?* Encourage students to produce another word that begins with the /l/ sound. Then repeat the activity with the words *workers/water* and *carrier/cards.*

Oral Language Development Card 24

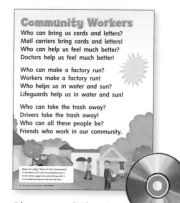

Rhymes and Chants Flip Chart, page 14

Center Time

> **Center Rotation** Center Time includes teacher-guided activities and independent activities. Refer to the **Learning Centers** on pages 62–63 for independent activity ideas.

small group · 60–90 minutes

Construction Center

☑ **Observe children participating in a conversation with their friends.**

Materials cardboard outlines of people (6"–8" tall), clay

Building a Parade Ask: *How do people look when they march in community parades?* (They are proud and happy.) *¿Cómo se ven las personas que marchan en los desfiles de la comunidad? (orgullosos y felices)*

- Have children draw clothing and faces on the figures.

- Help them stick their figures into balls of clay and arrange the people in a parade. Have them make up stories about the figures they created, drawing from personal experience with parades they have participated in or watched.

Center Tip

If...children have difficulty making up stories, **then...** encourage them to begin by making a name for a person and deciding what kind of job that person has.

ABC Center

☑ **Watch as children offer compliments to one another.**

☑ **Track children's ability to identify the sounds /s/, /l/, and /t/.**

Materials a cardboard outline of a tree with three branches, paper leaves, crayons, pictures from the *Photo Library CD-ROM*

Matching Initial Sounds Glue each of the following pictures to a branch of the tree: socks, a ladder, and a tent. Name and label the pictures, emphasizing the beginning sounds /s/, /l/, and /t/. Point out that *tree* begins with /t/ and *leaf* begins with /l/.

- On paper leaves, have children draw pictures of things that begin with the same sound as *sock, ladder,* or *tent.*

- Have children tape their pictures to the appropriate branch. Remind children to find opportunities to compliment classmates on their artwork.

Center Tip

If...children have difficulty tearing tape off a roll, **then...** hang short pieces of tape near the tree for them to use.

Learning Goals

Social and Emotional Development
- Child shows empathy and care for others.

Language and Communication
- Child begins and ends conversations appropriately.

Emergent Literacy: Reading
- Child produces words with the same beginning sound.

Differentiated Instruction

Extra Support

ABC Center

If...children have difficulty thinking of pictures to draw on leaves, **then...**make available a collection of picture dictionaries and mark the appropriate pages with sticky notes.

 Enrichment

Construction Center

Challenge children to color figures of themselves and their friends and place them next to the parade as observers.

Accommodations for 3's

Construction Center

If...it is difficult for some children to color the figures, **then...**make flags for them to color and add to the parade.

Focus Question

How does a community help me?

¿Cómo me ayuda una comunidad?

Learning Goals

Language and Communication
• Child demonstrates an understanding of oral language by responding appropriately.

Emergent Literacy: Reading
• Child names most upper- and lowercase letters of the alphabet.

• Child identifies the letter that stands for a given sound.

• Child asks and answers questions about books read aloud (such as, "Who?" "What?" "Where?").

Vocabulary

community	comunidad
construction worker	trabajadores de la construcción
healthy	saludable
neighborhood	vecindario
neighbors	vecinos
sidewalks	aceras
trash	basura
uniform	uniforme

Differentiated Instruction

 Extra Support

Learn About Letters and Sounds
If...children are having difficulty identifying the letters and sounds, **then...**name the letter and say its sound as you roll them the ball.

 Enrichment

Learn About Letters and Sounds
Invite children to play the game in small groups, using balls with the letters *Tt, Ll, Ss,* and *Ee.*

♥ **Special Needs**

Cognitive Challenges
If...children have difficulty understanding the book, **then...**paraphrase the story as you display the pictures.

Literacy Time

 Read Aloud

✓ **Can children respond appropriately to questions about community helpers?**

✓ **Do children ask questions about the pictures in the book?**

Build Background Remind children that a community is a place where people live and work. Ask children to tell what they have learned about communities. If necessary, prompt a discussion with these questions.

● Ask: **What buildings are in a community?** *¿Qué edificios hay en una comunidad?*

● Say: **Name some community helpers who keep people healthy and safe.** *¿Quiénes son algunos de los trabajadores de la comunidad que ayudan a mantener a las personas sanas y seguras?*

Listen for Understanding Display *Concept Big Book 2: In the Community* and read the title aloud. Ask children to use their own words to explain what a community is.

● Conduct a picture walk through the book. Ask children to point out buildings and community workers. Encourage children to ask questions about the pictures.

● Read the book aloud, stopping to assess children's comprehension of vocabulary words such as *neighbors, healthy, sidewalks,* and *trash.* Give child-friendly explanations of vocabulary words as needed.

Respond to the Book Discuss the book. Say: **We all live together in a community. What people in our community help us every day?** *Todos vivimos en una comunidad. ¿Qué personas de nuestra comunidad nos ayudan todos los días?*

ELL Model using complete sentences to identify items. Have children point to a familiar item in an illustration and say a related sentence, such as: **This is a car.**

Learn About Letters and Sounds

✓ **Can children identify letters and their sounds?**

Review the Letters *Tt* and *Ee* Review the letter shapes *T, t, E,* and *e* and the sounds /t/, /ē/, and /ĕ/.

● Write the letters *T, t, E,* and *e* one each on four ping pong balls. Display the letters and discuss the similarities and differences between the upper case and lower case letters.

● Sit in a circle and roll one of the labeled balls to a child. Have the child name the letter, say its sound or sounds, and say a word that begins with that sound. Have the children sitting next to that child each name another word that begin with the same sound.

In the Community
En la comunidad

Math Time

Building Blocks

Online Math Activity

Children can complete Party Time 2 and Memory Number 1 during computer time or Center Time.

Observe and Investigate

 Can children count jumps?

Let's Jump! Lead children in a game of "jumping" to a count of numbers.

● Show a Numeral Card 1 to 8. Have children say the numeral on the card.

● Then have the children jump as many times as indicated on the card. Say: **Let's jump (given number) times!** *¡Saltemos este número de veces!* after the children have said the number on the card. Count the jumps in unison.

● Repeat with a different numeral. You may wish to use other movements that the children would enjoy, such as clapping or squatting.

ELL Before you begin the activity, provide support by modeling jumping as you say the word.

✖✖✖ Social and Emotional Development

Making Good Choices

 Do children show an understanding of how to be nice to one another?

Caring for Others Ask children what makes them sad and what friends or classmates can do to cheer up one another.

● Point to the illustration on the *Making Good Choices Flip Chart,* page 14. Say: **Let's pretend that (Dog Puppet 1's name) and (Dog Puppet 2's name) are in this classroom.** *Imaginemos que el Perro 1 y el Perro 2 están en el salón de clase.* Refer to the chart scenarios and have children role-play scenes such as the following.

Dog Puppet 1: **You look sad. Why are you so sad?** *Pareces triste. ¿Por qué estás así?*

Dog Puppet 2: **I spilled some water and made a mess.** *Es que derramé el agua y está todo hecho un lío.*

Dog Puppet 1: **Do you want me to help you clean it up? Then maybe we can play. Do you want to do a puzzle with me?** *¿Quieres que te ayude a limpiar? Luego tal vez podemos jugar juntos. ¿Quieres armar un rompecabezas conmigo?*

Making Good Choices Flip Chart, page 14

Learning Goals

Social and Emotional Development
• Child shows empathy and care for others.

Mathematics
• Child counts 1–10 concrete objects correctly.
• Child recognizes and names numerals 0 through 9.

Vocabulary

cheer up	alegrar	community	comunidad
crying	llanto	feelings	sentimientos
jump	saltar	twirl	girar

Differentiated Instruction

 Extra Support

Observe and Investigate

If...children need help keeping count during the jumping game, **then...**use smaller numbers.

Enrichment

Making Good Choices

Ask children to act as one of the puppets in the role-play activity.

Accommodations for 3's

Observe and Investigate

If...children need help knowing how many times to jump, **then...**show the number of times with your fingers.

Focus Question
How does a community help me?
¿Cómo me ayuda una comunidad?

Learning Goals

Social and Emotional Development
• Child shows eagerness, curiosity, and confidence while learning new concepts and trying new things.

Language and Communication
• Child names and describes actual or pictured people, places, things, actions, attributes, and events.

Social Studies
• Child identifies common areas and features of home, school, and community.

Vocabulary

apartment	edificio de apartamentos
building	edificios
fire station	estación de bomberos
grocery store	tienda de alimentos
house	casa
next to	junto a
park	parque

Differentiated Instruction

 Extra Support
Understand and Participate
If...children don't join in the activity on their own, **then...**direct questions to them, such as: *Joe, what building should we put next to the grocery store? [Nombre], ¿qué podemos colocar junto a la tienda de alimentos?*

⭐ **Enrichment**
Understand and Participate
Challenge children to add other kinds of buildings.

Accommodations for 3's
Understand and Participate
If...building a whole neighborhood seems like an overwhelming task, **then...**help children build a neighborhood with just houses and a school.

Social Studies

large group 20 minutes

Language and Communication Skills Model how to politely listen to other's contributions and compliment them on their ideas.

Oral Language and Academic Vocabulary

☑ **Can children identify buildings in a community and create models of the buildings?**

☑ **Can children stay focused on the activity from the beginning to the end?**

Buildings in the Community Display pages 6 and 7 of *Concept Big Book 2: In the Community.*

● Ask: **What buildings are there in a community?** *¿Qué lugares recuerdan de esta comunidad?* Guide children to name a school, a store, and homes.

Understand and Participate

☑ **Can children use words to compare the size of community buildings?**

Filling Community Buildings Make cardboard outlines of buildings in your community, such as a school, several stores, a firehouse, and houses and apartment buildings. On sheets of newsprint taped together, draw appropriate community features, such as a park, a pond, and railroad tracks.

● Display the building outlines, using the words *smaller* and *larger.* Then ask: **Which one might be a house? Which one might be a school? Which one might be a store?** *¿Cuál podría ser una casa? ¿Cuál debería ser una escuela? ¿Cuál podría ser una tienda?*

● Place the school on the paper background. Say: **This is the school in our community. What building should we put next to it?** *Ésta es la escuela de nuestra comunidad. ¿Qué establecimiento deberíamos colocar junto a ella?* Continue until all the buildings have been placed. When the community is finished, ask children to talk about what happens in each building.

ELL To help children use comparison words, practice talking about *smaller* and *larger.* Display the building outlines and say: **This building is smaller than this building. Which building is smaller? Which building is larger?** Prompt children to make comparisons.

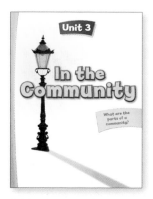

In the Community
En la comunidad

Center Time

> **Center Rotation** Center Time includes teacher-guided activities and independent activities. Refer to the **Learning Centers** on pages 62–63 for independent activity ideas.

 small group | 30 minutes

Construction Center

✓ **Observe children caring for one another's feelings as they play.**

✓ **Track children's participation in the group activity.**

Materials cardboard building shapes from the Social Studies activity, background from Day 2, people figures

Role-Playing in the Community Have children use the materials to reconstruct a community. Tell them it does not have to be the same as the community they built yesterday.

● Tell children to role-play the people in the community using the figures. Remind them to let everyone participate and not to hurt people's feelings as they play together.

● Model sentences to show how the community is helpful to the people: *I need to buy apples. I'm going into this store. An old building is on fire! Firefighters will come from the fire station!* *Necesito comprar manzanas. Voy a entrar a esta tienda. ¡Un viejo edificio está en llamas! ¡Los bomberos saldrán de la estación!*

Center Tip

If…children have difficulty beginning the activity, **then…** place a few buildings in the community for them to build around.

✓ Learning Goals

Social and Emotional Development
● Child initiates interactions with others in work and play situations.
● Child shows empathy and care for others.

Emergent Literacy: Writing
● Child uses scribbles, shapes, pictures, symbols, and letters to represent language.

Writing

Talk about the different kinds of things people would buy in the community grocery store. Have children draw a picture of something their family buys at the store. Label their pictures and have children trace the letters with colored crayons.

Purposeful Play

✓ **Observe whether or not children are being kind to one another as they play.**

Children choose an open center for free playtime. Suggest they play together, pretending that they are working in a store, a school, or a fire station.

Let's Say Good-Bye

 large group | 15 minutes

 Read Aloud Revisit "Why Goldfinches Are Yellow Like the Sun"/"Por qué los jilgueros son amarillos como el sol" for your afternoon Read Aloud. Remind children to listen for words that describe people in a community.

 Home Connection Refer to the Home Connections activities listed in the Resources and Materials chart on page 59. Remind children to tell their families about how the community helps them. Sing the "Good-Bye Song"/ "Hora de ir a casa" as children prepare to leave.

Focus Question

How does a community help me?

¿Cómo me ayuda una comunidad?

Learning Goals

Language and Communication
• Child uses oral language for a variety of purposes.

Emergent Literacy: Reading
• Child produces words with the same beginning sound.

Vocabulary

make-believe   imaginario   real   real

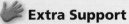

Differentiated Instruction

 Extra Support

Oral Language and Vocabulary
If...children have difficulty identifying real and make-believe characters, **then...**provide additional practice by showing them books with pictures of real and make-believe characters.

⭐ **Enrichment**

Phonological Awareness
Ask children to think of other animal names that begin with the /t/ sound.

Accommodations for 3's

Oral Language and Vocabulary
If...children cannot name things that real animals can and cannot do, **then...**ask specific questions, such as: *Can real animals run? Can they talk? Can they fly? Do they laugh? ¿Los animales reales pueden correr? ¿Hablar? ¿Pueden volar? ¿Se ríen?*

Let's Start the Day

▶ **Opening Routines and Transition Tips**
For **Opening Routines** and **Transition Tips** turn to pages 178–181 and visit DLMExpressOnline.com for more ideas.

 Read **"The Great Big Turnip"/**"El nabo gigante" from the *Teacher's Treasure Book*, page 243, for your morning Read Aloud.

large group   15 minutes

Language Time

👥 **Social and Emotional Development** Encourage children to compliment classmates on their ideas.

Oral Language and Vocabulary

✓ **Can children suggest ways that animals could help each other?**

Animals That Help Remind children that people in a community often help each other. Ask whether, in some stories, animals help each other.

● Ask: *Are these kinds of stories about real animals or make-believe animals? Why do you think that? ¿Estos tipos de cuentos son sobre animales reales o imaginarios? ¿Cómo lo saben?*

● Discuss what real animals can do and what they cannot do.

Phonological Awareness

✓ **Can children identify words with the same initial sound?**

Review Initial Sounds Tell half of the class that they are on the Tall Toad team. *Ask: What sound do you hear at the beginning of the words* tall *and* toad? *¿Qué sonido escuchan al comienzo de las palabras* tall *y* toad? Tell children to hop like a toad. Tell the other children that they are on the Easy Eagle team. *Ask: What sound do you hear at the beginning of the words* easy *and* eagle? *¿Qué sonido escuchan al comienzo de las palabras* easy *y* eagle? Tell them to flap their arms like an eagle. Say words that begin with /t/ and /ē/. Tell children to move when they hear a word that begins with the same sound as their team name.

ELL Show children pictures of a toad and an eagle and model the movements they make. Then make the motions and tell children to say *toad* or *eagle*.

Center Time

▶ **Center Rotation** Center Time includes teacher-guided activities and independent activities. Refer to the **Learning Centers** on pages 62–63 for independent activity ideas.

 small group 60–90 minutes

Learning Goals

Social and Emotional Development
• Child maintains concentration/attention skills until a task is complete.

Language and Communication
• Child uses oral language for a variety of purposes.

Emergent Literacy: Writing
• Child uses scribbles, shapes, pictures, symbols, and letters to represent language.

Writer's Center | Center Tip

☑ Observe children to see if they can write letters that represent sounds they know.

Materials drawing paper, crayons

Make-Believe Animals Remind children that many stories they hear are about make-believe animals. These animals do things that real animals can't do.

● Have children draw pictures of animals doing things that real animals cannot do.

● Ask them to say a word that tells what the make-believe animal is doing, such as *reading* or *cooking*. Tell children to write letters that they hear in the word.

Center Tip

If...children have a difficult time getting started on the activity, **then...** brainstorm ideas with the class, offering suggestions of things real animals do not do, such as play games and cook.

Differentiated Instruction

 Extra Support
Writer's Center
If...children can't sound out letters in the words they write, **then...**write the words for them and have them trace the letters.

 Enrichment
Library and Listening Center
After children have listened to the story, have them draw a picture of their favorite part of the story. Challenge them to write a word or phrase that describes their picture.

Accommodations for 3's
Writer's Center
If...children can't think of ideas for their drawings, **then...**have them browse through books to find pictures of make-believe animals doing things that real animals can't do.

Library and Listening Center | Center Tip

☑ Listen for the use of the oral vocabulary words *real* and *make-believe* as children discuss the book.

☑ Observe to see if children can sustain focus on the activity and not be distracted by other activities in the room.

Materials audio recorder, book about make-believe animals

Listening to a Story Record a book about the adventures of make-believe animals, such as *Sheep in a Jeep* by Nancy Shaw, or *Bear Snores On* by Karma Wilson.

● Have children listen to the recording.

● Have pairs of children discuss the story and talk about all the things the make-believe animals did that real animals cannot do.

Center Tip

If...you want to have children look at the book's illustration as they listen to the story, **then...** include page turning instructions in your recording.

Learning Goals

Language and Communication
• Child demonstrates an understanding of oral language by responding appropriately.

Emergent Literacy: Reading
• Child names most upper- and lowercase letters of the alphabet.
• Child identifies the letter that stands for a given sound.

Vocabulary

burro	*burro*	bushel	*fanega*
chile	*chile*	patch	*sembrado*
ram	*carnero*		

Differentiated Instruction

 Extra Support

Learn About Letters and Sounds
If...children have a difficult time remembering the directions, **then...**say a word followed by the question: *Does it begin with the same sound as* **ear** *or* **elbow**? *¿Comienza con el mismo sonido que* ear *o que* elbow?

Enrichment
Read Aloud
Invite children to retell the story in their own words using the flannel board characters.

Literacy Time

large group 15 minutes

📖 Read Aloud

☑️ **Can children recall story characters?**

Build Background Tell children that you will be telling them a story about some animals that tried to help a little boy solve a problem.

● Ask: *Do you think this story will be about make-believe animals or real animals? Why? ¿Creen que el cuento será sobre animales reales o ficticios? ¿Por qué?*

Listen for Enjoyment Tell children that they are going to listen to a story called "The Ram in the Chile Patch"/"El carnero en el sembrado de chiles" (*Teacher's Treasure Book,* page 283). Explain that a chile patch is a small garden where people grow a vegetable called chile peppers.

● Introduce the flannel board characters. Explain that a ram is a sheep, a cock is a rooster, and a burro is a donkey.

● Tell children to listen closely to find out which animal is able to help the boy solve his problem.

● Read the story aloud, using the flannel board characters to act out events.

Respond to the Story Discuss the story. Help children recall all the animals that tried to help the little boy. Ask: *How are the animals in the story like neighbors? ¿Cómo son los animales del cuento como vecinos?*

ELL Use the flannel board animals to reinforce common animal names, such as *dog, cow,* and *ant.* Display the figures and ask: *Which one is the dog?* Have children point to the dog and say: *This is the dog.*

Learn About Letters and Sounds

☑️ **Can children identify words with the initial sounds of /ē/ and /ĕ/?**

Review the Letter *Ee* Review the sounds of /ē/ and /ĕ/ by using the *ABC Big Book* pictures for *eraser* and *egg.*

● Tell children to touch their ears. Say: *The first sound you hear in* **ear** *is /ē/. El primer sonido que escuchan en* ear *es /ē/.* Tell children to touch their elbows. Say: *The first sound you hear in* **elbow** *is /ĕ/. El primer sonido que escuchan en* elbow *es /ĕ/.*

● Say words that begin with /ē/ or /ĕ/. Tell children to touch their ears when they hear words that begin with /ē/ and to touch their elbows when they hear words that begin with /ĕ/.

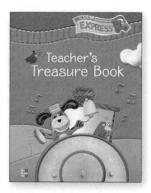

Teacher's Treasure Book, page 283

ABC Big Book

Math Time

Math and Science Flip Chart, page 24

large group 15 minutes

Observe and Investigate

✓ **Can children count to 8?**

Numeral 8 Explore the numeral 8 with children.

- Display the *Math and Science Flip Chart,* page 24. Ask: **What are there eight of on the chart? Point to the 8.** *¿De qué hay ocho en el cuadro? Señalen el 8.*

- Say: **This is how we draw an 8.** *Así dibujamos un 8.* Practice drawing the numeral 8 in the air with children.

Sing "Little Bird"

- This lesson repeats the activity introduced on Day 2. Add to the "Little Bird" finger play by adding these lines to the end of the song:

> Seven little birds think they are just great, one more came,
> And now there are eight. *(Show fingers extended on one hand and three fingers extended on the other.)*
> Eight little birds just as happy as can be,
> Eight little birds singing songs for you and me.

 Review the entire "Little Bird" finger play with children and help them match the numbers they hear with the corresponding numerals.

large group 15 minutes

✗✗✗ Social and Emotional Development

Making Good Choices

✓ **Do children understand how to be empathetic?**

Being Empathetic Use the Dog Puppets to model showing caring.

- Dog Puppet 1 says: **What's wrong with Cara? She looks very sad.** *¿Qué le pasa a Cara? Parece muy triste.*

- Dog Puppet 2 answers: **I don't know, but that's how I look when I feel sad. Come on. Let's do a puzzle together.** *No lo sé, pero así me veo yo cuando estoy triste. Vamos, armemos juntos un rompecabezas.*

- Dog Puppet 1 responds: **Let's invite Cara to do the puzzle. I think that might cheer her up.** *Invitemos a Cara a armarlo con nosotros. Tal vez eso la alegre un poco.*

- Ask: **What would you do if a classmate looked sad?** *¿Qué harías si un compañero estuviera triste?*

- Encourage children to take turns using the puppets to show other ways someone can be caring and empathetic.

Online Math Activity

Children can complete Party Time 2 and Memory Number 1 during computer time or Center Time.

✓ Learning Goals

Social and Emotional Development
- Child shows empathy and care for others.

Language and Communication
- Child begins and ends conversations appropriately.

Mathematics
- Child counts 1–10 concrete objects correctly.
- Child recognizes and names numerals 0 through 9.

Vocabulary

cheer up	alegrar	eight	ocho
great	genial	happy	alegre
sad	triste		

Differentiated Instruction

✋ **Extra Support**

Observe and Investigate
If...children have difficulty with the finger play, **then...**go slowly.

★ **Enrichment**

Making Good Choices
Invite children to use the puppets to act out their own scenes about caring for others.

♥ **Special Needs**

Hearing Impairments
If...children have difficulty following along with the song and actions, **then...**make sure they are seated closely enough to you to clearly see your face and fingers.

Learning Goals

Social and Emotional Development
• Child uses classroom materials carefully.

Language and Communication
• Child exhibits an understanding of instructional terms used in the classroom.

Mathematics
• Child demonstrates that, when counting, the last number indicates how many objects were counted.

• Child recognizes and names numerals 0 through 9.

Vocabulary

| players | jugadores | race | carrera |
| space | espacio | | |

Differentiated Instruction

 Extra Support

Math Time
If...children have difficulty making strategic choices, **then...**provide individual support.

 Enrichment

Math Time
Ask children questions about how many spaces they would need to reach the end of the game.

Accommodations for 3's

Math Time
If...children have difficulty determining whether their opponent has said the correct number, **then...**state the correct number, and ask if that's the number their opponent said.

Math Time

large group 20 minutes

Numeral Train Choice Invite children to play Numeral Train Choice. Tell them they are going to race along the game track by rolling a number cube.

● Play the game together as a whole group, then organize the class into pairs to play. Provide a game board (*Teacher's Treasure Book,* page 505), two number cubes, and two Farm Animal Counters per pair.

● Explain the rules to children. Say: **Player One, roll both cubes. Choose a number on one of the cubes. Say the number aloud.** *Jugador uno, lanza los dos cubos. Elije un número de uno de los cubos. Di el número en voz alta.*

● Then direct your attention to Player Two. Say: **Player Two, has Player One said the correct number?** *Jugador dos, ¿el jugador uno dijo el número correcto?* If so, Player One moves that many spaces. Say: **Player Two, if Player One said the correct number, say "Numeral Train!"** *Jugador dos, si el jugador uno ha dicho el número correcto, di "¡carrera de espacios!".*

● Help children understand that it might be better to choose a smaller number if it lands them on a frog space instead of a bee space. A frog action space moves a player forward; a bee space moves a player backward. Say: **If you land on a frog space, roll one number cube and move forward that many spaces. If you land on a bee space, roll one number cube and move backward that many spaces. If you land on a white space, stay there until your next turn.** *Si caen en el casillero de la rana, lancen un cubo y avancen ese número de casilleros. Si caen en el casillero de la abeja, lancen un cubo y retrocedan ese número de casilleros. Si caen en un casillero en blanco, deben esperar hasta el próximo turno.*

● Players switch roles, and the game continues until both players reach the end.

 Tell students that that the word *space* has multiple meanings. One meaning is "an area." Another meaning refers to where planets, such as Earth, are found.

Center Time

▶ **Center Rotation** Center Time includes teacher-guided activities and independent activities. Refer to the **Learning Centers** on pages 62–63 for independent activity ideas.

  small group 30 minutes

Math and Science Center

Center Tip

 Encourage children to match Numeral Cards with the correct number of counters.

Materials Numeral Cards, counters

Match the Card Display Numeral Cards and counters on a table. Ask children to choose Numeral Cards and place the correct number of counters over them.

- Say: *What is the number on the card? How many counters go on the card?* *¿Qué número dice la tarjeta? ¿Cuántas fichas deben colocarse en la tarjeta?*

- Have children choose several cards.

If...children have difficulty choosing the correct number of counters, **then...** ask yes/no questions about whether the number of counters is correct as you add counters to the card.

Purposeful Play

 Look for and acknowledge children who play responsibly and respect other people's personal space.

 Observe to see if children initiate social interactions, join in activities, and contribute to the group.

Children choose an open center for free playtime. Encourage children to work in small groups and act out the story of "The Ram in the Chile Patch." Remind children to "play act" and not really kick, push, or bite one another as they act out the story.

Let's Say Good-Bye

  large group 15 minutes

Read Aloud Revisit "The Great Big Turnip"/"El nabo gigante" for your afternoon Read Aloud. Tell children to think about what the story has to do with a neighborhood or community.

Home Connection Refer to the Home Connections activities listed in the Resources and Materials chart on page 59. Remind children to tell their families about how the community helps them. Sing the "Good-Bye Song"/ "Hora de ir a casa" as children prepare to leave.

Learning Goals

Social and Emotional Development
- Child participates in a variety of individual, small- and large-group activities.
- Child initiates interactions with others in work and play situations.

Emergent Literacy: Writing
- Child uses scribbles, shapes, pictures, symbols, and letters to represent language.

Mathematics
- Child demonstrates that, when counting, the last number indicates how many objects were counted.
- Child recognizes and names numerals 0 through 9.

Writing

Remind children that several animals in "The Ram in the Chile Patch" tried to help the boy, but it was only the tiny ant that could make the ram go away. Help children brainstorm times they were able to help someone else. Have children draw one of those times. Label children's pictures and have them copy familiar letters in the word.

DAY 5

Let's Start the Day

Focus Question

How does a community help me?

¿Cómo me ayuda una comunidad?

Learning Goals

Language and Communication
• Child uses newly learned vocabulary daily in multiple contexts.

Emergent Literacy: Reading
• Child produces words with the same beginning sound.

Vocabulary

community	comunidad
doctor	médico
driver	conductor
lifeguards	guardavidas
mail carrier	cartero

Differentiated Instruction

✋ Extra Support
Phonological Awareness
If...children can't think of a word with the same initial sound as the one in the rhyme, **then...** name two words and have children choose the one that corresponds.

⭐ Enrichment
Oral Language and Vocabulary
Challenge children to think of community helpers not mentioned in the rhyme, such as police officers, nurses, and teachers.

Accommodations for 3's
Phonological Awareness
If...children have difficulty identifying initial sounds, **then...**emphasize the initial sound of several words in the rhyme.

▶ **Opening Routines and Transition Tips**
For **Opening Routines** and **Transition Tips** turn to pages 178–181 and visit **DLMExpressOnline.com** for more ideas.

 Read **"Keiko's Good Thinking"/**"Keiko resuelve un problema" from the *Teacher's Treasure Book,* page 169, for your morning Read Aloud.

Language Time

large group   15 minutes

👪 **Social and Emotional Development** Encourage children to be good listeners when you or classmates are talking.

Oral Language and Vocabulary

✅ Can children use words about the community to describe the illustration on the *Rhymes and Chants Flip Chart?*

Help in the Community Remind children that they have been learning about ways people in the community help us. Ask: **What buildings in our community help you? What people in our community help you?** *¿Qué edificios de nuestra comunidad te ayudan? ¿Qué personas de nuestra comunidad te ayudan?*

● Display the *Rhymes and Chants Flip Chart,* page 14. Point to each community helper in the illustration and ask questions such as: **What would we do if we didn't have a police officer in our community? What would happen if no one took our trash away?** *¿Qué haríamos si no tuviéramos oficial de policía en la comunidad? ¿Qué sucedería si nadie recogiera la basura?*

ELL Use the *Rhymes and Chants Flip Chart* to revisit the words *mail carrier, doctor, worker, lifeguard,* and *driver.* To extend oral language, help children tell what each helper does in a simple sentence, such as: **Mail carriers bring letters. Lifeguards keep us safe.**

Phonological Awareness

✅ Can children produce words with matching initial sounds?

Review Initial Sounds Display the *Rhymes and Chants Flip Chart* to revisit the initial sounds of /l/, /t/, and /s/. Say *lifeguard, take,* and *sun,* emphasizing the initial sounds, and have children produce more words that begin with those sounds.

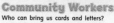
Rhymes and Chants
Flip Chart, page 14

Center Time

▶ **Center Rotation** Center Time includes teacher-guided activities and independent activities. Refer to the **Learning Centers** on pages 62–63 for independent activity ideas.

 small group 60–90 minutes

Learning Goals

Social and Emotional Development
• Child shows empathy and care for others.

Language and Communication
• Child begins and ends conversations appropriately.

Emergent Literacy: Reading
• Child produces words with the same beginning sound.

Pretend and Learn Center | Center Tip

 Look for and acknowledge children who are following everyday classroom routines.

 Observe to see if children can carry on meaningful conversations.

Materials toy telephones, *Rhymes and Chants Flip Chart,* page 14.

Calling Community Helpers Show children the illustration on the *Rhymes and Chants Flip Chart* and review the people who help them in the community.

• Have pairs of children sit together, each with a phone. One child calls a community helper and states what kind of help he or she needs, such as: *I need someone to come and get my garbage.*

• The community helper responds and states what he or she can do to help, such as: *I will drive the garbage truck to your house to get your garbage.* Have children switch roles.

Center Tip

If...children don't remember the different kinds of community helpers there are, **then...** display pictures of community helpers in the center.

Differentiated Instruction

✋ Extra Support
Creativity Center
If...children have difficulty matching pictures with the same initial sound, **then...**remind them to "stretch out" or repeat the first sound of the words to see if they match.

⭐ Enrichment
Creativity Center
When children "connect" the dominoes, matching a pair of words that share the same initial sound, encourage them to say out loud another word with that initial sound.

Accommodations for 3's
Creativity Center
If...the activity is too challenging, **then...**help children put two dominoes together, matching only one initial sound.

Creativity Center | Center Tip

 Look for children who help others play the game.

 Listen for children to identify the /t/, /l/, and /s/ sounds.

Materials picture dominoes made from pieces of cardboard and pictures of words that begin with the sounds /t/, /l/, and /s/ from the *Photo Library CD-ROM*

Playing with Dominoes Glue a picture on the ends of each piece.

• Have children work with a partner to arrange the dominoes so that pictures with the same initial sound are next to each other. For example, dominoes could be arranged in this order: toe/leg – ladder/sun – sock/leg – lips/turtle.

Center Tip

If...children end the game after they have matched only two pictures, **then...** point out how more dominoes can be added.

Focus Question

How does a community help me?

¿Cómo me ayuda una comunidad?

Learning Goals

Emergent Literacy: Reading

• Child independently engages in pre-reading behaviors and activities (such as, pretending to read, turning one page at a time).

• Child names most upper- and lowercase letters of the alphabet.

• Child identifies the letter that stands for a given sound.

• Child asks and answers questions about books read aloud (such as, "Who?" "What?" "Where?").

Vocabulary

bridge	puente	rush hour	hora pico
sidewalk	acera	taxi	taxi
tunnel	túnel		

Differentiated Instruction

 Extra Support

Read Aloud

If...children have difficulty answering the Build Background questions, **then...**browse through the book with them and ask the questions again.

 Enrichment

Read Aloud

Have children browse the book to find vehicles that they have ridden on or in. Then have them draw a picture of themselves in or on the vehicle.

 Special Needs

Cognitive Challenges

If...children cannot understand the book, **then...**paraphrase the text as you take a picture walk through the book.

Literacy Time

 large group   15 minutes

📖 Read Aloud

✅ Do children know to read from top to bottom of a page and from front to back of a book?

✅ Can children answer questions about the book?

Build Background Display *Rush Hour* and read the title aloud.

● Ask: *What is rush hour? What do people do during rush hour?* *¿Qué es la hora pico? ¿Qué hace la gente durante la hora pico?*

● Ask: *Does everyone walk to work and school during rush hour? How else do they get to these places?* *¿Camina la gente para ir al trabajo y a la escuela durante la hora pico? ¿De qué otra manera llegan las personas a esos lugares?*

Listen for Understanding I'm going to begin reading the book. Ask: *Where should I begin to read?* *¿Por dónde debo comenzar a leer?*

● Read the book aloud. At the end of each page, say: *I read to the bottom of the page. What do I do now?* *Leí hasta la parte inferior de la página. ¿Qué debo hacer ahora?* Invite a child to show you where to continue the story.

Respond and Connect Remind children that a community is a place where people live and work together. Ask: *What things in a community help people get to work and school?* *¿Qué cosas de una comunidad ayudan a la gente a llegar al trabajo y a la escuela?* Guide children to say that there might be buses, subways, and trains in a community. There might be bus drivers and taxi drivers. There are roads and sidewalks, and sometimes bridges and tunnels. Help them understand that these things help people get to work and school.

ELL Use the colorful illustrations to reinforce color vocabulary words. Point to pictures and say: *This is red*. Have children repeat the sentence. Then ask: *What color is this?*

Learn About Letters and Sounds

✅ Can children identify the /t/, /ē/, and /ĕ/ sounds?

Review Letters *Tt* **and** *Ee* Using masking tape, form a large *T* and large *E* on the floor. Have children sit in a circle around the letters

● Put pictures of items that begin with the sounds /t/, /ē/, and /ĕ/ in a pile.

● Have children take turns taking a picture from the pile, naming the picture, and placing it next to the letter that makes that sound.

TIP Remind children that the letter *E* can make the /ē/ sound and the /ĕ/ sound, so they will be placing words with different beginning sounds on the *E*.

Rush Hour
Hora pico

Math Time

 large group 15 minutes

Observe and Investigate

✓ **Can children add and subtract single-digit numerals?**

How Many Now? Invite children to play a counting game with hidden counters.

● Show children a number of counters. Say: *How many counters are there? ¿Cuántas fichas hay?* Cover the counters.

● Ask again: *How many counters are there? ¿Cuántas fichas hay?* Uncover the counters to check, and then show the matching Numeral Card.

● Add or subtract one counter. Cover the counters again. Ask: *How many counters are there now? ¿Cuántas fichas hay ahora?* Uncover the counters to check, and then show the matching Numeral Card.

● Repeat the process, adding and subtracting a different number of counters.

ELL Provide support by demonstrating with your fingers how many counters there are.

 large group 15 minutes

✕✕✕ Social and Emotional Development

Making Good Choices

✓ **Do children assume responsibilities in the classroom?**

✓ **Can children think of examples of when they were kind to each other?**

Being Responsible in School Display the *Making Good Choices Flip Chart,* page 14, and discuss the illustration.

● Say: *Let's review what you see happening here. When it comes to helping, how does our classroom compare with the picture? Do we seem to be like them or are we different? What do you do to help others? Vamos a recordar qué pasaba aquí. ¿En qué se parece nuestra clase a la de la ilustración? ¿Somos diferentes o parecidos a estos niños? ¿Cómo ayudan ustedes a otros?* Have children give examples.

 Building Blocks

Online Math Activity

Children can complete Party Time 2 and Memory Number 1 during computer time or Center Time.

Making Good Choices Flip Chart, page 14

Vocabulary

feelings	sentimientos	helpful	útil
hidden	oculto	kind	amable
now	ahora	more	más

Differentiated Instruction

✋ Extra Support
Observe and Investigate
If...children have difficulty adding and subtracting counters, **then...**use fewer counters.

★ Enrichment
Observe and Investigate
Increase the number of counters you add and subtract (for totals up to 10) to challenge children.

Accommodations for 3's
Observe and Investigate
If...children have trouble telling how many counters there are when the counters are covered, **then...**allow them more time to see the counters.

Learning Goals

Social and Emotional Development
• Child is aware of self in terms of abilities, characteristics and preferences, and respects personal boundaries.

Language and Communication
• Child names and describes actual or pictured people, places, things, actions, attributes, and events.

Fine Arts
• Child expresses thoughts, feelings, and energy through music and creative movement.

Vocabulary

drum	tambor	horn	corneta
march	marchar	parade	desfile

Differentiated Instruction

✋ Extra Support

Explore and Express

If...children don't feel the strong beat of the marching music, **then...**tap the beat on a drum as the music plays.

⭐ Enrichment

Explore and Express

Give children materials to make a flag for the marching band and tell them to include a picture or symbol that shows something about the class.

Accommodations for 3's

Explore and Express

If...children have difficulty marching around the room as they play their instruments, **then...**have them march in place.

Music and Movement Time

large group | 20 minutes

Social and Emotional Skills In an exaggerated, comical fashion, model how to take part in the activity without bumping into other people or classroom furniture.

Oral Language and Academic Vocabulary

✓ **Can children use words to talk about parades?**

Talk about Parades Display the picture on *Oral Language Development Card 24*. Guide children to use vocabulary words to describe the picture.

● Ask: *What people do you see in the parade? What else do you see in the parade?*
¿Qué personas ves en el desfile? ¿Qué otras cosas ves en el desfile?

Oral Language Development Card 24

Explore and Express

✓ **Can children feel the rhythm of marching music?**

✓ **Can children respect personal boundaries as they move around the room?**

March in a Band Discuss that many parades have marching bands and that band members march while they play musical instruments. Say: *Some kinds of music make people want to march. Algunos tipos de música hacen que la gente desee marchar.*

● Play recorded marching music. Ask: *How does this music make you want to move your feet? ¿Cómo quisieran mover los pies con esta música?* Allow students to demonstrate. Then model how to march in place to the beat, lifting your feet high.

● Hand out empty coffee cans and cardboard tubes for children to use as drums and horns. Lead a parade around the room as children play their instruments to the music. Remind children not to bump into others as they march.

ELL Show children a picture of a marching band and point out the instruments and uniforms.

Center Time

▶ **Center Rotation** Center Time includes teacher-guided activities and independent activities. Refer to the **Learning Centers** on pages 62–63 for independent activity ideas.

Writer's Center

☑ **Listen for children using oral vocabulary words to talk with each other about parades.**

☑ **See if children can write their own names.**

Materials paper, crayons, photos of and books about parades

My Parade Provide children with pictures of parades and books that contain images of parades. Tell children that they will draw a picture of themselves marching in a parade or watching a parade in their community.

● Encourage children to describe their pictures to other children in the center and to share ideas.

● Ask children to label themselves in the picture with their names. Have them add the first letter of their last names.

Center Tip

If...children cannot write their full first name, **then...**ask them to write the first letter of their name.

Purposeful Play

☑ **Observe how children are careful not to hurt classmates' feelings.**

Children choose an open center for free playtime. Remind them to try to make classmates feel better if they are sad.

Let's Say Good-Bye

large group   15 minutes

 Read Aloud Revisit "Keiko's Good Thinking"/"Keiko resuelve un problema" for your afternoon Read Aloud. Tell children to listen for words that begin with the sounds of /t/, /ē/, and /ĕ/.

 Home Connection Refer to the Home Connections activities listed in the Resources and Materials chart on page 59. Remind children to tell their families how the community helps them. Sing the "Good-Bye Song"/"Hora de ir a casa" as children prepare to leave.

 Learning Goals

Social and Emotional Development
• Child shows eagerness, curiosity, and confidence while learning new concepts and trying new things.

Language and Development
• Child begins and ends conversations appropriately.

Emergent Literacy: Writing
• Child writes own name or a reasonable approximation of it.

• Child writes some letters or reasonable approximations of letters upon request.

Fine Arts
• Child expresses thoughts, feelings, and energy through music and creative movement.

Writing

Help children recall some of the words they used this week that began with the sounds /t/, /ē/, and /ĕ/. If necessary, provide riddles or prompts, such as *This animal has a hard shell.* Record their answers on chart paper or an interactive whiteboard. Read the words back as you track the print.

Week 3

Focus Question

Who helps the community?
¿Quién ayuda a la comunidad?

This week children will learn about community workers and what they do for the community. They will listen to a counting song about little birds, work together to build a community out of scrap materials, and help Mr. Mix-Up straighten out his counting.

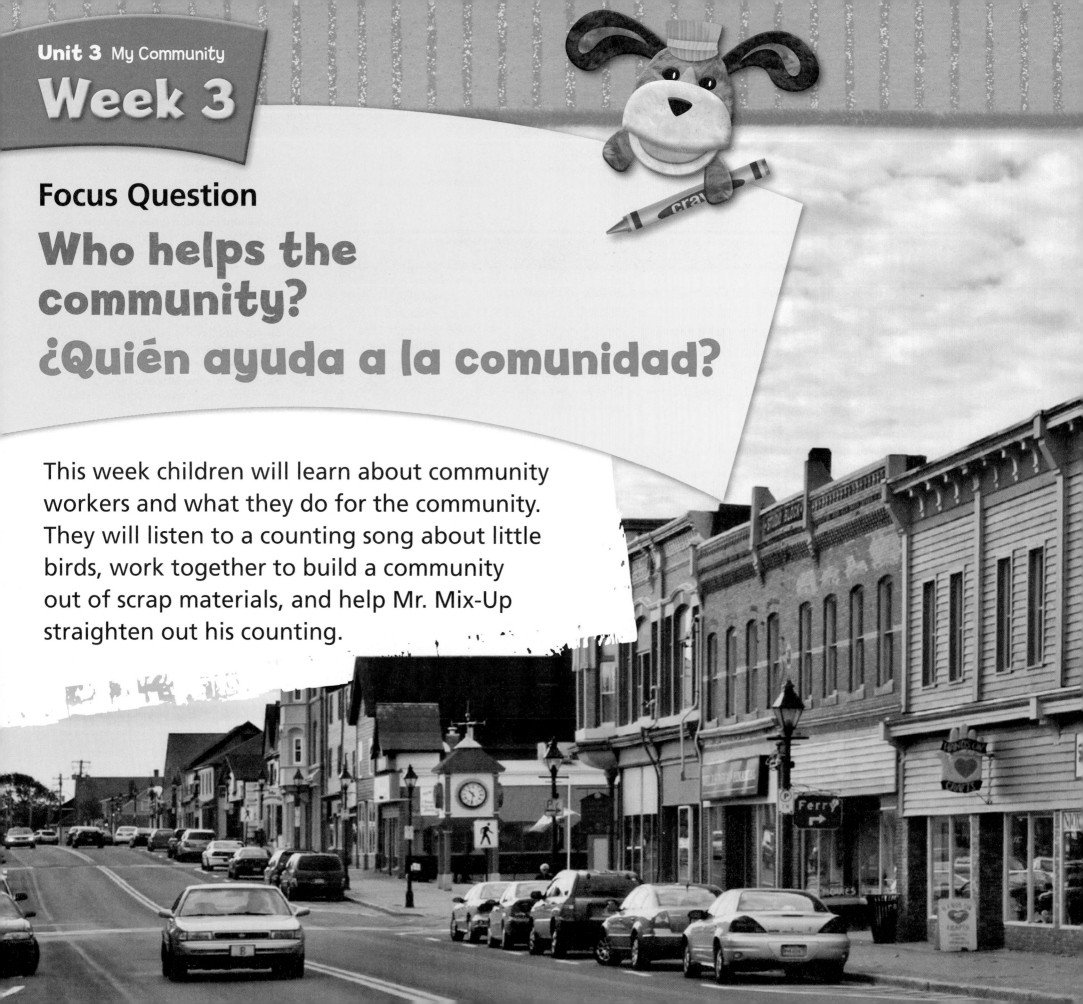

Social and Emotional Development	Day 1	2	3	4	5
Child uses classroom materials carefully.	✓	✓			✓
Child participates in a variety of individual, small- and large-group activities.	✓	✓	✓	✓	✓

Language and Communication	1	2	3	4	5
Child speaks in a way that is understood by children, teachers, or other adults.		✓			
Child names and describes actual or pictured people, places, things, actions, attributes, and events.		✓	✓		✓
Child uses newly learned vocabulary daily in multiple contexts.	✓		✓	✓	✓
Child uses words to identify and understand categories.	✓				
Child uses complex sentences that include many details, tell about one topic, and communicate meaning clearly.		✓			

Emergent Literacy: Reading	1	2	3	4	5
Child produces words with the same beginning sound.	✓	✓	✓	✓	✓
Child names most upper- and lowercase letters of the alphabet.			✓	✓	✓
Child identifies the letter that stands for a given sound.			✓	✓	✓
Child retells or reenacts poems and stories in sequence.	✓	✓	✓	✓	✓
Child asks and answers questions about books read aloud (such as, "Who?" "What?" "Where?").				✓	✓

Emergent Literacy: Writing	1	2	3	4	5
Child participates in free drawing and writing activities to deliver information.	✓	✓	✓		✓
Child uses scribbles, shapes, pictures, symbols, and letters to represent language.			✓	✓	✓

Mathematics	Day 1	2	3	4	5
Child uses words to rote count from 1 to 30.		✓		✓	
Child counts 1–10 items, with one count per item.		✓		✓	✓
Child counts up to 10 items, and demonstrates that the last count indicates how many items were counted.			✓		
Child recognizes one-digit numerals, 0–9.	✓		✓		
Child sorts objects that are the same and different into groups and uses language to describe how the groups are similar and different.		✓		✓	

Science	1	2	3	4	5
Child follows basic health and safety rules.					✓

Social Studies	1	2	3	4	5
Child understands and discusses roles, responsibilities, and services provided by community workers.			✓		
Child identifies the U.S. Flag and state flag.			✓		
Child recites the Pledge of Allegiance.			✓		

Fine Arts	1	2	3	4	5
Child expresses ideas, emotions, and moods through individual and collaborative dramatic play.					✓

Materials and Resources

	DAY 1	DAY 2	DAY 3	DAY 4	DAY 5
Program Materials	• Teacher's Treasure Book • Oral Language Development Card 25 • Rhymes and Chants Flip Chart • *Quinito's Neighborhood* Big Book • ABC Big Book • Numeral Cards • Online Building Blocks Math Activities • Making Good Choices Flip Chart • Math and Science Flip Chart • Home Connections Resource Guide	• Teacher's Treasure Book • Concept Big Book 2 • Dog Puppet 1 and 2 • *Quinito's Neighborhood* Big Book • ABC Picture Cards • Numeral Cards • Online Building Blocks Math Activities • Making Good Choices Flip Chart • Dot Cards • Math and Science Flip Chart • Home Connections Resource Guide	• Teacher's Treasure Book • Oral Language Development Card 26 • Rhymes and Chants Flip Chart • Concept Big Book 2 • ABC Big Book • Numeral Cards • Making Good Choices Flip Chart • Dog Puppet 1 and 2 • Home Connections Resource Guide	• Teacher's Treasure Book • Flannel Board Characters for "The Little Red Hen" • Dog Puppet 1 and 2 • ABC Big Book • Numeral Cards • Making Good Choices Flip Chart • Home Connections Resource Guide	• Teacher's Treasure Book • Rhymes and Chants Flip Chart • Photo Library CD-ROM • *Quinito's Neighborhood* Big Book • Making Good Choices Flip Chart • Home Connections Resource Guide
Other Materials	• dress-up clothes • paper, pencils, stickers • props for community helpers • markers, crayons • craft sticks • scissors, glue • magazines • paper plates, string	• blocks • cardboard boxes • scissors, tape • paper, pencils, markers, crayons • small boxes, objects for sorting (many of each kind)	• paper, pencils, markers, crayons • cardboard, tape, scissors • paper towel tubes • glue • books, magazines with photos of police officers, firefighters, community helpers	• dress-up clothes • props; ordinary classroom materials • paper, pencils, markers, crayons • small boxes, objects for sorting (many of each kind) • sets of tactile numerals • muffin pans or paper cups	• crayons, paper • cardboard tubes, boxes • tape, glue, decorating materials • markers • penny • red checker
Home Connection	Tell children to show their families which things around their houses are living and nonliving. Send home the following materials. Weekly Family Letter, Home Connections Resource Guide, pp. 33–34	Invite children to count up to 20 for their families.	Encourage children to tell their families about different community helpers and what they do.	Invite children to tell their families what happened between the Dog Puppets and how it was resolved. Storybook 8, Home Connections Resource Guide, pp. 109–112	Have children choose one community helper and model their job for their families.

Assessment

As you observe children throughout the week, you may fill out an Anecdotal Observational Record Form to document an individual's progress toward a goal or signs indicating the need for developmental or medical evaluation. You may also choose to select work for each child's portfolio. The Anecdotal Observational Record Form and Weekly Assessment rubrics are available in the assessment section of DLMExpressOnline.com.

More Literature Suggestions

• **The Bus for Us/Nuestro autobús** by Suzanne Bloom
• **Trashy Town** by Andrea Zimmerman
• **Walter the Baker** by Eric Carle
• **Oficios en mi vecindario** por Gladys Rosa-Mendoza
• **Ayudantes del vecindario** por Jennifer Blizin Gillis

Week 3

Daily Planner

		DAY 1	DAY 2
Let's Start the Day **Language Time**	large group	**Opening Routines** p. 102 **Morning Read Aloud** p. 102 **Oral Language and Vocabulary** p. 102 Community Helpers **Phonological Awareness** p. 102 Match the Sound	**Opening Routines** p. 108 **Morning Read Aloud** p. 108 **Oral Language and Vocabulary** p. 108 Community Helpers **Phonological Awareness** p. 108 Words That Begin with the Same Sound
Center Time	small group	**Focus On:** **Pretend and Learn Center** p. 103 **Creativity Center** p. 103	**Focus On:** **Construction Center** p. 109 **Writer's Center** p. 109
Circle Time **Literacy Time**	large group	**Read Aloud** *Quinito's Neighborhood/ El vecindario de Quinito* p. 104 **Learn About Letters and Sounds: Learn About the Letters** *Gg* **and** *Rr* p. 104	**Read Aloud** *Quinito's Neighborhood/ El vecindario de Quinito* p. 110 **Learn About Letters and Sounds: Learn About** *Gg* **and** *Rr* p. 110
Math Time	large group	**Numeral 9** p. 105	**Sort and Label** p. 111
Social and Emotional Development	large group	**Materials** p. 105	**Using Materials Correctly** p. 111
Content Connection	large group	**Science:** **Oral Language and Academic Vocabulary** p. 106 **Observe and Investigate** p. 106	**Math:** **Mr. Mixup** p. 112
Center Time	small group	**Focus On:** **Math and Science Center** p. 107 **Purposeful Play** p. 107	**Focus On:** **Math and Science Center** p. 113 **Purposeful Play** p. 113
Let's Say Good-Bye	large group	**Read Aloud** p. 107 **Writing** p. 107 **Home Connection** p. 107	**Read Aloud** p. 113 **Writing** p. 113 **Home Connection** p. 113

DAY 3

Opening Routines p. 114

Morning Read Aloud p. 114

Oral Language and Vocabulary
p. 114 Firefighting

Phonological Awareness
p. 114 Words That Begin with
the Same Sound

Focus On:

ABC Center p. 115

Creativity Center p. 115

Read Aloud
*In the Community/En la
comunidad* p. 116

**Learn About Letters and
Sounds: Learn About
Letters *Gg* and *Rr* p. 116**

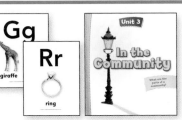

Ten Little Birdies p. 117

Using Materials Correctly p. 117

Social Studies:

Oral Language and Academic Vocabulary
p. 118 Community Workers

Understand and Participate
p. 118 Class Book

Focus On:

Library and Listening Center p. 119

Purposeful Play p. 119

Read Aloud p. 119

Writing p. 119

Home Connection p. 119

DAY 4

Opening Routines p. 120

Morning Read Aloud p. 120

Oral Language and Vocabulary
p. 120 Lessons in Folktales

Phonological Awareness
p. 120 Words That Begin with
the Same Sound

Focus On:

Pretend and Learn Center p. 121

Writer's Center p. 121

Read Aloud
"The Little Red Hen"/
"La gallinita roja" p. 122

**Learn About Letters and
Sounds: Learn About Letters
and Sounds** p. 122

Sort and Label p. 123

Using Materials Fairly p. 123

Math:

Mr. Mixup p. 124

Focus On:

Math and Science Center p. 125

Purposeful Play p. 125

Read Aloud p. 125

Writing p. 125

Home Connection p. 125

DAY 5

Opening Routines p. 126

Morning Read Aloud p. 126

Oral Language and Vocabulary
p. 126 Community Helpers

Phonological Awareness
p. 126 Words with Initial /h/

Focus On:

ABC Center p. 127

Construction Center p. 127

Read Aloud
*Quinito's Neighborhood/
El vecindario de Quinito*
p. 128

**Learn About Letters and Sounds:
Learn About the Alphabet** p. 128

Ten Little Birdies p. 129

**Review the Making Good Choices
Chart** p. 129

Dramatic Play Time:

Oral Language and Vocabulary
p. 130 Communities and Community Helpers

Explore and Express
p. 130 Act Out Community Helpers

Focus On:

Writer's Center p. 131

Purposeful Play p. 131

Read Aloud p. 131

Writing p. 131

Home Connection p. 131

Week 3

Learning Centers

Math and Science Center

Living Things
Children sort pictures of living and non-living things, p. 107.

Match the Dots
Children match dots and numerals, p. 113.

Sort!
Children sort numerals, p. 125

How Many?
Place 1–10 counters in paper bags. Distribute the bags and have children count how many counters are in their bag. Have children report their number to a partner. Together, they count aloud as they remove each counter from the bag.

Count Up and Down:
Count aloud from one to ten and have children hop or jump forward once for each number. Then count backward and have them hop backward as you count down.

ABC Center

Letters and Sounds
Children draw things that begin with /f/, p. 115.

Find /h/ Items
Children identify objects that begin with /h/, p. 127.

Connect the Dots
Model how to place dots, using stickers or dot pens, to form the letter G. Show children how to connect the dots. Have children make dot patterns for the letters G and R.

Letter Flowers
Group children in pairs. Have pairs trace letters to make groups of flowers. For example, a flower's center might be an O and the petals Vs.

Creativity Center

Draw Helpers at Work
Children draw pictures of community helpers, p. 103.

Make Firefighting Equipment
Children make firefighting equipment, p. 115.

New Uniform
Explain that community workers often wear a uniform so you can recognize them. Have children design and draw a new uniform for a community worker of their choice.

Counting Book
Provide folded books with a numeral 1–10 on each page. Children use stickers, stamps, or other materials to make the corresponding number of items on each page.

Library and Listening Center

Telling Stories
Children make a class book about community helpers, p. 119.

Little Helpers
Children browse through children's books and magazines and point out pictures of children helping out in their community. Encourage them to tell one another about a time they helped out as in the picture.

Name That Story
Children listen to an excerpt from a familiar story. They guess which story it is and tell what will happen next. They continue listening so they can check their retelling.

Construction Center

Build a Neighborhood
Children build a neighborhood out of boxes and blocks, p. 109.

Build a Fire Station
Children make a community building, p. 127.

Our Building
Have children group chairs to make a "building" inside the classroom. Have them make a sign for their building.

A Nest or a Hive
Children build a nest and a hive out of building materials. Then they tell what they know about groups of animals that might live in each home.

Writer's Center

Write About a Community Helper
Children make up stories about a community helper, p. 109.

Write a Story
Children write a story with a lesson, p. 121.

My Friend the Community Helper
Children write about a friend who role-played a community helper, p. 131.

The Flag
Children draw a picture of someone pledging to the American flag. Have them write to complete the sentence frame: *I _____ allegiance to the _____ of the United States of America.*

Library Roles:
Children tell about what roles they play as a student, friend, and helper when they are in the library. Have them draw a picture to illustrate carrying out that role.

Pretend and Learn Center

Act Like a Community Helper
Children pretend to be community helpers, p. 103.

The Little Red Hen
Children act out roles from the story, p. 121.

Community Worker Interview
Have children talk about different community workers they've met. Have pairs take turns pretending to be a reporter and a community helper being interviewed.

Librarians
Provide props found in a library. Children discuss what librarians do. Have them role-play going to the library and checking out materials, asking a librarian for help, and so on.

DAY 1

Let's Start the Day

Focus Question
Who helps the community?
¿Quién ayuda a la comunidad?

Opening Routines and Transition Tips
For **Opening Routines** and **Transition Tips** turn to pages 178–181 and visit DLMExpressOnline.com for more ideas.

Read **"Mail Carrier"**/"La cartera" from the *Teacher's Treasure Book*, page 98, for your morning Read Aloud.

Learning Goals

Social and Emotional Development
• Child participates in a variety of individual, small- and large-group activities.

Language and Communication
• Child uses newly learned vocabulary daily in multiple contexts.

Emergent Literacy: Reading
• Child produces words with the same beginning sound.

Vocabulary

address	dirección	deliver	entregar
helper	ayudando	letter	carta
mail	correo	package	paquete
send	enviar		

Differentiated Instruction

Extra Support
Phonological Awareness
If...children have difficulty isolating the initial sound of *doctor* and *dentist*, **then...**repeat the sound several times, such as : /d/ /d/ /d/ *doctor*. Have children pay attention to the shape and position of your mouth.

Enrichment
Phonological Awareness
Challenge children to name words that end with the sound /d/ or include /d/ in the middle.

Accommodations for 3's
Oral Language and Vocabulary
If...children have trouble remembering the names of helpers, **then...**allow them to act out or describe what the people do.

Language Time

15 minutes large group

Social and Emotional Development Help children understand that they can help their classmates and get help from them as well.

Oral Language and Vocabulary

Can children identify and name people who are community helpers?

Track new words children use to describe community helpers.

Community Helpers Talk about people who help others. Ask: ***Do you know a person whose job is to help other people?*** *¿Conocen a alguna alguien que tenga el trabajo de ayudar a otras personas?* Explain that mail carriers deliver letters that help us keep in touch with our friends and family. Ask: ***Have you ever received a letter with your name and address on it? How did you feel when you got it? Who was it from? Who delivered it to you?*** *¿Alguna vez han recibido una carta? ¿Cómo se sintieron cuando la recibieron? ¿De quién era? ¿Quién les entregó esa carta?*

• Explain that grown-ups are not the only people who can be helpers—children can be helpers too. Ask: ***Who do you know who is a helper?*** *¿Conocen a alguien que trabaje ayudando?*

• Display *Oral Language Development Card 25*. Help children name the community helper in the photograph and identify what he is carrying. Then follow the suggestions on the back of the card.

ELL Act out the words *help* and *helper* with the assistance of children. Drop a piece of paper on the floor and ask children for help picking it up. Then say: ***Thank you! It was nice of you to help me. You're a good helper.*** For additional suggestions on how to meet the needs of children at the Beginning, Intermediate, Advanced, and Advanced-High levels of English proficiency, see pages 184–187.

Phonological Awareness

Can children name words that start with the same /d/ sound as a given pair of words?

Match the Sound Display the *Rhymes and Chants Flip Chart*. Say the rhyme on page 15 with children. Then say the words *doctor* and *dentist*. Point out that they both start with the same sound, /d/. Say *deliver, wires,* and *day,* and have children stand when they hear a word beginning with /d/. Then help children name other words that begin with /d/, such as *dog* and *duck*.

Oral Language Development Card 25

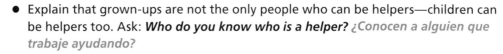

Rhymes and Chants Flip Chart, page 15

Center Time

▶ **Center Rotation** Center Time includes teacher-guided activities and independent activities. Refer to the **Learning Centers** on pages 100–101 for independent activity ideas.

 small group 60–90 minutes

Learning Goals

Social and Emotional Development
• Child participates in a variety of individual, small- and large-group activities.

Language and Communication
• Child uses newly learned vocabulary daily in multiple contexts.

Pretend and Learn Center

☑ Track children's understanding of community helper names, roles, and responsibilities.

☑ Look for and acknowledge children who are assuming various roles and responsibilities as part of the classroom community.

Materials dress-up clothes, paper, pencils, stickers, and various other objects to be used as props

Act Like a Community Helper Have children name and identify community helpers. Have them use props and dress-up clothes to act out what the community helpers do.

● Encourage children to work with other children in the group.

● Ask: *Is a dentist a community helper? Is a truck driver a helper? ¿Un dentista ayuda a su comunidad? ¿Y el conductor de un camión?* Help children name community helpers whose titles begin with /d/.

Center Tip

If...children have difficulty focusing on a particular community helper to act out, **then...** name a series of community helpers and give them a choice.

Differentiated Instruction

✋ **Extra Support**
Pretend and Learn Center
If...children are uncertain what a particular helper does, **then...**provide books and illustrations of the helpers in action.

⭐ **Enrichment**
Creativity Center
Help children write labels to show the names of the helpers and what they are doing.

💜 **Special Needs**
Vision Loss
If...children cannot easily make their drawings on regular-sized sheets of paper, **then...**provide them with larger sheets of paper.

Creativity Center

☑ Look for children to show helpers from the community and in their own lives.

☑ Listen for use of oral vocabulary as children talk about their pictures.

Materials paper, pencils, markers, crayons

Draw Helpers at Work Ask children to draw a picture of a helper doing his or her job.

● Have children think of all the helpers in the community. Prompt them to include themselves or friends if they are helpers.

● Ask them to choose one helper and draw a picture of that helper doing something to help others.

● Have children tell partners about their pictures.

Center Tip

If...children have difficulty explaining what is happening in their picture, **then...**draw a picture yourself and model explaining it.

Focus Question
Who helps the community?
¿Quién ayuda a la comunidad?

Circle Time

Learning Goals

Emergent Literacy: Reading
• Child produces words with the same beginning sound.
• Child retells or reenacts poems and stories in sequence.

Vocabulary

abuelo	abuelo	bodega	bodega
carpenter	carpintero	dentist	dentista
muralist	muralista	neighbors	vecinos
tia	tía		

Differentiated Instruction

 Extra Support

Learn About Letters and Sounds
If...children have difficulty distinguishing /g/ from /r/, **then...**say several words beginning with each sound and have children repeat them.

 Enrichment

Read Aloud
Ask children to describe how their neighborhoods are like Quinito's neighborhood and how they are different. Have them use the words *like* and *different*.

Literacy Time

large group   15 minutes

📖 Read Aloud

✓ **Can children retell and reenact what community helpers do in the story?**

Build Background Tell children that this book is about a child's neighborhood and the people who work there. Ask children what they know about neighborhoods.

● Ask: **Who are some people who live in your neighborhood?** *¿Quiénes son algunas de las personas que viven en su vecindario?*

● Ask: **Tell us some good things about the neighborhood you live in.** *¿Qué les gusta del vecindario donde viven?*

Listen for Enjoyment Display *Quinito's Neighborhood* and read the title. Remind children that the book tells about the neighborhood where a boy named Quinito lives.

● Walk through the pictures with children. Ask: **Who do you see? Does your neighborhood look like this? Do you see people doing these things in your neighborhood?** *¿Qué ven? ¿Su vecindario tiene este aspecto? ¿Ven personas que hagan estas cosas en su vecindario?*

● Read the book aloud. Emphasize the names of the helpers and what they do; for example, a muralist paints pictures, a dentist helps keep people's teeth healthy.

Respond to the Story Discuss the story. Help children recall the various people in the neighborhood and have them reenact what each one does. Ask: **How does _____ help the neighborhood?** *¿De qué manera _____ ayuda al vecindario?*

💡 **TIP** Connect the book to children's own lives by asking if they know people in their neighborhoods who are truck drivers, shopkeepers, and so on. Use vocabulary, such as *bank* and *crossing guard*, when possible.

ELL To support comprehension, have children act out or mime the things the characters in the story are doing. Have them say the job of the person as they act it out (for example, they say *crossing guard* as they hold up a pretend stop sign).

Learn About Letters and Sounds

✓ **Can children identify the letters Gg and Rr and sounds /g/ and /r/?**

Learn About the Letters Gg and Rr Display the picture of the girl and the picture of the ring from the *ABC Big Book*.

● Tell children that one of these words begins with the sound /g/ and the other begins with the sound /r/. Remind children that the letters for these sounds are *g* and *r*.

● Say *girl* and *garden* and show the pictures. Help children think of other words beginning with /g/. Repeat with *ring*, *rabbit*, and other words that begin with /r/.

Quinito's Neighborhood
El vecindario de Quinito

ABC Big Book

large group 15 minutes

Math Time

Observe and Investigate

 Can children correctly identify numerals from 1–9?

 Do children recognize that the last number counted is how many jumps were made?

Numeral 9 Explore the numeral 9 with children. Say: *This is how we draw a 9. Así dibujamos un 9.* Practice drawing the number 9 in the air with children. Then tell children that you are going to show them how to play the Jumping game. Lead children in a game of jumping to a count of numbers.

- Show a Numeral Card between 1 and 9. Have children say the numeral on the card. Hold up a card with a number and say: *Let's jump this many times!*

- Allow children to choose Numeral Cards and suggest the movements.

ELL Before you begin the activity, provide support by modeling jumping as you say the word.

Online Math Activity

Introduce Space Race: Number Choice from the Building Blocks online software. Discuss with children directions and strategies as appropriate. Each child should complete the activity this week.

large group 15 minutes

✳✳✳ Social and Emotional Development

Making Good Choices

 Do children know why they should take care of classroom materials?

Materials Have children name art materials they have used in the classroom. Ask if they have ever shared these materials. Then display the *Making Good Choices Flip Chart,* page 15.

- Point to the children in the front of the picture. Ask: *What are these children doing? What materials are they using? Why are they sharing materials?* ¿Qué están haciendo estos niños? ¿Qué materiales están usando? ¿Están compartiendo los materiales? ¿Cómo lo saben?

- Point to the child in the background. Ask: *How did she know where the scissors were kept?* ¿Cómo sabía la niña dónde estaban guardadas las tijeras?

- Point to the two children making the puzzle. Ask: *Why is it a good idea to put materials away when you are finished using them?* ¿Por qué es buena idea guardar los materiales cuando terminan de usarlos?

ELL Display common classroom materials. Hold them up one at a time, name them, and use the words in brief sentences, such as: *You cut with scissors*. Have children repeat by holding up the objects and having children name them and use the words in sentences.

Making Good Choices Flip Chart, page 15

Learning Goals

Social and Emotional Development
- Child participates in a variety of individual, small- and large-group activities.

Mathematics
- Child recognizes and names numerals 0 through 9.

Vocabulary

community	comunidad
glue	pegamento
jump	saltar
markers	marcadores
materials	materiales
scissors	tijeras
share	compartir

Differentiated Instruction

✋ **Extra Support**
Observe and Investigate
If...children need help during the Jumping game, **then**...use smaller numbers.

⭐ **Enrichment**
Making Good Choices
Challenge children to count sets of nine art materials, such as crayons and paintbrushes.

Accommodations for 3's
Observe and Investigate
If...children need help knowing how many times to jump, **then**...show the number of times with your fingers.

Focus Question
Who helps the community?
¿Quién ayuda a la comunidad?

Social and Emotional Development
• Child uses classroom materials carefully.

Language and Communication
• Child understands or knows the meaning of many thousands of words, many more than he or she uses.

Vocabulary

animals	animales	change	cambiar
grow	crecer	living	con vida
move	moverse	nonliving	sin vida
plants	plantas		

Differentiated Instruction

 Extra Support

Observe and Investigate
If...children have difficulty differentiating living from nonliving things, **then...**have them think about whether the item needs water or air.

 Enrichment

Oral Language and Academic Vocabulary
Challenge children to form one sentence that names a living thing and another that identifies something nonliving. For example: *A tree is a living thing. A rock is a nonliving thing.*

Science Time

Health Skills Model good habits of nutrition by eating and providing healthful snacks.

Oral Language and Academic Vocabulary

✓ **Can children distinguish between living and nonliving things?**

Point to the outdoor scene in the *Math and Science Flip Chart,* page 25. Say: *There are both living and nonliving things in the picture. En la ilustración hay cosas con vida y cosas que no están vivas.*

● Explain that all living things grow and change. Say: *The word* nonliving *means "not living." Nonliving things may change, but they do not grow on their own. Las cosas que no tienen vida pueden cambiar, pero no crecen solas.*

● Point to a living thing in the picture. Explain that living things need certain things, such as food and water, to live. Ask: *What do people need to have every day to live? ¿Qué necesitan las personas todos los días para vivir?* Have children identify other living things in the scene.

● Point to a nonliving thing in the picture. Explain that the nonliving thing does not need food or water. Have children identify other nonliving things in the scene.

Observe and Investigate

✓ **Can children identify living and nonliving things in the classroom?**

Provide each child with two craft sticks or strips of paper in different colors. Explain that one color will be used to identify living things and the other color will be used to identify nonliving things. You may wish to label the sticks or strips with the letters *L* and *N* prior to distributing them.

● Tell children to walk around the classroom or the schoolyard and place the sticks or strips near living and nonliving things. Encourage children to identify objects that have not already been identified. If needed, children can put the sticks near a window to indicate something outdoors.

● Have children look at all the living things. Ask: *What are the two main kinds of living things?* (plants and animals) *¿Cuáles son las dos clases principales de cosas con vida? How are plants and animals alike? How are they different? ¿En qué se parecen las plantas y los animales? ¿En qué se diferencian?* Talk about how animals can move from place to place on their own, while plants cannot. Discuss how plants need soil or water in which to live.

ELL Ask children questions linked to the characteristics of living things, such as: *Do you need food to live? Do you need water? Can you move from place to place? Do you grow?* Say: *You are a living thing.* Then display a book and ask the same questions. Say: *A book is a nonliving thing.*

Math and Science Flip Chart, page 25

Center Time

▶ **Center Rotation** Center Time includes teacher-guided activities and independent activities. Refer to the **Learning Centers** on pages 100–101 for independent activity ideas.

small group 30 minutes

Math and Science Center

☑ **Observe whether children can identify categories of living things.**

Materials child-friendly magazines, scissors, paper plates, glue, string

Living Things Tell children they will look for pictures of living things and separate them into two groups: plants and animals.

- Have children look through the magazines for pictures of plants and animals. Encourage children to find at least three different examples for each group.

- Have children glue all the animals on one side of a plate and all the plants on the other side. Help children label their groups. Attach string to the plates so they can be hung to show both sides.

Center Tip

If...children have difficulty finding plants, **then...** encourage them to look at the background of the pictures to find them.

Purposeful Play

☑ **Observe to see if children assume responsibility for classroom materials they use.**

Children choose an open center for free playtime. Encourage responsible use of classroom materials. If necessary, remind children to put away items before they leave the Center.

Let's Say Good-Bye

large group 15 minutes

 Read Aloud Revisit "Mail Carrier"/"La cartera" for your afternoon Read Aloud. Have children listen for the /g/ sound and the /r/ sound.

Home Connection Refer to the Home Connections activities listed in the Resources and Materials chart on page 97. Remind children to tell their families about different community helpers. Sing the "Good-Bye Song"/"Hora de ir a casa" as children prepare to leave.

✓ Learning Goals

Social and Emotional Development
- Child participates in a variety of individual, small- and large-group activities.

Language and Communication
- Child uses words to identify and understand categories.

Emergent Literacy: Writing
- Child participates in free drawing and writing activities to deliver information.

Writing

Recap the day. Ask: *Can you name some community helpers you learned about today?* Record their answers. Have children draw a picture showing a helper of their choice. Have them label the picture with the name of the helper, using letters, words, or scribbles. Tell children to take the pictures home and discuss community helpers with their family.

Focus Question

Who helps the community?

¿Quién ayuda a la comunidad?

✓ Learning Goals

Social and Emotional Development
• Child participates in a variety of individual, small- and large-group activities.

Language and Communication
• Child names and describes actual or pictured people, places, things, actions, attributes, and events.

Emergent Literacy: Reading
• Child produces words with the same beginning sound.

• Child retells or reenacts poems and stories in sequence.

Vocabulary

community	comunidad
healthy	saludable
neighborhood	vecindario
neighbors	vecinos
safe	seguro
sidewalk	acera
trash	basura

Differentiated Instruction

 Extra Support

Phonological Awareness

If...children have difficulty producing another word with the initial /g/ sound, **then...**say the words *girl* and *sit*, exaggerating the initial sound, and have children identify which of the words begins the same way as *go* and *get*.

 Enrichment

Oral Language and Vocabulary

Have children present a brief skit involving two or more of the community members described in *In the Community*.

Let's Start the Day

▶ **Opening Routines and Transition Tips**

For **Opening Routines** and **Transition Tips** turn to pages 178–181 and visit **DLMExpressOnline.com** for more ideas.

 Read **"The Traveling Musicians"**/*"Los músicos viajeros"* from the *Teacher's Treasure Book,* page 297, for your morning Read Aloud.

Language Time

`large group` 🕐 **15 minutes**

👪 **Social and Emotional Development** Encourage children to take on the role of helping other children in the classroom understand what happens in a community.

Oral Language and Vocabulary

✓ **Look for examples of children using a variety of words to name people in a community and what they do.**

Community Helpers Review what you discussed about community helpers on the previous day. Ask: **Who are some helpers in your community?** *¿Quiénes son algunas de las personas que brindan ayuda en su comunidad?*

● Read aloud *Concept Big Book 2: In the Community.* Say: **I will stop after I read the name of each community helper. You say the helper's name when I stop.** *Me detendré después de leer el nombre de cada persona que trabaja en la comunidad. Luego, ustedes dirán el nombre cuando yo me detenga.*

● Then have children act out what each pictured community member is doing. Have them complete the following sentence frame as they act out each helper: *I am a _____ and I help people stay healthy.*

ELL Help children with vocabulary by touching pictures in *Concept Big Book 2: In the Community* to illustrate words you read aloud. For example, touch the sidewalk and say: **This is a sidewalk. It is a path where people can walk safely**.

Phonological Awareness

✓ **Can children name a word that begins with the same sound as a given pair of words?**

Words That Begin with the Same Sound Display the Dog Puppets. Tell children that the puppets have been thinking about different words that begin with the same sound.

● Have one puppet say **go** and then have the other say **great.** Next, say the words in your normal voice and point out that each word starts with /g/.

● Help children come up with other words that begin with /g/, such as *game* and *give*. Repeat with the word pairs *rug/red* and *mat/mop*.

● Encourage children to use the puppets and create new word pairs that begin with one of the target sounds.

In the Community
En la comunidad

Center Time

▶ **Center Rotation** Center Time includes teacher-guided activities and independent activities. Refer to the **Learning Centers** on pages 100–101 for independent activity ideas.

 small group   60–90 minutes

Construction Center | Center Tip

 Do children speak well enough for others to understand them?

Materials blocks, cardboard boxes, scissors, tape

Build a Neighborhood Tell children they will build a neighborhood.

- Have children name buildings in their neighborhood. Have them share ideas with other children in their group.

- Say: *Decide with your group which building you want to build. Decidan en grupo qué edificio van a construir.* Have groups build with blocks and construct with cardboard boxes.

- Have children describe their neighborhood. Ask: *What building did you make? Who lives or works there? ¿Qué edificio hicieron? ¿Quiénes viven o trabajan allí?*

Center Tip

If...children have difficulty recalling the name of a neighborhood building or person, **then...**prompt them by giving clues, such as: *This store is where your family goes to buy groceries. It is a _____.*

Writer's Center | Center Tip

 Look for use of vocabulary words and complex sentences that include details relating to neighborhoods.

 Track children's abilities to produce coherent narratives.

Materials paper, pencils, markers, crayons

Write About a Community Helper Ask children to name community helpers they discussed previously. Have them choose one of the helpers. Then have them make up a story about a person who has that job.

- Ask children to write or draw their story. Take dictation as needed.

- Have children tell their story to a classmate, using the pictures and words as a guide.

Center Tip

If...children have difficulty writing their story, **then...**write dotted letters for them to trace.

Learning Goals

Social and Emotional Development
- Child participates in a variety of individual, small- and large-group activities.

Language and Communication
- Child speaks in a way that is understood by children, teachers, or other adults.
- Child uses complex sentences that include many details, tell about one topic, and communicate meaning clearly.

Differentiated Instruction

🖐 **Extra Support**

Writer's Center

If...children's stories make little sense, **then...** ask guiding questions such as: *What did the firefighter do first? What did the firefighter do next? ¿Qué hizo primero el bombero? ¿Qué hizo después el bombero?*

⭐ **Enrichment**

Construction Center

Have children make up and tell a story about what happens in the buildings of the neighborhood they created.

💜 **Special Needs**

Delayed Motor Development

If...children cannot cut and tape pieces of cardboard, **then...**do the cutting and taping yourself, asking them to use words to tell you what they want you to do.

Focus Question
Who helps the community?
¿Quién ayuda a la comunidad?

Learning Goals

Language and Communication
• Child names and describes actual or pictured people, places, things, actions, attributes, and events.

Emergent Literacy: Reading
• Child retells or reenacts poems and stories in sequence.

Vocabulary

abuelo	abuelo	carpenter	carpintero
dentist	dentista	muralist	muralista
neighbors	vecinos	tia	tía

Differentiated Instruction

✋ Extra Support
Learn About Letters and Sounds
If...children have difficulty producing the /r/ sound, **then...**say *rain, rose,* and *read,* emphasizing the initial sound and having children look closely at the position of your mouth and lips.

⭐ Enrichment
Read Aloud
Have children think of other community helpers who might live in Quinito's neighborhood. Have them name the jobs and act out doing them.

Literacy Time

large group • 15 minutes

📖 Read Aloud

☑ Can children retell parts of *Quinito's Neighborhood*?

☑ Track children's use of various words to describe Quinito's neighborhood.

Build Background Review what children have learned about communities and neighborhoods.

● Ask: *Remember when I asked you who lives in your neighborhood? What do you like best about the neighborhood where you live?* ¿Quién vive en su vecindario? ¿Qué es lo que más les gusta de su vecindario?

Listen for Understanding Display *Quinito's Neighborhood*. Read aloud the title and author's name. Open the book at random and point to the text. Track the print to show the direction in which the words are read.

● Tell children that you will read the book. Explain that you will ask children to retell and act out parts of the story when you are finished.

● Read the book aloud. Review job titles and restate what the people do.

Respond to the Story Discuss the book. Have children take turns retelling things they remember about the story while others listen. Ask: *What job does _____ do to help the neighborhood?* ¿Qué trabajo hace _____ para ayudar al vecindario?

💡 TIP Help children focus on the characters and the setting as you talk about the book.

Learn About Letters and Sounds

☑ Can children identify the letters *Gg* and *Rr* and the sounds /g/ and /r/?

Learn About *Gg* and *Rr* Display the *ABC Picture Cards* for *Gg* and *Rr*.

● Touch the letters and have children name them.

● Tell children that one of the letters goes with the sound /r/. Have children make the sound /r/. Say: *When you say /r/ /r/ /r/ it sounds like a /r/ /r/ /r/ rocket taking off.* Cuando dicen /r/ /r/ /r/ suena como el /r/ /r/ /r/ ruido de un cohete al despegar.

● Then have children identify the letter that goes with /g/. Say *girl* and *garden* and show the pictures. Encourage children to think of other words beginning with /g/.

● Repeat with *ring, rabbit,* and other words that begin with /r/.

ELL Note that many languages do not have an exact equivalent for the English sound /r/. Check children's ability to identify /r/ by saying /r/ along with another sound, such as /l/, /w/, or /d/. Ask children to nod their heads when you say /r/ and shake them when you say another sound.

Quinito's Neighborhood
El vecindario de Quinito

ABC Picture Cards

Math Time

Observe and Investigate

☑ **Can children sort and label objects?**

Sort and Label Give children small boxes to sort their objects.

● Provide a variety of objects for children. Make sure that each object has several variations of its kind, such as several different dolls.

● Give each child a group of objects. Say: ***Make two groups. Put all the blue crayons in one box and all the blue markers in another.*** *Formen dos grupos. Coloquen todos los crayones azules en una caja y todos los marcadores azules en otra.*

● Once children have finished sorting their objects, help them label each box with the correct numeral to tell how many there are. Provide Numeral Cards for labeling. Say: ***How many blue markers are in this box? Place that Numeral Card in front of the box.*** *¿Cuántos marcadores azules hay en esta caja? Coloquen esa tarjeta de número en el frente de la caja.*

Building Blocks

Online Math Activity

Introduce Dinosaur Shop 1: Label Boxes. In this activity, children work in a store that sells toy dinosaurs, and they help label boxes with numerals to tell how many dinosaurs are in each box. Each child should complete the activity this week.

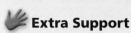

ᛘᛘᛘ Social and Emotional Development

Making Good Choices

☑ **Can children explain how to use and share classroom materials?**

Using Materials Correctly Display the *Making Good Choices Flip Chart,* page 15. Then display the two Dog Puppets. Say: ***The puppets aren't sure what the picture is all about. Let's explain it to them.*** *Los perritos no están seguros de qué pasa en esta ilustración. Expliquemos a los perritos qué sucede.*

● Say to Dog Puppets 1 and 2: ***Look at the children in the picture.*** *Miren a los niños de la ilustración.* Ask the dogs: ***Do you know what they're doing?*** *¿Saben qué están haciendo?* Ask children: ***What are some encouraging things you can say to them?*** *¿Qué cosas alentadoras pueden decirles?* Say: ***They are taking care of things they use in class.*** *Están cuidando los materiales que usan en clase.*

● Guide children to tell the puppets about the importance of taking care of classroom materials, sharing with others, and putting materials away.

● Play the song "We'll Take Good Care"/"Las cuidaremos" from the Making Good Choices Audio CD.

Making Good Choices Flip Chart, page 15

Learning Goals

Social and Emotional Development
● Child uses classroom materials carefully.
● Child participates in a variety of individual, small- and large-group activities.

Mathematics
● Child counts 1–10 concrete objects correctly.
● Child sorts objects and explains how the sorting was done.

Vocabulary

glue	pegamento	label	rotular
markers	marcadores	materials	materiales
objects	objetos	scissors	tijeras
share	compartir	sort	agrupar

Differentiated Instruction

✋ Extra Support

Observe and Investigate
If...children have difficulty labeling their boxes, **then...**count the numbers of objects in the boxes with them.

⭐ Enrichment

Making Good Choices
Have children work together to make a booklet or poster that tells class members how to care for materials properly. Have children draw pictures and write or dictate text to go with it.

Focus Question
Who helps the community?
¿Quién ayuda a la comunidad?

Learning Goals

Mathematics
• Child recites number words in sequence from one to thirty.

Vocabulary

correct	correcto	help	ayudar
mistake	error	mixup	confundir
Mr.	señor		

Differentiated Instruction

 Extra Support

Math Time
If...children have trouble correcting Mr. Mixup, **then...**clearly exaggerate the mistakes while using numbers less than 5.

 Enrichment

Math Time
Challenge children by using greater numbers for Mr. Mixup's mistakes.

 Special Needs

Behavioral Social/Emotional
If...children appear to be frustated following the more complex number-pattern mistakes, **then...**use simpler examples of number-pattern mistakes and repeat them.

Math Time

large group — 15 minutes

Mr. Mixup Introduce *Mr. Mixup* to children. Invite them to help Mr. Mixup find and correct his mistakes.

● Display the *Math and Science Flip Chart,* page 26. Say: *This is Mr. Mixup. He's always making mistakes! He needs our help. Éste es el Sr. Confundido. ¡Siempre comete errores! Necesita que lo ayudemos.*

● Instruct children to listen to Mr. Mixup's counting. Say: *Listen as Mr. Mixup counts. If he makes a mistake, say STOP! Escuchen mientras el Sr. Confundido cuenta. Si comete un error, digan ¡ALTO!* Begin counting, using the first row on the chart. Disguise your voice as Mr. Mixup.

● Say: *Hello, I am Mr. Mixup. Let me count for you! 1, 2, 3, 4, 6, 5.... "Hola, soy el Sr. Confundido. ¡Permítanme que cuente por ustedes! 1, 2, 3, 4, 6, 5..."* Continue until children yell: *Stop!* If children don't pick up on the mistake, ask them if 6 comes before 5. Say: *Hold on. Does 6 come before 5? Esperen. ¿6 está antes que 5?* Have children count from 1 to 6 correctly.

● Continue with the third row on the chart. Say: *Oops! I made a mistake. Let me try counting again. 1, 2, 3, 4, 5, 6, 8, 7. ¡Epa! Cometí un error. Permítanme que intente contar de nuevo: 1, 2, 3, 4, 5, 6, 8, 7.* Give children enough time to catch the mistake. Have them repeat the sequence correctly.

● Continue the activity with skipped numbers, such as 1, 2, 4, 5, and repeated numbers, such as 1, 2, 2, 3. If children are ready, use numbers higher than 10, such as the sequences on the second and fourth row of the chart.

*Math and Science
Flip Chart, page 26*

Center Time

> **Center Rotation** Center Time includes teacher-guided activities and independent activities. Refer to the **Learning Centers** on pages 100–101 for independent activity ideas.

 small group 30 minutes

Math and Science Center | Center Tip

☑ **Children match Dot Cards and Numeral Cards.**

Materials one set of Dot Cards (*Teacher's Treasure Book,* page 508) and one set of Numeral Cards (*Teacher's Treasure Book,* page 510) per child

Match the Dots Give each card set to children, making sure to keep each set separate.

● Say: *Place your cards face down. Flip over a Dot Card. Then flip over Numeral Cards until you have found the number that matches the number of dots. Have fun!* *Coloquen sus tarjetas mirando hacia abajo. Levanten las tarjetas de números hasta encontrar el número que coincida con la cantidad de puntos. ¡A jugar!*

● Encourage children to count out loud to check that they have the correct amount of dots.

● If children would like to play with partners, give one child the Dot Cards and the other the Numeral Cards.

Center Tip

If...children have difficulty reading numerals, **then...** place small dots on the side of the card with the numeral.

✓ Learning Goals

Emergent Literacy: Writing
● Child participates in free drawing and writing activities to deliver information.

Mathematics
● Child recites number words in sequence from one to thirty.

Writing

Recap what children told the puppets about how to care for materials in the classroom. Say: *Draw a picture showing how you take care of classroom materials.* *Hagan un dibujo para mostrar cómo cuidan los materiales del salón de clases.* Then ask them to tell what their pictures show. Record their answers. Read them back and have them write the words. Encourage all levels of writing.

Purposeful Play

☑ **Observe children as they count aloud to match cards.**

Children choose an open center for free playtime. Encourage children to use other manipulatives to match the dots.

Let's Say Good-Bye

 large group 15 minutes

 Read Aloud Revisit "The Traveling Musicians"/"Los músicos viajeros" for your afternoon Read Aloud. Help children listen for the /g/ sound and the /r/ sound.

 Home Connection Refer to the Home Connections activities listed in the Resources and Materials chart on page 97. Remind children to tell their families who helps the community. Sing the "Good-Bye Song"/"Hora de ir a casa" as children prepare to leave.

Let's Start the Day

Focus Question

Who helps the community?
¿Quién ayuda a la comunidad?

> **Opening Routines and Transition Tips**
> For **Opening Routines** and **Transition Tips** turn to pages 178–181 and visit **DLMExpressOnline.com** for more ideas.

📖 Read **"The Ram in the Chile Patch"**/"El carnero en el sembrado de chiles" from the *Teacher's Treasure Book,* page 283, for your morning Read Aloud.

 **Learning Goals**

Social and Emotional Development
• Child participates in a variety of individual, small- and large-group activities.

Language and Communication
• Child uses newly learned vocabulary daily in multiple contexts.

Emergent Literacy: Reading
• Child produces words with the same beginning sound.

Vocabulary

equipment	equipo	fire	incendio
firefighter	bombero	ladder	escalera
helmet	casco	hose	manguera

Differentiated Instruction

 Extra Support
Oral Language and Vocabulary
If...children have difficulty saying or using the word *firefighter*, **then...**have children say *fire*, then *fighter*, and repeat several times before joining the words to form *firefighter*.

 Enrichment
Oral Language and Vocabulary
Have children play I Spy with the *Oral Language Development Cards.* Ask them to take turns studying a picture and saying: *I spy with my little eye something that is red,* and so on. Have other children guess the object.

Language Time

 large group — 15 minutes

👥 **Social and Emotional Development** Check for understanding and recall of children's rules about talking and listening by asking children about taking turns talking and listening to each another when they are carrying out roles in the classroom.

Oral Language and Vocabulary

✓ **Can children use new vocabulary words to talk about fires and firefighters?**

Firefighting Talk about fires and the people who put them out. Ask: *What is a fire? What does a fire look like? What do you know about fires? ¿Qué es un incendio? ¿Cómo es un incendio? ¿Qué saben sobre los incendios?* Explain or elicit that fires can be dangerous. Ask: *Which community helpers put out fires? What tools do these helpers use? ¿Quiénes apagan los incendios? ¿Qué equipo usan estas personas?*

● Display *Oral Language Development Card 26.* Point to the firefighter and tell children that this is a firefighter. Point to and identify the different equipment, such as the helmet and the fire truck. Use the suggestions on the back of the card to generate discussion about fires and firefighting.

ELL Provide children with sentence starters to help them structure their ideas. Useful sentence starters for this activity might include *I see a ____;* and *A firefighter might use a ____.*

Phonological Awareness

✓ **Can children identify words that begin with the same sound as *fight* and *fires*?**

Words That Begin with the Same Sound Display the *Rhymes and Chants Flip Chart,* page 15. Read aloud the rhyme "Neighborhood Helpers."

● Focus on the words *fight* and *fires.* Have children say the words. Point out that the words begin with the same sound, /f/. Say /f/ and point to the position of your teeth and lips. Ask children what other words they know that begin with /f/. If necessary, point to your fingers and feet to elicit the words *fingers* and *feet.*

● Tell children that you will say some words. Explain and model that they should put their /f/ /f/ /f/ fingers on their /f/ /f/ /f/ feet if the word begins with the same sound as *fight* and *fires.*

● Say: **fine, rake, fun, fish, white, fur.**

Oral Language Development Card 26

Rhymes and Chants Flip Chart, page 15

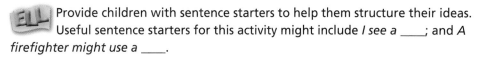

Center Time

Center Rotation Center Time includes teacher-guided activities and independent activities. Refer to the **Learning Centers** on pages 100–101 for independent activity ideas.

 small group · 60-90 minutes

ABC Center

Center Tip

 Assess children's ability to isolate initial sounds.

Materials markers, crayons, paper, pencils

Letters and Sounds Have children draw pictures of things that begin with the same sound as *firefighters*. Take dictation or help children write the word *firefighter*. Then encourage children to think of other words that begin with /f/. Have them draw and label these words.

● Have children share their drawings with the class.

If...children have trouble determining other words that begin with /f/, **then...** describe things that begin with /f/, such as *farm, food,* and *foot.* Have children name each item you describe.

Creativity Center

Center Tip

 Listen for use of vocabulary words that relate to firefighting.

Materials cardboard, paper-towel tubes, paper, scissors, markers, tape, glue

Make Firefighting Equipment Have children name some of the equipment used by firefighters. Then have children use materials to create and decorate their own hoses, fire engines, ladders, and so on.

● Have children talk about what they are making and how a firefighter might use it.

● Allow children to make objects that are either two- or three-dimensional.

● Encourage children to play the role of helper when other children are having difficulty identifying firefighter equipment.

● Suggest that children act out how each item might be used.

If...children have trouble remembering what equipment firefighters might use, **then...**display the picture of the firefighter on *Oral Language Development Card 26.*

Learning Goals

Social and Emotional Development
• Child participates in a variety of individual, small- and large-group activities.

Language and Communication
• Child uses newly learned vocabulary daily in multiple contexts.

Emergent Literacy: Reading
• Child produces words with the same beginning sound.

Differentiated Instruction

 Extra Support

ABC Center
If...writing the letter *f* is difficult for children, **then...**have them practice by using their arms and hands to write it in the air or on an interactive whiteboard.

 Enrichment

Creativity Center
Challenge children to discuss and then draw or build models of safety gear for firefighters. Have them explain and demonstrate what it does and how it works.

Special Needs

Behavioral Social/Emotional
If...children start drawing or creating objects unrelated to fires and firefighting, **then...** gently bring them back to the assignment by asking, *How would a firefighter use that? ¿De qué manera podría usar esto un bombero?*

Focus Question
Who helps the community?
¿Quién ayuda a la comunidad?

Learning Goals

Language and Communication
• Child names and describes actual or pictured people, places, things, actions, attributes, and events.

Emergent Literacy: Reading
• Child names most upper- and lowercase letters of the alphabet.

• Child identifies the letter that stands for a given sound.

• Child retells or reenacts poems and stories in sequence.

• Child asks and answers questions about books read aloud (such as, "Who?" "What?" "Where?").

Vocabulary

community	comunidad
construction workers	trabajadores de la construcción
neighborhood	vecindario
neighbors	vecinos
sidewalks	aceras
trash	basura

Differentiated Instruction

 Extra Support

Read Aloud
If...children have trouble using new vocabulary words from the book, **then...**have them point to the pictures in the book that they want to describe, and help them by supplying the beginning sounds of the words (such as /f/ for *firefighter* or /n/ for *neighbors*).

 **Enrichment**

Learn About Letters and Sounds
Give children simple picture books. Ask them to find upper and lower case *Gg* and *Rr*. Have them mark the letters wth sticky notes.

Literacy Time

large group   15 minutes

Read Aloud

✅ **Can children retell and act out information in the story about communities and neighborhoods?**

Build Background Display *Concept Big Book 2: In the Community* and remind children that the book tells about neighborhoods and communities.

● Ask: *What have we learned about communities? What have we learned about neighborhoods? ¿Qué hemos aprendido sobre las comunidades? ¿Qué hemos aprendido sobre los vecindarios?*

Listen for Understanding Ask children to listen for the names of community helpers and the different things people do when they live together in a neighborhood.

● Read the book aloud. Emphasize the names and jobs of the community helpers.

● Check children's knowledge periodically by making true and false statements about a community, such as: *A community has many families* or *A community has one home. En una comunidad viven muchas familias. Una comunidad está formada por un solo hogar* Have children put their thumbs up when you say a true statement and down when you say a false one.

Respond to the Story Discuss the story. Help children recall information about neighborhoods and communities. Have children act out some of the activities mentioned in the text, such as planting flowers or placing trash in a trashcan.

Learn About Letters and Sounds

✅ **Can children identify and write the letters *Gg* and *Rr*?**

Learn About Letters *Gg* and *Rr* Display the *ABC Big Book* page for *Gg*.

● Touch the letter. Have children name it.

● Remind children that *Gg* makes the sound /g/. Have children say the names of the pictures on the *ABC Big Book* page for *Gg*. Emphasize the initial /g/ in each word.

● Have children write *G* and then *g* in the air or on an interactive whiteboard. Guide their arms and hands if needed the first time through. Give children a simple chant to help them remember the motion, such as: *Around, around, around—and down!* for lower case *g*.

● Repeat with *Rr*. Then have children write *Gg* and *Rr* with their fingers in sand or on a table surface.

ELL Look for opportunities to single out English learners as experts and to send other children to them for help. For example, a child with limited English proficiency can become the class expert in writing lower case *g*.

In the Community
En la comunidad

ABC Big Book

large group 🕐 **15 minutes**

Math Time

Observe and Investigate

✓ **Can children recognize numerals 1–9?**

Ten Little Birdies Invite children to listen to a song about "Ten Little Birdies."

● As each bird "flies" away, "fly" both hands and return, one less finger up.

Ten Little Birdies

Ten little birdies chirping just fine. One flew away, then there were nine.
Nine little birdies wait, wait, wait. One flew away, then there were eight.
Eight little birdies, not quite eleven. One flew away, then there were seven.
Seven little birdies in a nest they fix. One flew away, then there were six.
Six little birdies see a busy hive. One flew away, then there were five.
Five little birdies watching others soar. One flew away, then there were four.
Four little birdies sitting in a tree. One flew away, then there were three.
Three little birdies love a sky of blue. One flew away, then there were two.
Two little birdies warm in the sun. One flew away, then there was one.
One little birdie having little fun. The birdie flew away, then there were none.

● Repeat the song as you hold up Numeral Cards.

● Allow children to hold up Numeral Cards as the group sings along with you.

ELL Provide visual support by positioning ten toy birds or images of birds on a surface and taking them away one by one as you recite the song.

large group 🕐 **15 minutes**

👫 Social and Emotional Development

Making Good Choices

✓ **Do children take care of classroom materials?**

Using Materials Correctly Display the *Making Good Choices Flip Chart*, page 15. Tell children they will use puppets to act out what is on the chart.

● Put on one of the puppets and have it say: **Let's draw. I'll get the markers.**
Dibujemos algo. Buscaré los marcadores.

● Have a child put on the other puppet and say something to match the flip chart, such as *I'll get the scissors.*

● Continue as above. Make sure that the children role-play fair use of materials, treating materials properly, and putting materials away.

● Repeat, with two children carrying out the role-play with both puppets.

Building Blocks

Online Math Activity

Children can complete Space Race: Number Choice and Dinosaur Shop 1 during computer time or Center Time.

Making Good Choices Flip Chart, page 15

✓ Learning Goals

Social and Emotional Development
• Child participates in a variety of individual, small- and large-group activities.

Mathematics
• Child demonstrates that, when counting, the last number indicates how many objects were counted.

• Child recognizes and names numerals 0 through 9.

Vocabulary

away	lejos
bird	pájaro
flew	volar
glue	pegamento
markers	marcadores
materials	materiales
scissors	tijeras
share	compartir

Differentiated Instruction

✋ **Extra Support**

Making Good Choices
If...children freeze while holding the puppet and can't think of anything to do or say, **then...** ask the puppet a question for the child to answer.

⭐ **Enrichment**

Observe and Investigate
Before you tell the next number of birds remaining, ask children to guess the number.

Accommodations for 3's

Making Good Choices
If...children lose track of the flip chart scenario while role-playing with puppets, **then...**gently redirect them by saying: **What will you do with those scissors?** *¿Qué harán con esas tijeras?* or **What materials should the puppets get out next?** *¿Qué materiales deben sacar los títeres ahora?*

Focus Question
Who helps the community?
¿Quién ayuda a la comunidad?

 Learning Goals

Social Studies
• Child understands and discusses roles, responsibilities, and services provided by community workers.

• Child identifies the U.S. Flag and state flag.

• Child recites the Pledge of Allegiance.

Vocabulary

flag   bandera   pledge   juramento

promise   promesa

Differentiated Instruction

 Extra Support

Understand and Participate
If...children have trouble remembering community helpers, **then...**display books and pictures to remind them of jobs they have learned about.

 Enrichment

Understand and Participate
Have children make a book that names and describes school helpers. Use the same format as the community helpers book in this activity.

Social Studies Time

 large group   20 minutes

Language and Communication Skills Have children identify the flags of their state and the United States. Have them face the United States flag. Lead them through the Pledge of Allegiance. Remind children that when they say the Pledge of Allegiance, they are saying they want to help their country and its people.

Oral Language and Academic Vocabulary

✓ **Can children identify community helpers and explain their own role in their school and home communities?**

Community Workers Review what a community is. Tell children that people have jobs to do in a community. Say: *Community workers spend a lot of time helping other people in the community.* *Las personas que trabajan en la comunidad dedican mucho tiempo a ayudar a otras personas de la comunidad.* Ask children how they can be community helpers too:

● *What do you do in school that helps our school community?* *¿Qué hacen en en la escuela para ayudar a la comunidad escolar?*

● *What do you do at home that helps your family?* *¿Qué hacen en casa para ayudar a su familia?*

Ask children to share with the class what they know about workers in their community.

Understand and Participate

✓ **What do children know about the names and duties of community helpers?**

Class Book Tell children that they will make a class book about community helpers.

● Ask children to name community helpers they have learned about during the week. Write the helpers' jobs or titles on the board.

● Choose one of the helpers listed. Ask children to tell you some things about that person and what he or she does. Write the ideas on chart paper or an interactive whiteboard. Use a different page for each helper.

● Continue with other workers and their jobs. Print and/or bind the pages. Use a page for the cover and write the title and authors.

TIP It will probably not be feasible to have children illustrate the book while you are taking dictation. Have children contribute pictures later on, and be sure to show the book again and read it aloud when all the pictures are complete.

ELL Model this sentence: *I help when I put away the markers.* Use a child's name and rephrase the sentence for the class: *Chen helps when he puts away the markers.* Emphasize the changes in pronouns and verbs.

Center Time

Center Rotation Center Time includes teacher-guided activities and independent activities. Refer to the **Learning Centers** on pages 100–101 for independent activity ideas.

Small Group | 30 minutos

Refer to the **Learning Centers** on pages 100–101

Library and Listening Center

✓ **Can children name the roles of community helpers?**

Materials books and magazines that contain pictures of police officers, firefighters, and other community helpers

Telling Stories Ask children to find pictures of community helpers in the books and magazines. Then have them use the pictures to make up and tell each other stories about the helpers.

- Have children focus on the helpers' actions and feelings as they tell their stories.

- Remind children that it is important to be good listeners as well as good storytellers.

Center Tip

If...children use vague terms in their stories when referring to the helpers (such as *her* or *the guy*), **then...**review the job titles of the helpers in the pictures and encourage children to use the titles as they talk.

Learning Goals

Emergent Literacy: Writing
• Child participates in free drawing and writing activities to deliver information.

Social Studies
• Child understands and discusses roles, responsibilities, and services provided by community workers.

Writing

Have children draw pictures of helping in the classroom or in their homes. Have them complete the following sentence frame: *I am helping to _____ at school/home.* Display the pictures in the Library and Listening Center.

Purposeful Play

✓ **Observe whether children play constructively and cooperatively with classmates.**

Children choose an open center area for free playtime. Encourage children to cooperate as they incorporate community helpers into their play, whether by acting out the work of these helpers or in some other way.

Let's Say Good-Bye

large group | 15 minutes

 Read Aloud Revisit "The Ram in the Chile Patch"/"El carnero en el sembrado de chiles" for your afternoon Read Aloud. Have children help you retell the story.

 Home Connection Refer to the Home Connections activities listed in the Resources and Materials chart on page 97. Remind children to tell their families about different community helpers. Sing the "Good-Bye Song"/"Hora de ir a casa" as children prepare to leave.

Focus Question

Who helps the community? ¿Quién ayuda a la comunidad?

Learning Goals

Language and Communication
• Child uses newly learned vocabulary daily in multiple contexts.

Emergent Literacy: Reading
• Child produces words with the same beginning sound.

• Child retells or reenacts poems and stories in sequence.

Vocabulary

bake	hornear		
folktale	cuento folclórico		
harvest	cosecha	help	ayudar
lesson	lección	market	mercado
wheat	trigo	wheelbarrow	carretilla

Differentiated Instruction

 Extra Support

Oral Language and Vocabulary
If...children have trouble following the story, **then...**read the story again and have them manipulate the flannel board pieces on the flannel board to match the words.

 Enrichment

Oral Language and Vocabulary
Have children discuss *What if* questions, such as: *What if the goose had helped the hen plant the seeds?* Encourage them to tell how the story would be different.

Accommodations for 3's

Oral Language and Vocabulary
If...children have difficulty remembering the various characters in the folktale, **then...**provide pictures of the various animal characters.

Let's Start the Day

▶ **Opening Routines and Transition Tips**
For **Opening Routines** and **Transition Tips** turn to pages 178–181 and visit **DLMExpressOnline.com** for more ideas.

 Read **"Engine Ninety-Nine"/**"La máquina noventa y nueve" from the *Teacher's Treasure Book*, page 250, for your morning Read Aloud.

Language Time

 large group 15 minutes

🧍🧍🧍 **Social and Emotional Development** Explain that because you are the teacher, it is your job to take care of the children in the class. Point out that you are helping them learn and stay safe.

Oral Language and Vocabulary

✓ **Can children identify the lesson of "The Little Red Hen"?**

Lessons in Folktales Tell children that you will be reading a kind of story called a folktale. Ask children if they know what a folktale is. (a story that often has a moral, or a lesson, that tells how people should behave)

● Read aloud "The Little Red Hen"/"La gallinita roja" from the *Teacher's Treasure Book*, page 288. Use the flannel board pieces to help you tell the story.

● Ask children questions about the story, such as: *What did the hen bake? ¿Qué horneó la gallinita?*

● Ask: *What might the animals do differently next time? What did they learn? What can you do when you are asked for help?* ¿Qué pueden hacer los animales la próxima vez? ¿Qué aprendieron? ¿Qué pueden hacer ustedes cuando alguien les pida ayuda?

● Have children use the flannel board pieces to retell and act out events in the story.

Phonological Awareness

✓ **Can children produce words that begin with the same sound as two given words?**

Words That Begin with the Same Sound Display the two Dog Puppets. Tell children that the puppets are eager to show what they know about words that begin with the same sound.

● Have one puppet say: *sing,* emphasizing the initial *s*. Have the other puppet say: *soft.* Then say: *sun.*

● Repeat, having the puppets say the word pairs *tie/toe, lake/leg,* and *more/me.*

● Encourage children to offer other words that start with the same sounds.

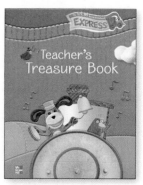

Teacher's Treasure Book, page 288

ELL Some languages don't have the /l/ sound. Exaggerate the sound and point out the position of your mouth and tongue to help children hear and pronounce /l/.

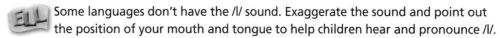

Center Time

▶ **Center Rotation** Center Time includes teacher-guided activities and independent activities. Refer to the **Learning Centers** on pages 100–101 for independent activity ideas.

small group 60–90 minutes

Pretend and Learn Center | Center Tip

 Assess children's ability to retell and re-enact a story.

 Listen for children's use of new vocabulary words.

Materials dress-up clothes, ordinary classroom materials to use as props

The Little Red Hen Have children act out parts of the story "The Little Red Hen."

- Ask children to pretend to be one or more of the characters in the story.

- Have children interact with each other to retell parts of the story.

Center Tip

If...several children want to play the same role, **then...** suggest that they take turns, or tell children that more than one child can play the role at the same time.

Writer's Center | Center Tip

 Monitor children's skill and comfort levels while they write.

Materials pencils, markers, crayons, paper

Write a Story Have children write and illustrate a story that has a lesson or moral.

- Ask children what they want their stories to teach readers.

- Have children write or scribble words. Take dictation if asked. Have them draw pictures. Help them put pages together into book form.

Center Tip

If...children are not sure what a moral or lesson is, **then...** review the moral of "The Little Red Hen." Give other examples as needed.

✓ Learning Goals

Social and Emotional Development
• Child participates in a variety of individual, small- and large-group activities.

Emergent Literacy: Reading
• Child retells or reenacts poems and stories in sequence.

Emergent Literacy: Writing
• Child uses scribbles, shapes, pictures, symbols, and letters to represent language.

Differentiated Instruction

🖐 Extra Support
Writer's Center
If...children are frustrated because their drawings do not look the way they planned, **then...**have them use stickers or magazine cutouts to illustrate their writing.

⭐ Enrichment
Pretend and Learn Center
Ask children to change the story so the little red hen is not making bread but is doing something else.

💜 Special Needs
Delayed Motor Development
If...writing and drawing are difficult for children, **then...**have them use large crayons with spongy grips and to take breaks as needed.

Circle Time

Learning Goals

Social and Emotional Development
• Child participates in a variety of individual, small- and large-group activities.

Emergent Literacy: Reading
• Child names most upper- and lowercase letters of the alphabet.

• Child identifies the letter that stands for a given sound.

• Child retells or reenacts poems and stories in sequence.

Vocabulary

bake	hornear
folktale	cuento folclórico
harvest	cosecha
help	ayudar
lesson	lección
market	mercado
wheat	trigo
wheelbarrow	carretilla

Differentiated Instruction

 Extra Support
Learn About Letters and Sounds
If...children are not certain of what it means for things or features to be alike, **then...**display two common classroom objects, such as two blocks, and explain how they are alike.

Enrichment
Learn About Letters and Sounds
Ask children to compare upper case *G* with other upper case letters, such as *C* or *I*. Repeat with other pairs of letters that include lower case *g* or upper/lower case *R*.

Accommodations for 3's
Read Aloud
If...it is hard for children to remember what happens next in the story, **then...**start reading the next part as a prompt.

Literacy Time

Read Aloud

Can children connect "The Little Red Hen" with the idea of community helpers?

Assess whether children can retell or reenact events in the story.

Build Background Display "The Little Red Hen"/"La gallinita roja" from the *Teacher's Treasure Book,* page 288, and read the title aloud. Remind children that this story is a folktale and that it has a moral.

● Say: *A moral is a lesson. Folktales are stories that have lessons. They are written to remind people how they should behave.* Una moraleja es una lección o una enseñanza. Los cuentos folclóricos son cuentos que tienen lecciones. Se han escrito recordar a las personas cómo se deben comportarse.

● Ask children how they can be good listeners as you read.

Listen for Enjoyment Have children listen for words and phrases that repeat, such as *Not I* and *And she did.*

● Read the story aloud. Encourage children to join you in saying some of the repeating expressions.

● Have children take turns acting out the story with flannel board pieces as you read.

Respond to the Story Explain that the animals in the story all live in the same house, so they are a community. Ask: *Do you think that the goose, dog, and cat were being good community helpers?* ¿Creen que la gansa, el perro y la gata se comportaron como buenos trabajadores comunitarios? Have children retell events in the story as they explain their thinking.

 Help children with homophones and words that have multiple meanings. Children may know the noun form of *plant* but not the verb form, for instance. Or they they may know *flower* but not *flour.* Use gestures, pictures, and simple definitions to help children learn these terms.

Learn About Letters and Sounds

Can children explain how the letters *Gg* and *Rr* are similar?

Learn About Letters and Sounds Write the upper case letters *G* and *R* on chart paper or an interactive whiteboard.

● Touch the letters. Have children name them.

● Help children say the sound /g/ for *g* and /r/ for *r*.

● Ask children how the letters are alike. Point out or elicit that they are both upper case letters and that they are about the same size. Encourage children to offer other ideas as well.

● Repeat with *g* and *r*.

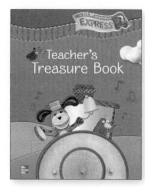

Teacher's Treasure Book, page 288

large group 15 minutes

Online Math Activity

Children can complete Space Race: Number Choice and Dinosaur Shop 1 during computer time or Center Time.

Math Time

Observe and Investigate

☑ **Can children sort and label objects?**

Sort and Label This lesson is a variation of the activity introduced on Day 2. Have children sort and label objects according to criteria that they determine. Give children small boxes to sort their objects.

- Provide a variety of objects for sorting. Make sure that there are several variations of each object, for example, different dolls or dinosaurs.

- Give each child a group of objects, or have them choose an object and find other objects that are similar. Tell children to collect as many of the object as they can.

- Prompt children by giving them ideas for sorting their groups. Say: *What do you notice about the dolls? What color hair do they have? OK, sort the dolls by hair color. Put all dolls with brown hair in this box.* ¿Qué color de cabello tienen las muñecas? Bien, agrupen las muñecas según el color del cabello. ¿Qué pueden notar sobre las muñecas? ¿Qué color de cabello tienen? Ahora, agrúpenlas según su color de cabello. Pongan todas las muñecas de cabello café en esta caja. Have children label each box with the correct numeral to tell how many there are.

- Provide Numeral Cards for labeling. Say: *How many dolls are in this box? Place the correct Numeral Card in front of the box.* ¿Cuántas muñecas hay en esta caja? Pongan la tarjeta de números correcta frente a la caja. Provide support by asking questions about the objects. For example, ask: *How many of these dolls have yellow hair?* ¿Cuántas de estas muñecas tienen cabello amarillo?

large group 15 minutes

✝✝✝ Social and Emotional Development

Making Good Choices

☑ **Can children recall and explain the proper use of classroom materials?**

Using Materials Fairly Remind children that they taught the puppets about the *Making Good Choices Flip Chart* picture two days earlier. Explain that you're not sure if the puppets understood.

- Put on both puppets. Have one say: *I want the blue marker! ¡Quiero el marcador azul!* Have the other explain that he is almost done with it. Have the first puppet try to grab the marker from the second puppet.

- Turn to the class and ask what happened. Then invite children to tell what the problem was and how the puppets might solve the problem.

- Repeat with other scenarios.

Making Good Choices Flip Chart, page 15

Learning Goals

Social and Emotional Development
- Child participates in a variety of individual, small- and large-group activities.

Mathematics
- Child counts 1–10 concrete objects correctly.
- Child sorts objects and explains how the sorting was done.

Vocabulary

box	caja	label	rotular
markers	marcadores	materials	materiales
share	compartir	sort	grupar

Differentiated Instruction

✋ **Extra Support**

Making Good Choices

If...children focus only on what the puppets should not be doing (*don't grab, don't drop them, don't throw them*), **then**...help children express their ideas in more positive ways (*share, take turns, put things away*).

⭐ **Enrichment**

Observe and Investigate

Ask children to think of other ways their objects could be sorted.

Accommodations for 3's

Observe and Investigate

If...children have difficulty sorting, **then**... provide individual support.

Focus Question
Who helps the community?
¿Quién ayuda a la comunidad?

Math Time

 large group · 15 minutes

Mr. Mixup Tell children they are going to help Mr. Mixup again. Talk about the importance of helping someone who makes mistakes.

● Display the *Math and Science Flip Chart,* page 26. Say: *Here's Mr. Mixup again. He's always making mistakes. He still needs our help.* *Aquí está el Sr. Confundido nuevamente. Siempre comete errores. Todavía necesita nuestra ayuda.*

● Continue making similar mistakes as before. Say: *Listen as Mr. Mixup counts. Remember, if he makes a mistake, say STOP!* *Escuchen mientras el Sr. Confundido cuenta. Recuerden, si comete un error, digan ¡ALTO!*

● Say: *"Hello, again! I am Mr. Mixup. Let me count for you! 1, 2, 3, 4, 5, 6, 8, 7... ."* *¡Hola! Aquí estoy de nuevo. Soy el Sr. Confundido. ¡Permítanme contar por ustedes! 1, 2, 3, 4, 5, 6, 8, 7...*Continue until children yell *Stop!* If children don't pick up on the mistake, ask them if 8 comes after 6. Say: *Hold on. Does 8 come after 6?* *Un momento. ¿El 8 viene después del 6?* Count from 1 to 8 correctly.

● If children are ready for numbers greater than 10, continue with another pattern. Say: *Oops! I made a mistake. Let me try counting again. 11, 12, 13, 14, 16.* *¡Epa! Cometí un error. Permítanme intentar contar de nuevo. 11, 12, 13, 14, 16.* Allow children enough time to catch the mistake, and then count the sequence correctly.

● Allow children to take a turn being Mr. Mixup.

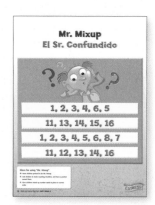

Math and Science Flip Chart, page 26

Center Time

▶ **Center Rotation** Center Time includes teacher-guided activities and independent activities. Refer to the **Learning Centers** on pages 100–101 for independent activity ideas.

  small group · 30 minutes

Math and Science Center | Center Tip

✓ **Can children sort and count numerals to 30?**

Materials several sets of tactile numerals, muffin pans or paper cups for sorting

Sort! Provide several sets of tactile numerals (magnetic, foam, and so on), and set up muffin tins or other containers for sorting.

- Tell children they will sort numerals into muffin tins. Model how to do the activity. Say: **How many 1's can we find? Let's put all the 1's in a muffin tin.** *¿Cuánto números 1 podemos encontrar? Coloquemos todos los números 1 en una bandeja.* Once you have sorted 1's, count them with children.

- Have children continue sorting numerals and counting groups. Periodically ask how many of a certain number children have sorted. From time to time, lead children in rote counting from 1 to 10, 1 to 20, or 1 to 30.

Center Tip

If...children have difficulty sorting, **then**...label paper cups with numerals.

✓ Learning Goals

Emergent Literacy: Writing
• Child uses scribbles, shapes, pictures, symbols, and letters to represent language.

Mathematics
• Child recites number words in sequence from one to thirty.

Writing

Recap the day. Help children recall the moral of "The Little Red Hen." Ask: **What is the moral, or lesson, of the story?** *¿Cuál es la moraleja o lección del cuento?* Record their answers on chart paper or an interactive whiteboard. Read them back as you track the print and emphasize the correspondence between speech and print. Encourage children to track their print along with you.

Purposeful Play

✓ **Observe children sorting numerals.**

Children choose an open center area for free playtime. Encourage children to help each other sort numerals.

Let's Say Good-Bye

 large group · 15 minutes

 **Read Aloud** Revisit "Engine Ninety-Nine"/"La máquina noventa y nueve" for your afternoon Read Aloud. Have children listen for words that begin with the same sound.

 Home Connection Refer to the Home Connections activities listed in the Resources and Materials chart on page 97. Remind children to tell their families about different community helpers. Sing the "Good-Bye Song"/"Hora de ir a casa" as children prepare to leave.

DAY 5

Let's Start the Day

Focus Question
**Who helps the community?
¿Quién ayuda a la comunidad?**

Learning Goals

Social and Emotional Development
• Child participates in a variety of individual, small- and large-group activities.

Language and Communication
• Child uses newly learned vocabulary daily in multiple contexts.

Emergent Literacy: Reading
• Child produces words with the same beginning sound.

Vocabulary

clerk	cajero
electrical	eléctrico
groceries	alimentos
roads	autopistas
sweepers	barrendero
truck	camión

Differentiated Instruction

 Extra Support

Phonological Awareness

If...children have trouble saying or identifying the sound /h/, **then...**tell them that /h/ is sometimes called the "puppy dog" sound and have them pant like a puppy before each new word you say.

 Enrichment

Oral Language and Vocabulary

Encourage children to memorize the first four or last four lines of the rhyme.

 Special Needs

Speech and Language Delays

If...three-year-olds have difficulty panting the /h/ sound, **then...**provide one-on-one help.

Opening Routines and Transition Tips

For **Opening Routines** and **Transition Tips** turn to pages 178–181 and visit **DLMExpressOnline.com** for more ideas.

 Read **"Helpful Friends"**/"Amigos útiles" from the *Teacher's Treasure Book, page 168,* for your morning Read Aloud.

Language Time

large group — 15 minutes

 Social and Emotional Development Ask children to think of some ways they can help each other in the classroom.

Oral Language and Vocabulary

 Can children use new vocabulary words to identify community helpers and tell what they do?

Community Helpers Tell children that today you will be talking about different kinds of community helpers.

● Display the *Rhymes and Chants Flip Chart,* page 15. Have children name and tell about each helper. Ask: ***What does this worker do in the community?*** *¿Qué hace este trabajador en la comunidad?*

● Then ask: ***What other community helpers can you name that are not in the rhyme?*** *¿Pueden nombrar a otras personas que trabajan en la comunidad?* Have children describe what those helpers do.

● Make a list of every community helper named. With the class, count the number of community helpers in the list.

ELL Review numbers in English before starting to count the helpers. Point out cognates, such as Spanish *seis* and English *six*.

Phonological Awareness

 Can children identify words with the same initial sound as *help* and *heavy*?

Words with Initial /h/ Make the sound /h/ several times in succession. Have children say the sound themselves.

● Display the *Rhymes and Chants Flip Chart,* page 15. Say the words *help* and *helpers,* emphasizing the initial /h/. Then say the word *happy.*

● Ask children to raise their "hands high" if *happy* begins with the same sound as *help* and *heavy.* Repeat with *hop, big, hole, cat,* and *hat.* Ask children to offer other words that begin with /h/.

Neighborhood Helpers
Electrical workers
Connect all the wires.
Firefighters help us
Fight dangerous fires.
Truck drivers deliver
Groceries and loads.
And street sweepers clean
Our streets and our roads.
A doctor, a dentist,
A teacher, a clerk,
They all help our neighborhood
Each day at work.

Rhymes and Chants Flip Chart, page 15

Center Time

 small group 60–90 minutes

ABC Center

✓ **Can children identify and produce words that begin with /h/?**

Materials *Photo Library CD-ROM*, crayons, paper

Find /h/ Items Display pictures from the CD-ROM of items community helpers might use. Half of the images should picture items that begin with the /h/ sound. Help children name each item.

● Hold up an /h/ item. Guide children to find other items with the same initial sound. Prompt them to name each item aloud.

● Ask children to draw pictures of a community worker using one of the items.

Center Tip

If...children have trouble naming items, **then...**have them pair with another child who can help them.

Construction Center

✓ **Can children assume a role in a group project?**

✓ **Track children's use of new vocabulary when describing their roles.**

Materials blocks, cardboard tubes and boxes, tape, glue, decorating materials

Build a Fire Station Have children build a fire station, police headquarters, dentist's office, or other building where community helpers might work.

● Have children work in small groups. Be sure that each group member assumes a role, such as a builder, decorator, or mover.

● Encourage children to present their structures to the class and to describe what community workers use their building and what they do to help their community.

Center Tip

If...children are not sure what a particular workplace looks like, **then...**have them look for ideas in books or magazines that tell about community helpers.

✓ Learning Goals

Language and Communication
• Child uses newly learned vocabulary daily in multiple contexts.

Emergent Literacy: Reading
• Child produces words with the same beginning sound.

Differentiated Instruction

 Extra Support
Construction Center
If...children are unfamiliar with places where community helpers work, **then...**provide them with pictures of community helpers at their places of work.

 Enrichment
ABC Center
Challenge children to name community-helper jobs that have the same initial sound, such as dentist/doctor and farmer/firefighter.

Accommodations for 3's
Construction Center
If...children are most familiar with teachers as community helpers, **then...**suggest that they look around and construct a teacher's workplace—a classroom.

Focus Question
Who helps the community?
¿Quién ayuda a la comunidad?

Literacy Time

 Read Aloud

 What do children know about family-related vocabulary?

Build Background Remind children that *Quinito's Neighborhood* describes neighbors who live near each other in the neighborhood. Explain that some of these people are members of Quinito's family.

- Say: ***Community helpers can be members of your family. Many of Quinito's family members work in his neighborhood.*** *Las personas que trabajan en la comunidad pueden ser miembros de su familia. Muchos de los familiares de Quinito trabajan en su vecindario.* Ask: ***Does someone in your family work in your neighborhood?*** *¿Alguno de sus familiares trabaja en el vecindario donde ustedes viven?*

Listen for Understanding Display *Quinito's Neighborhood* and read the title. Explain that some of the words in the book are Spanish. Have children listen for the Spanish words and raise their hands when they hear them.

Respond to the Story Ask children to retell the story of Quinito's neighborhood. Ask: ***Can you name one thing you like about Quinito's neighborhood? Which person in the book would you like to meet? Retell the part of the story that makes you want to meet this person.*** *¿Pueden mencionar algo que les guste del vecindario de Quinito? ¿Qué persona del libro desearían conocer? Vuelvan a contar la parte en que se menciona a esa persona.* Have children retell or re-enact parts of the story.

TIP Look to Spanish-speaking members of the class to help native English speakers learn words such as *tio* and *tia*.

Quinito's Neighborhood
El vecindario de Quinito

Learn About Letters and Sounds

 Can children explain how the letters *Gg* and *Rr* are different?

Learn About the Alphabet Write upper case letters *G* and *R* on the board.

- Touch the letters. Have children name them.

- Help children say /g/ for *g* and /r/ for *r*.

- Ask children how the letters are different. Point out that one starts with a curve and the other starts with a straight line. Encourage children to offer other ideas.

- Repeat with *g* and *r*.

ELL To model how two things can be different, display a penny and a red checker. Tell children that they are different colors and different sizes. Help children form their own sentences with the word *different*.

Learning Goals

Emergent Literacy: Reading
- Child names most upper- and lowercase letters of the alphabet.
- Child identifies the letter that stands for a given sound.
- Child retells or reenacts poems and stories in sequence.
- Child asks and answers questions about books read aloud (such as, "Who?" "What?" "Where?").

Vocabulary

abuela	abuela	cousin	primo
mami	mami	muralist	muralista
neighbors	vecinos	papi	papi
tia	tía	tio	tío

Differentiated Instruction

 Extra Support
Read Aloud
If...children do not raise their hands when they hear Spanish words, **then...**alert children when a Spanish word will appear on a following page so they will be ready for it.

 Enrichment
Read Aloud
Ask children to determine which people in the story are related to Quinito, and which are not.

large group 15 minutes

Math Time

Observe and Investigate

☑️ **Can children count 1–10 items?**

Ten Little Birdies Tell children they will listen to the song "Ten Little Birdies" again. Explain that this lesson repeats the activity you introduced to them a few days ago.

- Say: *Today I will ask you to guess the number of birds before I say it.* Hoy les pediré que adivinen la cantidad de pájaros antes de que yo la diga. Model the first two lines before you begin.

Ten Little Birdies

Ten little birdies chirping just fine. One flew away, then there were nine.
Nine little birdies wait, wait, wait. One flew away, then there were eight.
Eight little birdies, not quite eleven. One flew away, then there were seven.
Seven little birdies in a nest they fix. One flew away, then there were six.
Six little birdies see a busy hive. One flew away, then there were five.
Five little birdies watching others soar. One flew away, then there were four.
Four little birdies sitting in a tree. One flew away, then there were three.
Three little birdies love a sky of blue. One flew away, then there were two.
Two little birdies warm in the sun. One flew away, then there was one.
One little birdie having little fun. The birdie flew away, then there were none.

large group 15 minutes

ᨬᨬᨬ Social and Emotional Development

Making Good Choices

☑️ **Do children take care of classroom materials?**

☑️ **Do children take on roles in the classroom community?**

Review the Making Good Choices Chart Display the *Making Good Choices Flip Chart*, page 15. Ask: **What do the pictures show?** ¿Qué muestra esta ilustración? Turn the chart away from the children and ask them to remember and describe what they can about the picture and situation.

- Have 2–3 pairs of children act out a situation using materials. Have one child describe the situation while the others act it out.

- Ask: **What does the chart remind us to do when we're done with materials?** ¿Qué nos recuerda el rotafolio que debemos hacer cuando terminamos de usar los materiales?

Making Good Choices Flip Chart, page 15

Building Blocks

Online Math Activity

Children can complete Space Race: Number Choice and Dinosaur Shop 1 during computer time or Center Time.

 Learning Goals

Social and Emotional Development
- Child uses classroom materials carefully.
- Child participates in a variety of individual, small- and large-group activities.

Mathematics
- Child counts 1–10 concrete objects correctly.

Vocabulary

away	lejos	bird	perriots
flew	volar	glue	pegamento
markers	marcadores	materials	materiales
scissors	tijeras	share	compartir

Differentiated Instruction

 Extra Support
Observe and Investigate

If...children have difficulty sitting still during the song, **then...**encourage them to repeat after you.

 Enrichment
Observe and Investigate

Ask children to show the number of birds with their hands and fingers.

 Special Needs
Hearing Impairments
If...children have difficulty hearing the song, **then...**use gestures to illustrate meaning as you sing.

Focus Question
Who helps the community?
¿Quién ayuda a la comunidad?

Learning Goals

Language and Communication
• Child names and describes actual or pictured people, places, things, actions, attributes, and events.

Science
• Child follows basic health and safety rules.

Fine Arts
• Child expresses ideas, emotions, and moods through individual and collaborative dramatic play.

Vocabulary

community	comunidad
equipment	equipo
helper	ayuda
neighborhood	vecindario
safety	seguridad

Differentiated Instruction

Extra Support
Explore and Express

If...children are self-conscious when in front of the group, **then...**consider having them use and speak through a puppet.

Enrichment
Explore and Express

Ask children to keep count of the number of community helpers children act out. Have them predict whether the number will be more or less than 10. Then have them check their prediction.

Dramatic Play Time

large group | 20 minutes

Health Skills Have children take turns telling how they keep themselves safe. Guide the discussion toward in-school issues, such as no overly boisterous play, and watching out for other people.

Oral Language and Academic Vocabulary

✓ **Do children use a variety of words to label and describe people, places, things, and actions?**

Communities and Community Helpers Ask children what a community is and what community helpers do for a community. Have children think of ways to act out what a helper does in a community as they answer these questions.

● *What have you learned about community helpers? ¿Qué han aprendido acerca de las personas que trabajan en la comunidad?*

● *Which community helpers would you like to be? ¿Qué persona de la comunidad les gustaría ser?*

● *How do community helpers keep people safe? ¿Qué personas de la comunidad los ayudan a mantenerse seguros?*

Explore and Express

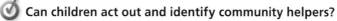

✓ **Can children act out and identify community helpers?**

Act Out Community Helpers Review the answers children gave to the questions above. Then have children take turns thinking of a community helper they would like to act out.

● Ask: *What does your community helper do?* Say: *Act out what that person does in his or her job. ¿Qué hace la persona que trabaja en la comunidad que eligieron representar? Actúen como esa persona en su trabajo.*

● Model pretending to be a crossing guard before children begin their dramatic play.

● Try having children act out helper roles with and without using their voices. Allow children to use props as they role-play.

● After children have acted out helper roles, ask: *What community helper was (Elizabeth) acting out? How do you know? ¿Qué persona que trabaja en la comunidad estaba representando [nombre de un niño]? ¿Cómo lo saben?*

ELL Help children complete sentence frames, such as: *(Franci) is a crossing guard* or *(Mark) is selling bread.*

Center Time

▶ **Center Rotation** Center Time includes teacher-guided activities and independent activities. Refer to the **Learning Centers** on pages 100–101 for independent activity ideas.

 small group 30 minutes

 Learning Goals

Social and Emotional Development
• Child participates in a variety of individual, small- and large-group activities.

Emergeny Literacy: Writing
• Child participates in free drawing and writing activities to deliver information.
• Child uses scribbles, shapes, pictures, symbols, and letters to represent language.

Writer's Center

	Center Tip

✓ **Do children use scribbles and writing to convey meaning?**

Materials paper, markers, crayons

My Friend the Community Helper Tell children they will write about a classmate who acted out the role of a community worker.

- Ask: *What community helper did your classmate act out? What did your classmate do to show the job the helper does in the neighborhood? Did he or she use any special equipment? ¿A qué persona que trabaja en la comunidad interpretó su amigo? ¿Qué hizo su amigo para mostrar el trabajo de esa persona en el vecindario? ¿Usó algún material para interpretarlo?*

- Say: *Draw a picture of your classmate as the community helper he or she acted out. Then write the name of your classmate and the name of the community helper. Dibujen a su amigo interpretando a la persona que trabaja en la comunidad que eligió. Luego, escribiremos el nombre de su amigo y el de la persona que trabaja en la comunidad.*

- Allow children to trace your letters if needed. Encourage all levels of writing.

Center Tip

If...children have difficulty writing letters, **then...**guide their hand as you help them with letter strokes.

 Writing

Have children decide what community helper they would most like to be. Ask them to draw themselves as that helper and to write a label for the picture.

Purposeful Play

✓ **Can children assume responsibilities in the classroom?**

Children choose an open center area for free playtime. Encourage children to assume responsibilities in the classroom when clean-up time comes and materials are to be put away.

Let's Say Good-Bye

 large group 15 minutes

 Read Aloud Revisit "Helpful Friends"/"Amigos útiles" for your afternoon Read Aloud. Review the initial sounds /g/ and /r/ with children in words where they appear.

 Home Connection Refer to the Home Connections activities listed in the Resources and Materials chart on page 97. Remind children to tell families about different community helpers. Sing the "Good-Bye Song"/"Hora de ir a casa" as children prepare to leave.

Focus Question

How can I help my community?

¿Cómo puedo ayudar a mi comunidad?

This week children will learn about helping others and how to care for the environment. They will make a recycling center, help the Dog Puppets to work together, and act out real and make-believe stories.

Social and Emotional Development

	DAY 1	2	3	4	5
Child is aware of self in terms of abilities, characteristics and preferences, and respects personal boundaries.					✓
Child identifies self by categories (such as gender, age, family member, cultural group).	✓				
Child follows simple classroom rules and routines.	✓	✓		✓	✓
Child participates in a variety of individual, small- and large-group activities.	✓	✓	✓	✓	✓
Child initiates interactions with others in work and play situations.	✓	✓	✓	✓	✓
Child initiates play scenarios with peers that share a common plan and goal.			✓	✓	
Child shows empathy and care for others.			✓	✓	
Child learns how to make and keep friends.	✓	✓		✓	✓

Language and Communication

	DAY 1	2	3	4	5
Child demonstrates an understanding of oral language by responding appropriately.	✓				
Child begins and ends conversations appropriately.					✓
Child names and describes actual or pictured people, places, things, actions, attributes, and events.	✓	✓	✓		
Child uses newly learned vocabulary daily in multiple contexts.	✓		✓	✓	✓
Child uses words to identify and understand categories.			✓		

Emergent Literacy: Reading

	DAY 1	2	3	4	5
Child independently engages in pre-reading behaviors and activities (such as, pretending to read, turning one page at a time).		✓			
Child produces words with the same beginning sound.	✓	✓	✓	✓	✓
Child names most upper- and lowercase letters of the alphabet.	✓	✓	✓	✓	
Child identifies the letter that stands for a given sound.	✓	✓			
Child produces the most common sound for a given letter.		✓		✓	✓
Child describes, relates to, and uses details and information from books read aloud.			✓	✓	
Child asks and answers questions about books read aloud (such as, "Who?" "What?" "Where?").	✓	✓			

Emergent Literacy: Writing

	DAY 1	2	3	4	5
Child participates in free drawing and writing activities to deliver information.		✓	✓	✓	✓
Child experiments with and uses some writing conventions when writing or dictating.	✓				

Mathematics

	DAY 1	2	3	4	5
Child recites number words in sequence from one to thirty.		✓			
Child demonstrates that the numerical counting sequence is always the same.				✓	
Child uses concrete objects or makes a verbal word problem to add up to 5 objects.	✓	✓	✓		
Child uses concrete objects or makes a verbal word problem to subtract up to 5 objects from a set.			✓		✓

Science

	DAY 1	2	3	4	5
Child knows the importance of and demonstrates ways of caring for the environment/planet.	✓				

Social Studies

	DAY 1	2	3	4	5
Child understands basic human needs for food, clothing, shelter.		✓			
Child understands basic concepts of buying, selling, and trading.		✓			

Physical Development

	DAY 1	2	3	4	5
Child engages in a sequence of movements to perform a task.					✓
Child completes tasks that require eye-hand coordination and control.					✓

Materials and Resources

DAY 1	DAY 2	DAY 3	DAY 4	DAY 5
Program Materials				
• Teacher's Treasure Book • Oral Language Development Card 27 • Rhymes and Chants Flip Chart • Making Good Choices Flip Chart • Connecting Cubes • Online Building Blocks Math Activities • *Flower Garden* Big Book • Math and Science Flip Chart • Home Connections Resource Guide	• Teacher's Treasure Book • *Flower Garden* Big Book • Dog Puppet 1 and 2 • Sequence Cards set: "Seed to Flower" • Online Building Blocks Math Activities • Making Good Choices Flip Chart • Connecting Cubes • Dot Cards • Home Connections Resource Guide	• Teacher's Treasure Book • Oral Language Development Card 28 • Rhymes and Chants Flip Chart • ABC Big Book • Concept Big Book 2 • Two-Color Counters • Numeral Cards • Making Good Choices Flip Chart • Dog Puppet 1 and 2 • Home Connections Resource Guide	• Teacher's Treasure Book • Dog Puppets 1 and 2 • ABC Big Book • Flannel Board Characters for "Three Billy Goats Gruff" • Dot Cards • Making Good Choices Flip Chart • Math and Science Flip Chart • Home Connections Resource Guide	• Teacher's Treasure Book • Rhymes and Chants Flip Chart • *Flower Garden* Big Book • ABC Big Book • Making Good Choices Flip Chart • Home Connections Resource Guide
Other Materials				
• letter stamps, stamp pads • paper, pencils, markers, crayons • large paper or cardboard • clay • ordinary objects • large trash bag • recycling symbol • various recyclable items or images of such items	• 2 red checkers, toy car • pencils, markers, crayons • large paper • scissors, tape, glue • ribbons, stickers • colored paper scraps • index cards printed with Tt, Ee, Gg, and Rr • small box lids • sand or clay • magazine pictures of items with initial t, e, g, and r	• books showing children interacting in various ways • paper, pencils, markers, crayons • dress-up clothes • toy dishes, food, tools, and so on, and pictures of each item	• dress-up clothes, stuffed animals, other props for dress-up • plasticene or modeling clay • alphabet books • sets of tactile numerals • muffin pans or paper cups	• cardboard and paper scraps • scissors, tape, glue • beads, decorating materials • pictures of recycling centers • paper, pencils, markers, crayons • books about trash cleanup • large paper, paint
Home Connection				
Encourage children to talk with their families about was they can recycle at home. Send home the following materials. Weekly Family Letter, Home Connections Resource Guide, pp. 35–36	Invite children to show their families how they made stairs in class with blocks.	Have children tell their families why people need food, clothing, and shelter.	Tell children to talk with their families about getting along and working together with other people. Storybook 9, Home Connections Resource Guide, pp. 113–116	Invite children to show their families how they moved during the outdoor play activity.

Assessment

As you observe children throughout the week, you may fill out an Anecdotal Observational Record Form to document an individual's progress toward a goal or signs indicating the need for developmental or medical evaluation. You may also choose to select work for each child's portfolio. The Anecdotal Observational Record Form and Weekly Assessment rubrics are available in the assessment section of DLMExpressOnline.com.

More Literature Suggestions

• **The Gardener/La jardinera** by Sarah Stewart
• **Jamaica Louise James** by Amy Hest
• **Frederick** by Leo Lionni
• **Five Little Monkeys with Nothing to Do/Cinco monitos sin nada que hacer** by Eileen Christelow
• **Mi jardín** por J. M. Parramón y Irene Bordoy

		DAY 1	**DAY 2**
Let's Start the Day Language Time	large group	Opening Routines p. 140 **Morning Read Aloud** p. 140 **Oral Language and Vocabulary** p. 140 Being a Helper **Phonological Awareness** p. 140 Same/Different Sounds	Opening Routines p. 146 **Morning Read Aloud** p. 146 **Oral Language and Vocabulary** p. 146 Being a Helper **Phonological Awareness** p. 146 Same and Different with the /r/ Sound
Center Time	small group	**Focus On:** **Writer's Center** p. 141 **Construction Center** p. 141	**Focus On:** **Creativity Center** p. 147 **ABC Center** p. 147
Circle Time Literacy Time	large group	**Read Aloud** *Flower Garden*/*Un jardín de flores* p. 142 **Learn About Letters and Sounds:** Learn About the Alphabet p. 142	**Read Aloud** *Flower Garden*/*Un jardín de flores* p. 148 **Learn About Letters and Sounds:** Learn About the Alphabet p. 148
Math Time	large group	Build Cube Stairs p. 143	Count and Move p. 149
Social and Emotional Development	large group	Working Together p. 143	Working with Others p. 149
Content Connection	large group	**Science:** Oral Language and Academic Vocabulary p. 144 Observe and Investigate p. 144	**Math:** Continuing Cube Stair Construction p. 150
Center Time	small group	**Focus On:** **Math and Science Center** p. 145 **Purposeful Play** p. 145	**Focus On:** **Math and Science Center** p. 151 **Purposeful Play** p. 151
Let's Say Good-Bye	large group	Read Aloud p. 145 **Writing** p. 145 **Home Connection** p. 145	Read Aloud p. 151 **Writing** p. 151 **Home Connection** p. 151

How can I help my community?
¿Qué son los animales salvajes?

DAY 3

Opening Routines p. 152
Morning Read Aloud p. 152
Oral Language and Vocabulary
p. 152 Helping at Home
Phonological Awareness
p. 152 Sounds and Words

Focus On:
Library and Listening Center p. 153
Pretend and Learn Center p. 153

Read Aloud
In the Community/*En la comunidad* p. 154
Learn About Letters and Sounds: Learn About the Alphabet
p. 154

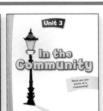

How Many Now? p. 155

Puppets Work Together p. 155

Social Studies:
Oral Language and Academic Vocabulary
p. 156 Food and Shelter
Understand and Participate
p. 156 Getting Food and Clothing

Focus On:
Writer's Center p. 157
Purposeful Play p. 157

Read Aloud p. 157
Writing p. 157
Home Connection p. 157

DAY 4

Opening Routines p. 158
Morning Read Aloud p. 158
Oral Language and Vocabulary
p. 158 Folktale
Phonological Awareness
p. 158 More Puppet Games

Focus On:
Pretend and Learn Center p. 159
ABC Center p. 159

Read Aloud
"The Three Billy Goats Gruff"/"Los tres chivitos Gruff" p. 160
Learn About Letters and Sounds: Learn About the Alphabet p. 160

Pick the Number in the Pattern p. 161

Puppets Play Again p. 161

Math:
Community Helpers p. 162

Focus On:
Math and Science Center p. 163
Purposeful Play p. 163

Read Aloud p. 163
Writing p. 163
Home Connection p. 163

DAY 5

Opening Routines p. 164
Morning Read Aloud p. 164
Oral Language and Vocabulary
p. 164 Being Helpful
Phonological Awareness
p. 164 Same and Different Game

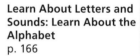

Focus On:
Construction Center p. 165
Library and Listening Center p. 165

Read Aloud
Flower Garden/*Un jardín de flores* p. 166
Learn About Letters and Sounds: Learn About the Alphabet
p. 166

Five Little Monkeys p. 167

Review the Chart p. 167

Outdoor Play Time:
Oral Language and Vocabulary
p. 168 Alone and with Partners
Move and Learn
p. 168 Outdoor Play

Focus On:
Creativity Center p. 169
Purposeful Play p. 169

Read Aloud p. 169
Writing p. 169
Home Connection p. 169

Learning Centers

Math and Science Center

Making a Poster
Children make a poster to encourage recycling, p. 145.

Order the Dots
Children order Dot Cards and count them, p. 151.

Sort!
Children sort numerals into muffin tins, p. 163.

Taking Inventory
Children count supplies and materials found in the classroom. Have them make a mark for each item. Then count the marks. Place one more mark and have them say how many there are now.

Bag Mystery
In a paper bag, place 1–9 small items. Children take turns reaching in and taking the items out one at a time as they count. When the bag is empty, the partner adds one more and says: *And one more is _____.*

ABC Center

Same or Different
Children identify letters, sounds, and upper case or lower case, p. 147.

Write and Say
Children find, write, and say letters, p. 159.

Telephone ABC
Children sit in a circle. One child draws a letter card from a pile. She/he whispers the letter and two words that begin with the letter into the ear of another child. That child passes on the "message" by whispering the letters and sounds to another child. The final child to receive the message says out loud what she or he heard.

T is For...
Display *ABC Picture Cards* and review the letters. Children draw a card, say a letter, and find it on the Alphabet Tree. Then they suggest a name that begins with it, such as **T** *is for Tara.*

Creativity Center

Garden Collage
Children use various supplies to make a garden collage, p. 147.

Make a Mural
Children paint about activities they did today, p. 169.

People's Needs Box
Provide a cardboard box, art supplies, and magazines. Children fill the box with images or items that all people need. Have them decorate the outside of their *People's Needs* box.

Leaf Rubbing
Children show how special leaves are by creating their patterns. They put a leaf on a sheet of paper, then cover it with another sheet of paper and rub a crayon horizontally on top of the image until it appears. Hang the leaf rubbings in the classroom.

Library and Listening Center

At Home
Children identify images of people helping one another, p. 153.

Keeping the World Clean
Children discuss recycling books and draw a picture, p. 165.

Predict it
Children browse through books about people from different cultures. Have them use the pictures to predict what the weather is like, what kind of transportation they have, and so on, in their community.

What Do You Hear?
Have children imitate sounds they've heard. Discuss which ones they are most likely to hear in a community, such as a police siren or a dog barking. Have them say which sounds are loud and which are soft.

Construction Center

Build a Classroom
Children use various materials to build a classroom, p. 141.

The Recycling Building
Children construct a recycling building, p. 165.

Trash or Treasure?
Have children use materials that are normally discarded to build a three-dimensional piece of art or clothing.

Museum of Touch
Organize children into small groups. One group builds a museum in the center. Others collect objects from the classroom with different textures. Children display their items in the museum and invite other children to touch their interactive display.

Recycle It!
Children recycle boxes, cups, wood scraps, foam pieces, and other buildable materials and build a Recycle It structure.

Writer's Center

Draw Yourself Helping
Children draw themselves helping someone in the classroom, p. 141.

Inside a Store
Children draw and write about going to a store, p. 157.

Recycle Here
Display signs and symbols children might see in the community that represent recycling. Discuss how community helpers collect recycling. Children make a sign that could go over a recycling area.

Forgetful Fernando
Tell children that Fernando has trouble remembering how to follow classroom rules. Children create images and signs to help him remember different classroom rules. Hang the signs around the room.

Pretend and Learn Center

Helping At Home
Children play different family members and demonstrate how they help one another, page 153.

Acting with Stuffed Animals
Children act out real and make-believe scenarios, p. 159.

Set Up Shop
Supply things you would find in a store. Children act out being a store owner and a consumer.

Recycle, Reuse
Children use stuffed animals to act out teaching about recycling and reusing paper, plastic containers, mailing envelopes, bags, and so on.

Focus Question

How can I help my community?

¿Cómo puedo ayudar a mi comunidad?

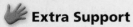

Learning Goals

Social and Emotional Development
• Child uses classroom materials carefully.

Language and Communication
• Child names and describes actual or pictured people, places, things, actions, attributes, and events.

Emergent Literacy: Reading
• Child produces words with the same beginning sound.

Vocabulary

clean	ordenar	help	ayudar
job	tarea	table	mesa
together	juntos	work	trabajo

Differentiated Instruction

✋ Extra Support

Phonological Awareness
If...children struggle to produce a word that begins with the same sound, **then...**say words that start with that sound, then point to something in the room which the child can identify that starts with the same sound.

⭐ Enrichment

Phonological Awareness
Ask children to produce sounds by clapping or humming. Then clap twice and ask children to make a sound that matches the sounds you made. Repeat, asking children to make a different pattern of sounds.

Let's Start the Day

▶ **Opening Routines and Transition Tips**
For **Opening Routines** and **Transition Tips** turn to pages 178–181 and visit **DLMExpressOnline.com** for more ideas.

📖 Read **"The Evil King"/"El rey malvado"** from the *Teacher's Treasure Book,* page 219, for your morning Read Aloud.

Language Time

 large group · 15 minutes

👥 Social and Emotional Development Ask children what their classroom rules are for listening to the teacher and following directions.

Oral Language and Vocabulary

✓ **Can children use a wide variety of words to describe ways they can be classroom helpers?**

Being a Helper Remind children that they learned about community helpers during the previous week. Explain that helpers do not have to be adults; children can be helpers too.

● Display *Oral Language Development Card 27.* Ask children what they see on the card. Elicit or explain that the children pictured are helping in their classroom. Ask children to tell about times when they have been helpers in the classroom. Then follow the suggestions on the back of the card.

ELL Children may confuse the terms *help* and *helper*. Mime helping someone and say *I can <u>help</u> Fazio.* Then point to yourself and say *I am a <u>helper</u>.* Provide practice with other pairs of this type, such as *teach/teacher* and *drive/driver*.

Phonological Awareness

✓ **Can children produce a word that begins with the same sound as a given pair?**

Same/Different Sounds Display the *Rhymes and Chants Flip Chart,* page 16. Read the rhyme aloud. Reread the first two lines, emphasizing the words *see* and *some*. Say: **The words** see **and** some **begin with the same sound.** *Las palabras* see *y* some *empiezan con el mismo sonido.* Ask: **Can you name another word that begins with this sound?** *¿Pueden decir otra palabra que empiece con este sonido?* Say: **trash and cup start with different sounds.** *Trash* y cup *empiezan con distintos sonidos.* Then say the following word pairs. Have children stand up and say another word with the sound if the word pairs start with the same sound: *cup, call; girl, boy; paper, parents.* Continue with other word pairs.

Oral Language Development Card 27

Rhymes and Chants Flip Chart, page 16

Center Time

▶ **Center Rotation** Center Time includes teacher-guided activities and independent activities. Refer to the **Learning Centers** on pages 138–139 for independent activity ideas.

 small group 60–90 minutes

Writer's Center

 Can children describe a time when they were helpful at school?

Materials paper, pencils, crayons or markers

Draw Yourself Helping Have children draw pictures of themselves helping another child or a teacher in the classroom.

- Have them tell you what they are doing and who they are helping.

- Write the words they dictate, and have them write letters they know.

Center Tip

If...children start to tell stories unrelated to helping someone else, **then...**gently but firmly steer them back by telling them that though it sounds like a great story, you want to know more about how they were helpful.

Construction Center

 Can children use a wide variety of words to identify, model, and talk about important parts of the classroom?

Materials large sheet of paper, modeling clay, ordinary objects

Build a Classroom Have children work as a team to build a model of a classroom.

- Spread out the paper on a table or the floor. Tell children to imagine it is their classroom.

- Have children use the materials to create models of tables, sinks, and other classroom features, and set them in places on the paper.

- Have children tell about the things they built. Ask in what parts of the room they have been helpers to teachers or other children.

Center Tip

If...children want to construct children to populate the classroom, **then...**encourage them to make themselves, but steer them away from making replicas of classmates; some children may not like the way they are portrayed.

 Learning Goals

Social and Emotional Development
- Child identifies self by categories (such as gender, age, family member, cultural group).

Emergent Literacy: Reading
- Child produces words with the same beginning sound.

Differentiated Instruction

✋ Extra Support

Writer's Center

If...children want to make the letters themselves but are dissatisfied with the way their letters look, **then...**consider giving them stamp pads and a set of letter stamps to use.

⭐ Enrichment

Writer's Center

Have children write about a time when someone else helped them, as well as writing about a time when they were helpful.

♥ Special Needs

Behavioral Social/Emotional

If...children have trouble talking about the things they built, **then...**ask encouraging questions, such as: *Who built a sink? ¿Quién construyó un fregadero?* and *What do you do at the sink? ¿Qué se hace en un fregadero?* and show interest in their responses.

Focus Question

How can I help my community?

¿Cómo puedo ayudar a mi comunidad?

Learning Goals

Language and Communication
• Child uses newly learned vocabulary daily in multiple contexts.

Emergent Literacy: Reading
• Child names most upper- and lowercase letters of the alphabet.
• Child identifies the letter that stands for a given sound.
• Child asks and answers questions about books read aloud (such as, "Who?" "What?" "Where?").

Vocabulary

flower	flores	garden	jardín
shopping	comprar	soil	tierra
stairs	escalera	trowel	palita

Differentiated Instruction

Extra Support
Learn About Letters and Sounds
If...children cannot match the four upper and lower case letter forms given, **then...**do the activity using only two letters at a time, then try it with three, and finally repeat it with four.

Enrichment
Read Aloud
Ask children to make a list or small drawings of all the places they have seen gardens.

Literacy Time

📖 Read Aloud

✅ Can children use content and pictures to answer appropriate questions about the story?

Build Background Ask children what they know about flowers and gardens.

● Ask: *Where have you seen a garden? What was growing in the garden? ¿Dónde han visto un jardín? ¿Qué plantas había en ese jardín?*

Listen for Enjoyment Display *Flower Garden* and read the title. Explain that this book tells about a very small garden with flowers.

● Say: *Look at the picture on the cover. Where do you think this garden might be? Have you ever made a garden? Why do you think people have gardens? Observen la ilustración de la portada. ¿Dónde creen que puede estar este jardín?¿Por qué creen que la gente tiene jardines?*

● Read the story aloud, tracking the text as you read.

Respond to the Book After reading the book, review children's predictions. Ask: *Where is the garden? Who helps make the garden? Why do the characters make the garden? ¿Dónde está el jardín? ¿Quién ayuda a hacer el jardín? ¿Por qué los personajes hacen el jardín?*

TIP Children may become worried about being wrong if what they predicted about the story missed the mark. Praise children for predictions that make sense, even if the book has different outcomes.

ELL English phrases such as *cardboard box* and *shopping cart* may present problems for children whose native language puts the noun first. You may wish to explain these terms as *a box made out of cardboard* or *a cart you use for shopping.*

Flower Garden
Un jardín de flores

Learn About Letters and Sounds

✅ Can children name upper case and lower case letters *Tt, Ee, Gg,* and *Rr* and produce their sounds?

Learn About the Alphabet Review the letters *T, E, G,* and *R* with children.

● Write upper case letters *T, E, G,* and *R* along one side of a large sheet of chart paper or an interactive whiteboard. Then write lower case letters *e, g, r,* and *t* along the other side of the paper. Name the letters with children and review their sounds. Help children draw lines to match the upper case and lower case letters.

large group · 15 minutes

Building Blocks

Online Math Activity

Introduce Build Stairs 1: Count Steps. In Build Stairs activities, characters need help climbing steps to get to a higher level. In this first level, children click on numerals to build the stairs. Each child should complete the activity this week.

large group · 15 minutes

Making Good Choices Flip Chart, page 16

Math Time

Observe and Investigate

☑️ **Can children use models to count?**

Build Cube Stairs Tell children they are going to be construction workers. Their task is to build a staircase. Talk about stairs and how we walk up and down stairs one step at a time.

● Say: ***Today we are going to be construction workers. We are going to build a staircase!*** *Hoy vamos a ser trabajadores de la construcción. Vamos a construir una escalera!* Display a set of Connecting Cubes.

● Say: ***Build your staircase one step at a time.*** *Construyan su escalera un escalón por vez.* Model building the staircase with one Connecting Cube for the first step, two Connecting Cubes for the second step, and so on. As children build, ask them how many cubes it will take to make the next step.

👫 Social and Emotional Development

Making Good Choices

☑️ **Can children tell what it means to be be responsible and work with others?**

Working Together Explain that sometimes your job is to work alone at school but other times it's your job to work and play with others. Display the *Making Good Choices Flip Chart,* page 16. Tell children the picture shows some children working together very well and some children who are having trouble working together.

● Ask: ***Which children are working together very well? What are they doing?*** *¿Qué niños están trabajando muy bien juntos? ¿Qué están haciendo?*

● Ask: ***Have you ever had trouble working or playing with other children? How did that make you feel? What did you do about it?*** *¿Alguna vez han tenido problemas para trabajar o jugar con otros niños? ¿Cómo se sintieron? ¿Cómo lo solucionaron?*

● Ask children to choose a song about having trouble working together, such as "Pushy, Pushy, Pushy"/"La cancion del empujon" or "Bossy"/"La mandona," from the Making Good Choices Audio CD.

ELL Knowing when to use verb forms with *-ing* can be hard for children. Model by holding up a pencil and saying: ***I will give this pencil to Ming.*** Emphasize the word *give*. Then hand the pencil to the child as you say ***I am giving this pencil to Ming.*** This time, emphasize the word *giving*. Repeat with other examples.

✔️ Learning Goals

Social and Emotional Development
• Child participates in a variety of individual, small- and large-group activities.

Language and Communication
• Child names and describes actual or pictured people, places, things, actions, attributes, and events.

Mathematics
• Child uses concrete objects or makes a verbal word problem to add up to 5 objects.

Vocabulary

down	bajar	feelings	sentimientos
stairs	escaleras	steps	escalones
together	juntos	up	subir
work	trabajar		

Differentiated Instruction

✋ **Extra Support**

Making Good Choices
If...children have difficulty identifying the emotions of the children in the picture, **then...**imitate the faces in the picture yourself, and ask children to name feeling words associated with your expressions.

⭐ **Enrichment**

Making Good Choices
Ask children to work in pairs to build a replica of the block building in the flip chart picture.

💜 **Special Needs**

Cognitive Challenges
If...children have difficulty connecting cubes, **then...**help them by modeling for them.

Learning Goals

Social and Emotional Development
• Child follows simple classroom rules and routines.

Language and Communication
• Child demonstrates an understanding of oral language by responding appropriately.

Science
• Child knows the importance of and demonstrates ways of caring for the environment/planet.

Vocabulary

can	lata
cardboard	cartón
conserve	onservar
environment	medio ambiente
glass	vidrio
plastic	plástico
recycle	reciclar

Differentiated Instruction

 Extra Support

Observe and Investigate

If...children have difficulty identifying what items can be recycled, **then...**help them look for the recycling symbol on recyclable items.

Enrichment

Observe and Investigate

Challenge children to set up a recycling project for the classroom, such as setting up a scrap-paper box and using both sides of paper.

Accommodation for 3's

Oral Language and Academic Vocabulary

If...children do not understand the word *environment*, **then...**explain that it refers to the natural things around them in the outdoors, such as trees in a forest, rivers, mountains, and oceans. Use pictures to help reinforce understanding.

Science Time

 large group · 20 minutes

Personal Safety Skills Model safe handling of trash and recyclable materials by carrying breakable items carefully and wearing gloves.

Oral Language and Academic Vocabulary

☑ **Can children show understanding by responding appropriately?**

Point to the boy brushing his teeth in the *Math and Science Flip Chart*, page 27. Say: *This child is saving, or conserving, water when he brushes his teeth.* *El niño está conservando el agua cuando se lava los dientes.*

● Explain that conserving water means using only what you need and not wasting it. Ask: *How is the child conserving water?* *¿Cómo está conservando el agua el niño?*

● Discuss other ways to conserve water, such as by taking shorter showers, turning off the water while soaping hands, and filling a sink to wash dishes instead of washing them under a running faucet.

Observe and Investigate

☑ **Can children demonstrate the importance of caring for the environment and the planet?**

Have children look at the *Math and Science Flip Chart*, page 27, and discuss other ways to care for the environment. Point out recycling and trash containers in the classroom or school and remind students to follow classroom and school rules about disposing of trash properly. Explain that some materials can be used again or recycled, and other materials are put in the trash.

● Take children on a walk to collect trash and recyclable materials around the school. Have children point out items for you to pick up and place in a bag.

● Look at the collected items and identify which can be recycled. Place those items in the proper containers.

● Discuss your school or community's recycling program. Most communities recycle plastic, paper, cardboard, glass, and aluminum cans. Discuss with children why recycling helps their community.

TIP Many towns distribute a printed trash and recycling guide. Bring in recycling containers and items to use as you talk about recycling.

ELL Explain that items that cannot be used or recycled are *trash* and the place where the items are put may also be called *the trash*. Help children identify the trash and recycling containers by labeling them with appropriate symbols or drawings.

Math and Science Flip Chart, page 27

Center Time

▶ **Center Rotation** Center Time includes teacher-guided activities and independent activities. Refer to the **Learning Centers** on pages 138–139 for independent activity ideas.

  small group 30 minutes

Math and Science Center

Center Tip

☑ Encourage children to demonstrate caring for the environment by identifying items that should be recycled.

☑ Observe examples of children initiating interaction and developing meaningful friendships by working together.

Materials recycling symbol; examples of recyclable items, such as aluminum cans, bottles, and cardboard; drawing paper; crayons

Making a Poster Tell children that they will make a poster to encourage recycling at home.

- Display the recycling symbol. Point out different items to recycle. Have children locate the recycling symbol on some of these items.

- Have children work with a friend to make a poster with drawings of different recyclable items around the recycling symbol. Suggest that pairs team up to draw a particular item. As children begin, remind them to follow classroom rules about sharing supplies.

If...children cannot draw the items, **then...**provide pictures or drawings that they can glue onto the posters.

 Learning Goals

Social and Emotional Development
- Child follows simple classroom rules and routines.
- Child initiates interactions with others in work and play situations.

Language and Communication
- Child uses newly learned vocabulary daily in multiple contexts.

Emergent Literacy: Writing
- Child experiments with and uses some writing conventions when writing or dictating.

Science
- Child knows the importance of and demonstrates ways of caring for the environment/planet.

 Writing

Ask children to name one thing they learned today. Provide prompts as needed, such as *Today I learned that...*or *Now I know how to...*Display items such as the book *Flower Garden* or the *Making Good Choices Flip Chart* to help remind children of their activities. Children write or dictate ideas for you to write on the board. Read them aloud, pausing between each idea.

Purposeful Play

☑ Observe children as they use new vocabulary to discuss recycling or caring for the planet.

Children can choose an open area for free playtime. Encourage children to create a dance or song to help them remember what items should be put in the trash or recycled.

Let's Say Good-Bye

  large group 15 minutes

  Read Aloud Revisit "The Evil King"/"El rey malvado" for your afternoon Read Aloud. Help children listen for the /t/ sound at the beginning of words.

Home Connection Refer to the Home Connections activities listed in the Resources and Materials chart on page 135. Remind children to tell families about different ways they can help in the community. Sing the "Good-Bye Song"/"Hora de ir a casa" as children prepare to leave.

Let's Start the Day

Focus Question

How can I help my community?

¿Cómo puedo ayudar a mi comunidad?

> **Opening Routines and Transition Tips**
> For **Opening Routines** and **Transition Tips** turn to pages 178–181 and visit DLMExpressOnline.com for more ideas.
>
> Read **"Stone Soup"**/"La sopa de piedra" from the *Teacher's Treasure Book*, page 315, for your morning Read Aloud.

Language Time

large group   15 minutes

 Social and Emotional Development Model for children being aware of and carrying out classroom rules and routines as you go through the day.

Oral Language and Vocabulary

✓ **Can children use a variety of words to describe how they can be helpers?**

Being a Helper Have children name ways they've learned to be helpers.

- Display *Flower Garden.* Conduct a brief picture walk to review what happens in the story. Then ask:

- *How does the girl help butterflies with her garden?* Con su jardín, ¿cómo ayuda la niña a las mariposas?

- *How does she help people who walk down the street?* ¿Cómo ayuda a la gente que camina por la calle?

- *How does she help her mother?* ¿Cómo ayuda a su mamá?

Flower Garden
Un jardín de flores

Phonological Awareness

✓ **Can children identify words that begin with the same sound as *run* and *rain*?**

Same and Different with the /r/ Sound Display Dog Puppet 1. Say: **run.** Then have the puppet say: **rain.** Ask children if the two words begin with the same sound or with a different sound.

- Have children run in place if the words begin with the same sound or stay seated if they begin with different sounds. Repeat the words slowly and draw out the beginning /r/ sound. Then have the puppet say other words and ask children to run in place if they hear the same initial /r/ sound as in *run* and *rain.* As they are running, have them shout out another word that begins with /r/.

ELL To help children with the meanings of *same* and *different,* give them visual models. Hold up two identical red checkers and say: **same.** Then hold up a checker and a toy car and say: **different.** Have children echo you. Repeat with different pairs of objects.

Learning Goals

- **Social and Emotional Development**
Child follows simple classroom rules and routines.

Language and Communication
- Child names and describes actual or pictured people, places, things, actions, attributes, and events.

Emergent Literacy: Reading
- Child produces words with the same beginning sound.

Vocabulary

butterflies	mariposas	ladybugs	catarinas
lift	levantar	meet	encontrar
rest	descansar	walkers	caminar

Differentiated Instruction

 Extra Support
Phonological Awareness
If...children have trouble isolating the initial sounds of the words, **then...**say the words with a distinct pause after the initial sound before saying the whole word, such as /r/-*ain, rain.*

Enrichment
Phonological Awareness
Challenge children to think of sentences that contain several words with the initial /r/ sound, such as *I run races in the rain.*

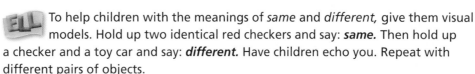

Center Time

▶ **Center Rotation** Center Time includes teacher-guided activities and independent activities. Refer to the **Learning Centers** on pages 138–139 for independent activity ideas.

Creativity Center

☑ **Encourage children to assume various roles and responsibilities while creating a collage.**

☑ **Observe examples of children initiating social interaction by working together.**

Materials large sheet of paper, markers or crayons, ribbons, stickers, scissors, tape, glue, colored paper scraps

Garden Collage Children work together to make a garden collage.

● Tell children they are going to work together to make a garden.

● Model how children can cut paper and other objects into different shapes and then glue or tape them to the large sheet of paper.

● Stress to children that they need to work together.

● When the collage is complete, ask: *What did you do to help make the collage? What was helpful about working together to make the collage? How did working together make you feel?* *¿Qué hicieron para ayudar a hacer el collage? ¿Qué resultó útil de trabajar juntos para hacer el collage? ¿Cómo los hizo sentir trabajar juntos?*

Center Tip

If...children have trouble talking about how they worked together, **then...**give them examples of what you noticed, such as: *I saw Bobby and Tanya making yellow flowers together; Bobby and Tanya, what did you like about that?* *Veo que Bobby y Tanya están haciendo flores amarillas juntos. Bobby y Tanya, ¿por qué les gusta hacer eso?*

ABC Center

☑ **Assess whether children identify letters and produce the correct sounds for letters.**

Materials index cards with printed letters *Tt, Ee, Gg,* and *Rr;* small box lids with sand covering the bottom; magazine pictures of items with initial *t, e, g,* and *r*

Same or Different? Have children write one upper case and one lower case letter at a time in the sand, using letter cards as models.

● Partners say the name of each letter and the sound it makes.

● Have them find a picture that begins with the same sound. Have them name the picture and say another word that begins with the sound. Extend the activity by adding letters from previous weeks.

Center Tip

If...children are tactile sensitive and will not work in the sand, **then...**have them use clay to form their letters or trace the cards with their finger.

✓ Learning Goals

Social and Emotional Development
• Child participates in a variety of individual, small- and large-group activities.

• Child initiates interactions with others in work and play situations.

Emergent Literacy: Reading
• Child names most upper- and lowercase letters of the alphabet.

• Child produces the most common sound for a given letter.

Differentiated Instruction

 Extra Support
ABC Center
If...children have difficulty determining how to form the letters, **then...**have them trace the strokes on the cards before they write each stroke in the sand.

 Enrichment
ABC Center
Have children say a word that begins with the letter they wrote, such as *rabbit* for *Rr.* Challenge them to try writing the entire word.

 Special Needs
Delayed Motor Development
If...children lack the motor skills needed to cut the paper the way they want, **then...**have them indicate how they want the paper cut and guide their hands or hold the paper as they use the scissors.

Focus Question

How can I help my community?

¿Cómo puedo ayudar a mi comunidad?

 Learning Goals

Emergent Literacy: Reading

• Child independently engages in pre-reading behaviors and activities (such as, pretending to read, turning one page at a time).

• Child names most upper- and lowercase letters of the alphabet.

• Child identifies the letter that stands for a given sound.

• Child asks and answers questions about books read aloud (such as, "Who?" "What?" "Where?").

Vocabulary

bus	autobús	garden	jardín
page	página	shopping cart	carrito
upright	vertical	upside down	al revés

 Differentiated Instruction

 Extra Support

Learn About Letters and Sounds

If...children have trouble hearing the initial sound of the word, **then...**simply say the sounds, such as /r/, /e/, and so on, and have children sit when you say the sound that goes with /g/.

Enrichment

Learn About Letters and Sounds

After you have modeled the activity several times, invite children to "be the teacher." Write a letter on the board and have children choose and say words for the class that do or do not have that initial letter.

Accommodations for 3's

Learn About Letters and Sounds

If...it makes children too distracted to walk in a circle with classmates, **then...**have them walk in place instead.

Literacy Time

 large group · 15 minutes

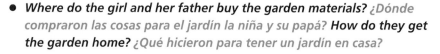 **Read Aloud**

✓ Do children know how to hold a book and turn the pages?

✓ Can children answer comprehension questions about a story?

Build Background Remind children that they read a story about gardens yesterday.

● Ask: *What do you know about gardens? ¿Qué saben sobre los jardines? What do you like about gardens? ¿Cuáles son las cosas que les gustan de los jardines?*

● Use the Sequence Cards set "Seed to Flower" to reinforce the concept of the life cycle of plants.

Listen for Understanding Display *Flower Garden* upside down and read the title. Draw out that you are holding the book upside down and ask children how they know. Model turning the pages three or four at a time; draw out that the pages should be turned one at a time or you'll leave out parts of the book. Then read the story aloud, asking children to look and listen for answers to these questions:

● *Where do the girl and her father buy the garden materials? ¿Dónde compraron las cosas para el jardín la niña y su papá? How do they get the garden home? ¿Qué hicieron para tener un jardín en casa?*

● *What does the mother do when she sees the garden? ¿Qué hizo la mamá cuando vio el jardín?*

Respond to the Book Ask children to act out the answers to the questions above. Have children act out other parts of the story they liked.

TIP If children don't notice that the book is upside down, display it both ways and ask children to look at the picture and the letters closely to help them see which way it should appear.

ELL It is fine for children to act out the story silently, but encourage them to make up and say dialogue using English vocabulary words.

Learn About Letters and Sounds

✓ Can children name the letters *t, e, g,* and *r* and produce their sounds?

Learn About the Alphabet Review *t, e, g,* and *r* with a game.

● Write *g* on the board. Say its name with children and say its sound, /g/, as well.

● Have children walk slowly in a circle. Say: *I will say some words. When I say a word that begins with* g, *sit down right where you are! Voy a decir algunas palabras. Cuando diga una palabra que empieza con g, ¡siéntense en su lugar!*

● Slowly say the words *road, tail, ray,* and *good.* Check that children sit down only after they hear the word *good.*

● Repeat with other words and letters.

Flower Garden
Un jardín de flores

Math Time

Observe and Investigate

 Can children use words to count?

Count and Move Invite children to count and move together.

● Say: *Let's count and move! Imagine you are climbing the stairs. ¡Contemos y movámonos! Imaginen que están subiendo las escaleras.* Have children march in place to mimic climbing stairs. Say: *Let's count as we climb the stairs. One stair, two stairs, three stairs.... Contemos mientras subimos las escaleras. Un escalón, dos escalones, tres escalones...* Continue counting with children to 10.

● Then say: *Next, let's creep forward and then creep back. Count and move with me! Ahora, arrastrémonos hacia adelante y después hacia atrás. ¡Cuenten y muévanse conmigo!* Have children creep forward and backward to the count of 10.

● Experiment with other movements that children like.

𝕏 Social and Emotional Development

Making Good Choices

 Can children begin to make friends by working and playing together?

Working with Others Display the *Making Good Choices Flip Chart,* page 16. Then hold up Dog Puppet 2. Tell children that Dog Puppet was absent yesterday and doesn't know about the flip chart yet. Ask them to teach the puppet about it. Guide the discussion by asking:

● *What are the children in the front of the picture doing? What are the children in the back doing? ¿Qué están haciendo los niños en la parte de adelante de la ilustración? ¿Qué están haciendo los niños en la parte de atrás?*

● *What can we learn from the picture about how to work and play together in school? Does it help us make friends if we can work together and help one another? ¿Qué podemos aprender sobre la manera de trabajar y jugar juntos en la escuela? Si trabajamos y nos ayudamos, ¿podemos hacernos amigos?*

ELL Provide sentence starters such as *You should (share, talk about your ideas, and so on)* and *You should not (grab things, yell, and so on)* to help children organize and express their ideas.

Making Good Choices Flip Chart, page 16

Building Blocks

Online Math Activity

Introduce Build Stairs 2: Order Steps. Children are given a group of steps in random order to put in proper order to build stairs. Each child should complete the activity this week.

Focus Question
How can I help my community?
¿Cómo puedo ayudar a mi comunidad?

Learning Goals

Mathematics
• Child uses concrete objects or makes a verbal word problem to add up to 5 objects.

Vocabulary

build	construir
tools	herramientas
staircase	escaleras

Differentiated Instruction

 Extra Support

Math Time

If...children have difficulty counting the cubes, **then...**count the cubes with them.

⭐ **Enrichment**

Math Time

Challenge children by adding up to 10 objects.

Accommodations for 3's

Math Time

If...children have difficulty connecting the cubes, **then...**help them by modeling for them how to count and connect the cubes.

Math Time

large group — 20 minutes

✓ **Can children use a model to add objects and recognize patterns?**

Continuing Cube Stair Construction Tell children they are going to continue building cube staircases.

● This activity is a variation of the activity introduced on Day 1.

● Construct five steps with Connecting Cubes. Display the steps one through three; hide steps four and five.

● Ask children to observe the steps and describe the pattern. Guide them to understand that each steps gets taller and each step has one more cube than the step before it.

● Ask children how many cubes the next step will have. Have them say the number of cubes in each step out loud with you. Continue counting beyond step 3 so children will hear how many cubes the next steps will have.

● Divide children into small groups and have them build their own sets of cube stairs. Supervise their work.

TIP Lead a follow-up discussion about which buildings in the community have staircases.

ELL Explain to students that the word *step* can mean a physical stair or the action of moving one foot forward or upward. Have students act out walking up steps slowly. Count with them *one step, two steps, three steps,* and so on.

Center Time

▶ **Center Rotation** Center Time includes teacher-guided activities and independent activities. Refer to the **Learning Centers** on pages 138–139 for independent activity ideas.

 small group · 30 minutes

Math and Science Center

	Center Tip

 Observe children using words to rote count.

Materials one set of Dot Cards for each child, 1–10

Order the Dots Prepare one set of Dot Cards for each child.

- Say: ***Place your cards face down. Flip over a Dot Card. Then flip over your Dot Cards until you find the next one in the pattern.*** *Coloquen sus tarjetas mirando hacia abajo. Levanten una tarjeta con puntos. Luego, den vuelta tus tarjetas con puntos hasta que encuentren la siguiente en el patrón.*

- Have children count the dots on the cards, then rote count to the same number.

- Have children place the Dot Cards in order.

Center Tip

If...children are having difficulty ordering the cards, **then...**have them work with a partner.

Learning Goals

Emergent Literacy: Writing
- Child participates in free drawing and writing activities to deliver information.

Mathematics
- Child recites number words in sequence from one to thirty.

Writing

Have children draw gardens from their imaginations. Then have them write or scribble a few words about the gardens. Help with dictation as needed; encourage children to write letters they know.

Purposeful Play

 Observe children ordering cards by numeral.

Children can choose an open center for free playtime. Encourage children to order Numeral Cards.

Let's Say Good-Bye

 large group · 15 minutes

 Read Aloud Revisit "Stone Soup"/"La sopa de piedra" for your afternoon Read Aloud. Have children count the first 10 pages aloud as you point to them.

 Home Connection Refer to the Home Connections activities listed in the Resources and Materials chart on page 135. Remind children to tell families what they learned about how they can help their community. Sing the "Good-bye Song"/"Hora de ir a casa" as children prepare to leave.

Let's Start the Day

Focus Question

How can I help my community?

¿Cómo puedo ayudar a mi comunidad?

 Learning Goals

Social and Emotional Development
• Child initiates interactions with others in work and play situations.

Language and Communication
• Child names and describes actual or pictured people, places, things, actions, attributes, and events.

Emergent Literacy: Reading
• Child produces words with the same beginning sound.

Vocabulary

bag	bolsa	helping	ayudar
home	casa	job	trabajo
leaves	hojas	neighborhood	vecindario
pile	pila	rake	rastrillo

Differentiated Instruction

 Extra Support

Phonological Awareness

If...children have trouble generating words that begin with /r/, **then...**give children hints, such as: *I'm thinking of a word that starts with /r/ and rhymes with light* and *I'm thinking of color that starts with /r/.*

 Enrichment

Oral Language and Vocabulary

Have children describe ways they can be helpful around their homes when they are older. Ask them to estimate how old they will be before they can do the things they named.

> **Opening Routines and Transition Tips**
> For **Opening Routines** and **Transition Tips** turn to pages 178–181 and visit **DLMExpressOnline.com** for more ideas.
>
> Read **"Ms. Bumblebee Gathers Honey/**"La abejorrita Zumbi lleva miel" from the *Teacher's Treasure Book,* page 207, for your morning Read Aloud.

large group | 15 minutes

Language Time

Social and Emotional Development Encourage children to look for ways to help others as they move through the day.

Oral Language and Vocabulary

 Can children use a wide variety of words to describe ways to be helpers at home?

Helping at Home Ask children some ways to be helpful at school that they have learned. Tell them they will now learn about ways to be helpful at home.

● Display *Oral Language Development Card 28*. Discuss with children what they see in the picture and how the children shown are being helpers. Ask: **What do you do at home to be helpful?** *¿Qué hacen para ayuda en su casa?* Then follow the suggestions on the back of the card.

ELL Work with children to distinguish the words *help, helper, helping,* and *helpful.* Use each in simple sentence structures (*I can help; she is helpful*). Have children repeat the sentences and then change them slightly (*We can help; you are helpful*).

Phonological Awareness

 Can children produce words that begin with the same sound as a given pair of words?

Sounds and Words Display the *Rhymes and Chants Flip Chart,* page 16. Read the rhyme with children. Ask them what they know about recycling. Then point out that *recycle* begins with the /r/ sound. Explain that *run* begins with the same sound as *recycle.* Help children generate other words with initial /r/ . Then have them generate /r/ words on their own. Continue by saying pairs of words that begin with the same sound, such as *trash/toys* and *parent/pick,* and have children think of another word that begins with the same sound.

Oral Language Development Card 28

Rhymes and Chants Flip Chart, page 16

Center Time

▶ **Center Rotation** Center Time includes teacher-guided activities and independent activities. Refer to the **Learning Centers** on pages 138–139 for independent activity ideas.

small group 60–90 minutes

Learning Goals

Social and Emotional Development
• Child initiates interactions with others in work and play situations.

Language and Communication
• Child uses newly learned vocabulary daily in multiple contexts.

Emergent Literacy: Reading
• Child produces words with the same beginning sound.

Library and Listening Center

Center Tip

 Track new vocabulary words children use as they discuss ways to be helpful.

Materials fiction and nonfiction books, paper, pencils, markers or crayons

At Home Provide children picture books that show children interacting and being helpful or not being helpful. Have pairs look at the books together.

• Say: *Discuss what the children in the pictures are doing. Tell your partner which activities you have done or would like to do.* *Observen qué están haciendo los niños de las ilustraciones. Cuenten a su compañero si alguna vez realizaron esas actividades y si les gustaría realizarlas.*

• Have children decide if the children in the pictures are working together and helping each other. Have them explain their ideas.

• Close by having children draw something they read about that they would like to do.

If...children are not sure if the children in the pictures are working together or not, **then...**encourage them to look at the facial expressions on the characters to see if that gives them a clue about how they are feeling.

Differentiated Instruction

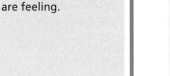 **Extra Support**

Library and Listening Center
If...children are not sure what they are supposed to do, **then...**model talking about one of the pictures, such as: *These two children are digging in the sand together. It looks like they are sharing the shovels. That's working together!*

 Enrichment

Library and Listening Center
Have children write words at the bottom of their pictures to show what is happening.

Accommodations for 3's

Pretend and Learn Center
If...children don't know all the names for the items, **then...**review all the items each time before they begin their play.

Pretend and Learn Center

Center Tip

 Observe children initiating social interactions.

✓ Track words that children produce that have the same initial sound as a given pair.

Materials dress-up clothes; toy household items, such as food, boxes, and so on; classroom materials; pictures of each item

Helping at Home Have children choose two pictures that begin with the same sound, such as *broom* and *box*. Have children pretend to be different family members and use the two items in their play. They supply another word or item that begins with the the same sound.

• Model carrying out ordinary activities with the items you choose as you interact with another child. For example, you might say: *Oh no, Jenny dropped a box of blueberries. I will clean them up with a broom.*

• Ask children if you were being helpful.

If...children cannot think of a word that begins with the same sound as a pair of words, **then...**name the two pictures and emphasize the initial sound.

Focus Question
How can I help my community?
¿Cómo puedo ayudar a mi comunidad?

Circle Time

Learning Goals

Language and Communication
• Child uses newly learned vocabulary daily in multiple contexts.

Emergent Literacy: Reading
• Child names most upper- and lowercase letters of the alphabet.
• Child describes, relates to, and uses details and information from books read aloud.

Vocabulary

community	comunidad
construction workers	trabajadores de la construcción
healthy	saludables
neighborhood	vecindario
neighbors	vecinos
sidewalks	aceras
safe	segura
trash	basura

Differentiated Instruction

 Extra Support

Learn About Letters and Sounds
If...children cannot reliably identify the letter when you come to the correct page,
then...give them a small card with the letter written on it and have them compare the letter on the card with the letter on the board.

 Enrichment

Learn About Letters and Sounds
Open the *ABC Big Book* to a random page. Point out the letter and sing "The ABC Song" with children. Ask them if the page with *E* comes before the page you're on or after it. Repeat with other pages and other letters.

Literacy Time

 large group 15 minutes

📖 Read Aloud

✓ **Can children relate the concepts in the book to their own lives?**

Build Background Explain that the book you're about to read tells about how people help their communities and their neighbors. Ask:

● *How many people have you helped today? Was it at school? At home? ¿A cuántas personas ayudaron hoy? ¿En la escuela? ¿En casa?*

● *How did you help those people? ¿Cómo ayudaron a estas personas?*

Listen for Understanding Display *Concept Big Book 2: In the Community* and read the title. Remind children that they have heard the book before.

● Ask children to help you remember important vocabulary words from previous discussions about the community and community helpers such as *firefighter* and *doctor*.

● On the last few pages, ask children to raise their hands if they have helped someone in the way described in the book.

Respond to the Book Ask children to name some ways that they can be helpful. Talk about how doing these things would help other people.

TIP To engage children in the discussion and keep them focused, have 2 or 3 children name ways that they have been helpful. Then challenge the class by asking questions, such as: *Who said she rakes leaves? ¿Quién dijo que recogió hojas con un rastrillo?*

Learn About Letters and Sounds

✓ **Can children identify upper case and lower case letters and their sounds?**

Learn About the Alphabet Write the letters *Tt*, *Ee*, *Gg*, and *Rr* on the board and review the names of the letters and their sounds.

● Display the *ABC Big Book*. Go through it slowly page by page, asking children to look for the page with *Tt*.

● Have children stop you when you get there by saying /t/ /t/ /t/.

● Review the pictures and words on the page.

● Continue with *Ee*, *Gg*, and *Rr*.

ELL You may find it helpful to preview the pictures on the *ABC Big Book* pages with children before doing this activity. Open the book to the *T, E, G,* and *R* pages and help children identify the pictures and words. When you do the activity above, they will be better able to participate if they have had an opportunity to preview.

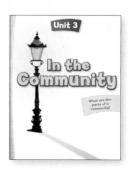

In the Community
En la comunidad

ABC Big Book

Math Time

Online Math Activity

Children can complete Build Stairs 1 and Build Stairs 2 during computer time or Center time.

Observe and Investigate

✓ **Can children use concrete models to add or subtract up to five objects?**

How Many Now? Invite children to play a counting game with hidden counters.

- Divide children in groups of 2 or 3 and give children copies of Numeral Cards.

- Show children a number of counters. Ask: *How many counters are there? ¿Cuántas fichas hay?* Have children hold up the corresponding Numeral Card.

- Cover the counters and add or subtract one counter. Uncover the counters and ask again: *How many counters are there? ¿Cuántas fichas hay?* Have children hold up the correct Numeral Card.

- Invite children to count the number of counters out loud to check their answers.

- Repeat the process, adding and subtracting counters.

⚥ Social and Emotional Development

Making Good Choices

✓ **Do children show a desire to be helpful and caring?**

Puppets Work Together Display the two Dog Puppets. Place the *Making Good Choices Flip Chart,* page 16, where children can refer to it. Explain that the puppets will try working together to move a block from one part of the meeting area to another.

- Have the puppets try to move the block without cooperating. Have them make comments such as *I want to pick up that end! ¡Yo quiero levantar esta punta!* and *Me first! ¡Yo primero!*

- Then have the puppets work together to move the block, saying, *Let's lift at the same time* and *Is it too heavy for you? ¡Levantémoslo al mismo tiempo! o ¿Es demasiado pesado para ti?*

- Have children tell what they saw and heard. Ask them to evaluate how well the puppets worked together each time. Ask children to discuss a time they solved a problem by working together.

ELL To help support comprehension, use gestures to model the meanings of words, such as *heavy,* used by the puppets.

Making Good Choices Flip Chart, page 16

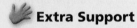
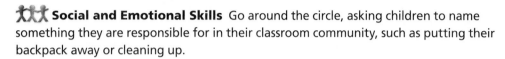

Social Studies Time

large group   20 minutes

👥 **Social and Emotional Skills** Go around the circle, asking children to name something they are responsible for in their classroom community, such as putting their backpack away or cleaning up.

Oral Language and Academic Vocabulary

✓ Can children use category labels to understand how the words *food, clothing,* and *shelter* relate to each other?

Food and Shelter Introduce the words *food, clothing,* and *shelter.* Ask children if they think all people need food, clothing, and shelter. Lead students to an understanding that the answer is yes, and then ask them to think of reasons why people might need these things.

● Review the words *food, clothing,* and *shelter* by playing a game. Tell children to say whether a thing you name is a type of food (such as carrots), a type of clothing (such as pants), or a type of shelter (such as a house).

● Repeat the activity with other examples.

Understand and Participate

✓ Can children use category labels to understand how the words *clerk* and *customer* relate to each other?

✓ Can children portray what it means to be a customer?

Getting Food and Clothing Ask children where their families get food and clothing. Explain or elicit that many people go to stores and use money to buy what they need. Introduce the vocabulary words *clerk* and *customer.*

● Help children understand the different roles performed by a clerk and a customer. Name activities, such as helping someone find shoes or buying a hat, and have students tell whether they apply to a clerk or a customer.

● Model being a store customer buying a shirt from a clerk. Have a child be the clerk.

● Then have pairs of children take turns role-playing being a customer buying goods from a clerk.

💡 **TIP** This activity may be more meaningful to children if you have them use play money and actual play items to "buy."

ELL Consonant blends such as /kl/ at the beginning of *clerk* and *clothing* may be difficult to pronounce for children from some language backgrounds. Help them by segmenting the words and repeating them.

Center Time

▶ **Center Rotation** Center Time includes teacher-guided activities and independent activities. Refer to the **Learning Centers** on pages 138–139 for independent activity ideas.

 **small group** 30 minutes

Refer to the **Learning Centers** on pages 138–139 for independent activity ideas.

✓ Learning Goals

Social and Emotional Development
• Child initiates interactions with others in work and play situations.

Emergent Literacy: Writing
• Child participates in free drawing and writing activities to deliver information.

Social Studies
• Child understands basic concepts of buying, selling, and trading.

Writer's Center

✓ **Encourage awareness of what it means to be a consumer by having children draw and tell about a visit they made to a store.**

Materials paper, pencils, crayons or markers

Inside a Store Have children write and draw about a time they went to a store.

• Have children describe what they did in pictures and in words. Take dictation or ask children to write on their own.

• Ask: *What kind of store was it? What did you see? What did you buy?*
¿Qué clase de tienda era? ¿Qué vieron? ¿Qué compraron?

• Have children initiate sharing their work with classmates. Encourage them to use vocabulary words in their discussions.

Center Tip

If...children are reluctant to do any writing on their own, **then...**encourage them to spell out words with plastic letters or have them make letters out of modeling clay.

Writing

Ask children to name things they have bought in a store with their families. Write the name of each item on the board, saying it slowly and asking children to help you identify some of the letters.

Purposeful Play

✓ **Observe children interacting with and playing productively with others to accomplish a goal.**

Children choose an open center for free playtime. Encourage children to share materials and work together to build a house or to put the letters of the alphabet in order.

Let's Say Good-Bye

  large group 15 minutes

 Read Aloud Revisit "Ms. Bumblebee Gathers Honey"/"La abejorrita Zumbi lleva miel" for your afternoon Read Aloud. Ask children to look for the letter *Ee* and listen for the sound /e/.

 Home Connection Refer to the Home Connections activities listed in the Resources and Materials chart on page 135. Remind children to tell families what they learned about how they can help their community. Sing the "Good-bye Song"/"Hora de ir a casa" as children prepare to leave.

Focus Question

How can I help my community?

¿Cómo puedo ayudar a mi comunidad?

Learning Goals

Social and Emotional Development
- Child participates in a variety of individual, small- and large-group activities.
- Child shows empathy and care for others.

Emergent Literacy: Reading
- Child produces words with the same beginning sound.
- Child describes, relates to, and uses details and information from books read aloud.

Vocabulary

folktale	cuento folclórico
make-believe	fantasía
pretend	simular
real	real
talking animals	animales que hablan

Differentiated Instruction

 Extra Support

Oral Language and Vocabulary
If...children have trouble distinguishing between real and make-believe, **then...**tell them something real and something make-believe and have them choose which is which; repeat several times.

Enrichment

Oral Language and Vocabulary
Have children think of stories they know. Ask them if the stories are real or make-believe. Have them tell how they know.

Let's Start the Day

 Opening Routines and Transition Tips
For **Opening Routines** and **Transition Tips** turn to pages 178–181 and visit **DLMExpressOnline.com** for more ideas.

 Read **"The Little Red Hen"/**"La gallinita roja" from the *Teacher's Treasure Book,* page 288, for your morning Read Aloud.

Language Time

large group   15 minutes

Social and Emotional Development Model taking on various roles and responsiblities throughout the day. Verbalize them so children can be guided by you while assuming roles and responsibilities for themselves.

Oral Language and Vocabulary

✓ **Can children use infomation learned from stories to distinguish between real and make-believe?**

Folktale Ask children if they remember hearing folktales before. Explain or have children explain that folktales are stories that have been told by many people for many years.

- Explain that some stories are real and others are make-believe, or pretend. Tell children that stories that are real could actually happen. They show people doing real things. Then say: *Folktales are usually make-believe. They are about talking animals, characters, or creatures that are not be real.* *Los cuentos folclóricos generalmente son de fantasía. Tratan sobre animales que hablan o personajes y criaturas que no son reales.*

- Have children tell about something that is real and then tell about something that is make-believe. Ask them to explain how they know.

ELL Not all cultures draw as sharp a distinction between *real* and *make-believe* as standard American culture does today. Be sensitive to children from backgrounds in which stories that may seem implausible are accepted as true.

Phonological Awareness

✓ **Can children name a word with the same initial sound as a pair of words?**

More Puppet Games Display the two Dog Puppets. Tell children that you are going to play a game with the puppets. When Dog Puppet 1 says two words that begin with the same sound, children should say a third word that starts with this same sound. When Dog Puppet 2 says two words that begin with the same sound, children should say a third word that starts with a different sound. Model this procedure; then play the game. Give children a chance to use the puppets.

Center Time

► **Center Rotation** Center Time includes teacher-guided activities and independent activities. Refer to the **Learning Centers** on pages 138–139 for independent activity ideas.

small group   60–90 minutes

Pretend and Learn Center

 Observe children initiating interaction and working together through pretend play.

 Assess whether children can use infomation learned from books to distinguish between real and make-believe.

Materials dress-up clothes, stuffed animals, other props

Acting with Stuffed Animals Have pairs of children dress up and use stuffed animals to act out real and make-believe scenarios from stories they know. Encourage each child to initiate a scenario.

● Children work with a partner to act out things that are real.

● Then, children work with a partner to act out things that are make-believe.

Center Tip

If...children get silly or frustrated after working with a certain partner for a while, **then**...rotate partners so children work with someone new.

ABC Center

 Assess whether children can identify the initial sound of a pair of words and produce another word with the same sound.

Materials plasticene or modeling clay, *ABC Big Book,* other alphabet books

Write and Say Partners find pictures they like in the alphabet books.

● Have one child say the word that names the picture and the initial sound of the word, *girl, /g/.* Then the other child finds another picture that begins with the same sound, *goat, /g/.*

● Partners find a third item together and then say the name of each picture followed by the initial sound of the words, *girl, /g/; goat, /g/; grass, /g/.*

● As you move through the room, ask children to name their sounds for you.

Center Tip

If...children are choosing pictures beginning with sounds they cannot pronounce, **then**... mark pages with sticky notes that have pictures of one or two sounds children are confident about.

Learning Goals

Social and Emotional Development
• Child initiates play scenarios with peers that share a common plan and goal.

Emergent Literacy: Reading
• Child identifies the letter that stands for a given sound.

• Child produces the most common sound for a given letter.

• Child describes, relates to, and uses details and information from books read aloud.

Differentiated Instruction

✋ **Extra Support**
Pretend and Learn Center
If...children are uncertain which activities are real and which are make-believe, **then**...ask questions such as: *Do you know anyone who owns a talking dog? Do you know anyone who has a garden?*

★ **Enrichment**
ABC Center
Challenge children to find pictures in magazines and make a letter-sound collage.

Accommodations for 3's
ABC Center
If...children have trouble thinking of make-believe stories, **then**...ask questions about stories or books you have read in class.

Focus Question
How can I help my community?
¿Cómo puedo ayudar a mi comunidad?

Learning Goals

Emergent Literacy: Reading
• Child names most upper- and lowercase letters of the alphabet.
• Child describes, relates to, and uses details and information from books read aloud.

Vocabulary

bridge	puente	goat	cabrito
grass	pasto	hooves	pezuñas
horns	cuernos	troll	gnomo

Differentiated Instruction

Extra Support

Read Aloud
If...children use vague words such as *they* for the goats and *the thing* for the bridge, **then...**say the actual words and help children use them in their sentences. For example, turn *They'll walk over the thing* into *The goats will walk over the bridge.*

Enrichment

Learn About Letters and Sounds
Give children picture books. Have them find all the *t*s they can on a given page. Repeat with other letters from the lesson.

Special Needs

Behavioral Social/Emotional
If...children have trouble sitting through and concentrating on the story, **then...**engage their bodies by having them clap their hands or bang their feet to demonstrate the noises the goats make when they cross the bridge.

Literacy Time

Read Aloud

 Can children use and understand vocabulary words from the lesson?

Build Background Ask children what they know about goats. Then ask children to tell what they know about bridges. Tell children that they will hear a folktale about some goats who try to cross a bridge.

• Ask children to act out what a goat sounds like and what a goat does.

• Have children use words and pictures to describe what a bridge is and what it is for.

Listen for Understanding Display "The Three Billy Goats Gruff"/"Los tres chivitos Gruff" (*Teacher's Treasure Book,* page 280) flannel board pieces. Read the title. Ask children to predict, or tell you what they think will happen, when the goats try to cross the bridge.

• Read the story aloud. Use the flannel board pieces to model story events.

• From time to time, invite children to make new predictions.

Respond to the Story Ask children to summarize what happened in the story. Ask them to explain why the story is make-believe. Ask children if the billy goats worked together in the story.

TIP Some children may have heard this story before. If children say they are familiar with the story, ask them to keep the ending a surprise for others. Remember that it can be hard for children not to share what they know.

Learn About Letters and Sounds

Can children find words beginning with the letters *Tt, Ee, Gg,* and *Rr*?

Learn About the Alphabet Children will look around the classroom for the letters *Tt, Ee, Gg,* and R*r*.

• Ask children to find words on the classroom walls or in books that begin with the letter *Tt.*

• When children find the letter, have them say: *I found a* t*!* As a class, look at the example provided by each child.

• Repeat the activity with the letters *Ee, Gg,* and *Rr.*

ELL Hearing and producing vowel sounds is often the most difficult aspect of learning a new language. Have children watch your mouth and lips as you say /e/ /e/ /e/. Help them distinguish, in particular, between /e/, /a/, and /i/.

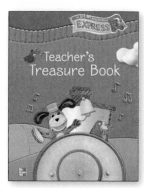

Teacher's Treasure Book, page 280

large group · 15 minutes

Math Time

Observe and Investigate

✓ **Can children order numbers?**

Predict the Number in the Pattern Invite children to predict the next number in a pattern.

- Display Dot Cards 1–5 in order from left to right. Say: *Look at the Dot Cards. Can you describe their pattern? Miren las tarjetas de puntos. ¿Pueden describir el patrón?*

- Talk about numbers in the community. Say: *What numbers do you see in your community? ¿Qué números ven en su comunidad?* Discuss, for example, address numbers on houses. Say: *The numbers on houses follow a pattern. When mail carriers deliver mail, they sort the mail to follow the patterns of numbers on the houses. Los números de las casas siguen un patrón. Cuando el cartero entrega el correo, sigue el patrón de números de las casas para agrupar las cartas.*

- Direct children back to the Dot Cards. Tell children to count aloud, predicting what number will be next.

Online Math Activity

Children can complete Build Stairs 1 and Build Stairs 2 during computer time or Center Time.

large group · 15 minutes

✗✗✗ Social and Emotional Development

Making Good Choices

✓ **Can children initiate ways to cooperate and get along with others?**

Puppets Play Again Ask children how, the previous day, the puppets had a hard time working together at first but did better the second time they tried.

- Explain that the puppets are friends that help one another, just like the children do, and they want to work together to make a block building like the one in the *Making Good Choices Flip Chart,* page 16.

- Have children initiate interactions using the puppets by guiding them in what to say and do.

- Show the puppets having trouble getting along once or twice, but allow children to guide the puppets back to working together.

ELL Help children understand that commands use special word order. Commands begin with verbs, as in: *Lift the block higher.* Most sentences typically have verbs later in the sentence, as in: *The puppet lifted the block higher.*

Making Good Choices Flip Chart, page 16

 Learning Goals

Social and Emotional Development
- Child initiates interactions with others in work and play situations.
- Child learns how to make and keep friends.

Mathematics
- Child demonstrates that the numerical counting sequence is always the same.

Vocabulary

cooperate	cooperar
get along	llevarse bien
number	número
pattern	patrón
predict	predecir
work together	trabajar juntos

Differentiated Instruction

✋ **Extra Support**

Observe and Investigate
If...children have difficulty predicting the next number, **then...**model counting from 1 to generate the next number.

⭐ **Enrichment**

Making Good Choices
Ask children to recall and describe how the puppets showed examples of working together. the previous day.

Accommodations for 3's

Making Good Choices
If...older children are dominating the discussion, **then...**go around the circle to give younger children a turn; this helps you know if these children are having difficulty understanding.

Mathematics

• Child demonstrates that the numerical counting sequence is always the same.

Vocabulary

bus driver	conductor
crossing guard	inspector de tránsito
help	ayudar
police officer	policía
teacher	maestro

 Extra Support

Math Time

If...children have difficulty with the Plus 1 pattern, **then...**review the Plus 1 pattern with them.

Enrichment

Math Time

Ask children to think of other community helpers. Have them give the next number after 10, and assign it to a new helper.

Accommodations for 3's

Math Time

If...children have trouble counting the higher-numbered helpers, **then...**invite them to come to the flip chart and touch each picture as they count.

Math Time

 large group 20 minutes

✅ **Do children show an understanding of counting sequences?**

Community Helpers Discuss with children all the different people in their community who help others. Ask children to think of why each person is important to the community.

● Display the *Math and Science Flip Chart,* page 28. Point to the title of the page. Say: *Here are some community helpers. Without them, our community would not work! Aquí hay algunas personas que trabajan en la comunidad. ¡Sin ellos, nuestra comunidad no podría funcionar!*

● Point to the numeral 1. Say: *Here is the numeral 1. What community helper is there one of? Éste es el número 1. ¿De qué tipo de persona que trabaja en la comunidad hay uno?* Allow children time to answer. If they have trouble, describe what the person does. Say: *This person delivers our mail. If there were none of these helpers, we would never get our mail! Esta persona reparte el correo. Sin una de estas personas, ¡nunca recibiríamos el correo!*

● Then go to numeral 2. Ask: *What is the next numeral? ¿Cuál es el siguiente número?* Point to the numeral 2. Say: *Yes! The next numeral is 2. The next numeral is one more than one. What community helper are there two of? ¡Sí! El número que sigue es el 2. El siguiente número es uno más que uno. ¿De qué tipo de persona que trabaja en la comunidad hay dos?*

● Continue this way for each numeral, emphasizing the Plus 1 pattern.

● Conclude by asking children to describe the Plus 1 pattern.

Math and Science Flip Chart, page 28

Center Time

> **Center Rotation** Center Time includes teacher-guided activities and independent activities. Refer to the **Learning Centers** on pages 138–139 for independent activity ideas.

 small group 30 minutes

Math and Science Center

Center Tip

Observe children's understanding of counting sequences through numeral sorting.

Materials several sets of tactile numerals, muffin pans or paper cups for sorting

Sort! Divide children into small groups. Provide several sets of tactile numerals, such as magnetic, foam, and so on. Set up muffin tins or other sorting containers for children.

- Ask: *How many numbers do you have? ¿Cuántos números tienen?*

- Say: *Sort the numbers in order. Start with 1, 2, 3, and so on. Agrupen los números en orden. Comiencen con 1, 2, 3, y sigan de esa manera.*

If...children have difficulty sorting, **then...**label the muffin pans or paper cups with numerals for extra support.

Learning Goals

Social and Emotional Development
- Child learns how to make and keep friends.

Emergent Literacy: Writing
- Child participates in free drawing and writing activities to deliver information.

Mathematics
- Child demonstrates that the numerical counting sequence is always the same.

Writing

Have children write and draw about teaching Dog Puppet 1 and Dog Puppet 2 how to work together and get along. Encourage them to form letters they know themselves. Ask them to share their work with a classmate.

Purposeful Play

✓ Encourage children to work with children they might not know well.

✓ Observe whether children work productively with children they often choose as companions.

Children can choose an open center for free playtime. Ask children to think about how they can make new friends and keep old friends while they are playing.

Let's Say Good-Bye

 large group 15 minutes

 Read Aloud Revisit "The Little Red Hen"/"La gallinita roja" for your afternoon Read Aloud. Have children listen to decide whether the story is real or make-believe.

 Home Connection Refer to the Home Connections activities listed in the Resources and Materials chart on page 135. Remind children to tell families what they learned about how they can help their community. Sing the "Good-bye Song"/"Hora de ir a casa" as children prepare to leave.

DAY 5

Let's Start the Day

Focus Question

How can I help my community?

¿Cómo puedo ayudar a mi comunidad?

Opening Routines and Transition Tips

For **Opening Routines** and **Transition Tips** turn to pages 178–181 and visit DLMExpressOnline.com for more ideas.

Read **"The Great Big Pumpkin"**/"La calabaza gigante" from the *Teacher's Treasure Book*, page 292, for your morning Read Aloud.

large group   15 minutes

Learning Goals

Social and Emotional Development
• Child follows simple classroom rules and routines.

Language and Communication
• Child names and describes actual or pictured people, places, things, actions, attributes, and events.

Emergent Literacy: Reading
• Child produces words with the same beginning sound.

Vocabulary

cleaner	limpio	cup	vaso
jug	envases	plastic	plástico
recycle	reciclar	trash	basura

Language Time

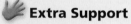 **Social and Emotional Development** Ask children what their rules are for following the routines of the classroom as they move through the day.

Oral Language and Vocabulary

Can children use vocabulary words to talk about trash and recycling?

Being Helpful Display the *Rhymes and Chants Flip Chart,* page 16. Read the poem aloud. Encourage children to say the parts they have learned. Then ask:

● *Why is it a good idea to ask a grown up before you pick up some trash? ¿Por qué es una buena idea preguntarle a un adulto antes de recoger basura?*

● *Why is it a good idea to recycle? ¿Por qué reciclar es una buena idea?*

● *Tell about some things you recycle. Where do you put them? What do you do with them then? Cuéntenme si reciclan algunas cosas. ¿Dónde las ponen? ¿Qué hacen con esas cosas?*

Phonological Awareness

Can children distinguish between words that begin with the same sound and words that begin with different sounds?

Same and Different Game Display the *Rhymes and Chants Flip Chart,* page 16. Tell children to stand in a circle and hold hands. When you say a pair of words from the rhyme that start with different sounds, they should drop their hands; when you say a pair of words that start with the same sounds, they should hold hands again. Say these word sets: *call/can; girls/things; parents/pick; make/milk; some/world.*

ELL Children may have difficulty determining if the initial sounds of word pairs are alike or different, especially if the sounds are not exactly the same as the sounds of their native language. You can help by exaggerating the positioning of your mouth with emphasis when you say the initial sounds. Have children repeat the sounds, imitating the position of your mouth.

Rhymes and Chants Flip Chart, page 16

Differentiated Instruction

✋ Extra Support

Phonological Awareness

If…children seem to be holding or dropping hands based only on what other children are doing, **then…**form smaller groups, including one made up only of children whom you think are struggling, and give each group a different word pair to work with.

⭐ Enrichment

Oral Language and Vocabulary

Help children make a tally chart showing objects in the classroom recycling container.

Center Time

► **Center Rotation** Center Time includes teacher-guided activities and independent activities. Refer to the **Learning Centers** on pages 138–139 for independent activity ideas.

 small group 60–90 minutes

Construction Center | Center Tip

✓ **Observe children to see if they use their imaginations to build a recycling center.**

✓ **Listen to note whether children use vocabulary words to talk about their work with others.**

Materials cardboard and paper scraps, scissors, tape, glue, beads and other decorations, pictures of recycling centers

The Recycling Building Ask children to talk about where recycled trash goes after it is picked up. Show children pictures of a recycling center. Have them construct a building where materials are recycled.

- Encourage children to work with a partner or with several other children.

- Have children explain to you or another child what the parts of their buildings are for and the steps involved in recycling. Check that they use terms such as *trash* and *recycling* as they talk.

Center Tip

If...children start building something different from the assignment, **then...**return them to the task at hand by giving them a gentle prompt, such as *That looks like a wonderful thing to build another time; for right now, let's think about recycling. Is there a place for the trucks to unload?*

Library and Listening Center | Center Tip

✓ **Listen to note if children can talk about trash and recycling.**

Materials books about trash, picking up trash, and keeping the world clean; pencils, paper, markers, or crayons

Keeping the World Clean Have children look through books about trash and recycling with a partner.

- Have them talk together about what they see and what they learn from the books.

- Ask them to draw and talk about what they can do to help make the world a cleaner place.

Center Tip

If...children want to learn more about recycling, **then...**look on the Internet to find child-friendly sites about the subject.

 Learning Goals

Social and Emotional Development
- Child initiates interactions with others in work and play situations.

Language and Communication
- Child uses oral language for a variety of purposes.
- Child uses newly learned vocabulary daily in multiple contexts.

Differentiated Instruction

 Extra Support

Construction Center
If...children can't sequence the events easily when they describe their work, **then...**provide the prompts *first, next,* and *last* and help children use them to order their descriptions.

⭐ **Enrichment**

Construction Center
Ask children to make up a story about something that might happen at a recycling center. Have them name some items they think may be made from recycled materials.

 Special Needs

Delayed Motor Development
If...children cannot cut and glue on their own, **then...**help them hold the scissors or glue while you guide them to cut in the right place or use the right amount of glue.

Focus Question
How can I help my community?
¿Cómo puedo ayudar a mi comunidad?

 Learning Goals

Emergent Literacy: Reading
• Child produces the most common sound for a given letter.

Vocabulary

bus	autobús	clerk	cajera
driver	conductor	flower	flor
garden	jardín	grocery	tienda

Differentiated Instruction

 Extra Support
Learn About Letters and Sounds
If...children cannot identify the initial letter based on the word, **then...**segment the word and say it in two parts, such as /t/ -op.

Enrichment
Read Aloud
Ask children what they think the other characters in the story might be thinking when they see the girl and her father.

Literacy Time

large group • 15 minutes

Read Aloud

✓ **Do children recognize the theme of helpfulness in the story *Flower Garden*?**

Build Background Ask children what they remember about gardens. Ask:

• *What can grow in a garden?*

• *How do you keep a garden growing?*

Listen for Understanding Display *Flower Garden* and read the title. Remind children that they read this story before. Explain that you will read the book again. Ask children to look and listen for ways people help each other in the book.

• Ask: ***Does the grocery store clerk help anybody? Does the bus driver help anybody?*** *¿La cajera de la tienda ayuda a alguien? ¿Y el conductor del autobús?*

• Say: ***I think most of the people in the story are helpful. Let's find out how.*** *Creo que la mayoría de la gente del cuento ayuda a alguien. Veamos de qué manera.*

Respond and Connect Read the book. Have children describe ways that people helped others in the book. For example, the bus driver gave the girl and her father a ride.

TIP Make the connections between the book and the theme of helpfulness as explicit as possible. If needed, you can extend the discussion above with questions such as: ***What might have happened if the bus driver hadn't helped them?*** *¿Qué habría sucedido si el conductor del autobús no los hubiera ayudado?* or ***What are some things you can only do if you have help?*** *¿Qué cosas sólo pueden hacer si tienen ayuda?*

ELL To help children grow used to the cadences of English, ask children to echo you as you read the story one line at a time. Check children's pronunciation, but focus on whether their intonation is correct.

Learn About Letters and Sounds

✓ **Can children identify initial letters when they hear words that start with the corresponding sound?**

Learn About the Alphabet Ask children to name the four letters they have been working on this week.

• Write the letters *Tt, Ee, Rr,* and *Gg* on the board. Read the letters with children and review the sounds that go with each letter. Have children produce the sounds with you.

• Open the *ABC Big Book* to the *Ee* page, but don't show it to children. Read one or two of the *Ee* words on the page. Challenge children to identify the initial letter. Show them the page when they have the correct answer.

• Repeat with *Tt, Rr,* and *Gg*.

Flower Garden
Un jardín de flores

ABC Big Book

Online Math Activity

Children can complete Build Stairs 1 and Build Stairs 2 during computer time or Center time.

Math Time

large group 15 minutes

Observe and Investigate

☑ **Can children subtract from 1 to 5 objects?**

Five Little Monkeys Invite children to join in the finger play Five Little Monkeys. The Spanish version of this finger play can be found in the *Teacher's Treasure Book*, page 80. Tell children that these monkeys are not careful. They are jumping on the bed. Discuss with children why it's not safe to jump on a bed.

● Open your hand, palm up, for the bed. Put your other hand's fingers up as the monkeys. Show the "monkeys" jumping on the "bed." As each monkey falls off the bed, fold that finger over. Invite children to join you by using their hands to represent the monkeys and the bed. Sing the following song:

> **Five little monkeys jumping on the bed; one fell off and bumped his head.** (*Lightly tap head.*)
> **We called for the doctor, and the doctor said,** (*Hold pretend phone to ear.*)
> **"No more monkeys jumping on the bed!"** (*Shake your head.*)

● Continue counting backward until there are no more monkeys. Encourage children to sing with you and participate in the finger play.

𝕏𝕏𝕏 Social and Emotional Development

large group 15 minutes

Making Good Choices

☑ **Do children remember strategies for working together with friends?**

Review the Chart Display *Making Good Choices Flip Chart*, page 16. Tell children that they did a great job of teaching the puppets about the chart.

● Then ask: *Who worked well with their friends this week? Who did you work with? What were you doing? ¿Quiénes trabajaron bien con sus amigos esta semana? ¿Con quién trabajaron? ¿Qué hicieron?*

● Wrap up by complimenting children on what they learned and noting that you saw many children working well together and making new friends.

ELL Provide choices for children with limited English proficiency. For instance, instead of simply asking the open-ended question *What were you doing*, ask: *Were you drawing, or were you playing dress-up?* Use gestures to help get across the meaning of those choices. Have children repeat the correct word or say a sentence, such as, *I was drawing.*

Making Good Choices Flip Chart, page 16

 Learning Goals

Social and Emotional Development
• Child initiates interactions with others in work and play situations.
• Child learns how to make and keep friends.

Mathematics
• Child uses concrete objects or makes a verbal word problem to subtract up to 5 objects from a set.

Vocabulary

bed	cama	friends	amigos
monkeys	monitos	playing	jugamos
working	trabajamos		

Differentiated Instruction

🖐 **Extra Support**

Making Good Choices

If...it is hard for children to remember when they worked well with someone, **then...**point to different parts of the room and ask: *Did you work well with someone in the block area? Did you work well with someone in the housekeeping center? Did you work well with someone at the science table? ¿Trabajaron bien con alguien en el área de los bloques? ¿Trabajaron bien con alguien en el centro de la casa de juguete? ¿Trabajaron bien con alguien en la mesa de ciencias?*

⭐ **Enrichment**

Observe and Investigate

Revise the finger play to include numbers up to 10.

Accommodations for 3's

Observe and Investigate

If...children have trouble manipulating their fingers, **then...**provide individual support.

Focus Question
How can I help my community?
¿Cómo puedo ayudar a mi comunidad?

 Learning Goals

Social and Emotional Development
• Child is aware of self in terms of abilities, characteristics and preferences, and respects personal boundaries.

Physical Development
• Child coordinates body movements in a variety of locomotive activities (such as walking, jumping, running, hopping, skipping, climbing).
• Child completes tasks that require eye-hand coordination and control.

Vocabulary

balance	equilibrio	partner	compañero
run	correr	stoop	inclinarse
tiptoe	puntas de pie	walk	caminar

Differentiated Instruction

 Extra Support

Move and Learn
If...children have difficulty balancing, **then...**have them stand on one foot while holding on to a piece of playground equipment; then have them slowly release their grip.

Enrichment

Move and Learn
Have children do some of these activities in groups of 3, finding two other children to join them.

Outside Play Time

  large group · 20 minutes

Social Emotional Skills Help children recognize where their bodies are in space and how they can respect the boundaries of others.

Oral Language and Vocabulary

Can children understand and use action words?

Alone and with Partners Introduce vocabulary by giving directions and leading children as they walk in place, run in place, tiptoe in place, stoop (squat), and balance (stand on one foot). Then model following each direction with a partner by holding hands with one child and repeating the actions with that child.

• Walk through the meeting area and have children name what you are doing. Repeat with the other actions.

Move and Learn

Can children carry out physical actions when the action is named?

Can children move through the play area without interfering with others?

Outdoor Play Have children spread out in the play area. Be sure no one is touching anyone else. Tell children that you will give them directions and that they need to listen closely. Explain that they should only touch other children if the direction includes the word *partner*. If they hear *partner*, they should follow the direction while holding a partner's hand. Explain that making sure you are not interfering with classmates is part of helping them.

• Tell children to tiptoe and check that they are doing so.

• Then tell them to tiptoe with a partner. Check that children follow the direction.

• Repeat with other actions. Cycle through all of the actions several times in random order, sometimes having the children do them with a partner and sometimes having the children do them alone.

TIP When modeling these activities indoors, it's best to have children walk, run, and tiptoe in place. Outdoors, however, you should encourage them to move around the play area as much as possible, while respecting the boundaries of others.

ELL Have English language learners repeat the directions after you say them to help them with the sounds and intonations of English words.

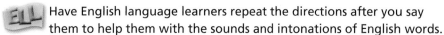

Center Time

Center Rotation Center Time includes teacher-guided activities and independent activities. Refer to the **Learning Centers** on pages 138–139 for independent activity ideas.

small group 30 minutes

Creativity Center

 Observe to see if children represent themselves doing the Outside Play activity.

 Observe to make sure children share materials and space as they paint.

Materials large paper, paint

Make a Mural Have children paint the activity they did outdoors.

- Ask children what they did outside.

- Have them paint on the paper with other children to show the activity. Remind them to work together and to share space.

- Have children share their work with classmates. Encourage them to use vocabulary words in their discussions.

Center Tip

If...children have trouble managing the paintbrushes, **then...**have them try paintbrushes of different sizes, or have them paint with sponges or other tools instead.

Social and Emotional Development
- Child is aware of self in terms of abilities, characteristics and preferences, and respects personal boundaries.

- Child initiates interactions with others in work and play situations.

Emergent Literacy: Writing
- Child participates in free drawing and writing activities to deliver information.

Writing

Ask children to think back about their week. Ask them to choose one thing they did that was especially fun for them. Have them write and draw about it and write some words they associate with the activity.

Purposeful Play

 See if children recognize where their bodies are in space and avoid unnecessary contact with others.

Children choose an open center for free playtime. Remind children to pay attention to where other children are in the center so they don't disturb others. Remind them that respecting the space of others is a kind of helping too.

Let's Say Good-Bye

large group 15 minutes

 Read Aloud Revisit "The Great Big Pumpkin"/"La calabaza gigante" for your afternoon Read Aloud. Have children listen for the sound of the letter *Tt*.

 Home Connection Refer to the Home Connections activities listed in the Resources and Materials chart on page 135. Remind children to tell families what they learned about how they can help their community. Sing the "Good-bye Song"/"Hora de ir a casa" as children prepare to leave.

In general, the purpose of assessing young children in the early childhood classroom is to collect information necessary to make important decisions about their developmental and educational needs. Because assessment is crucial to making informed teaching decisions, it is necessarily a vital component of *DLM Early Childhood Express.* The guidelines and forms found online allow the teacher to implement assessment necessary in the pre-kindergarten classroom.

Effective assessment is an ongoing process that always enhances opportunities for optimal growth, development, and learning. The process of determining individual developmental and educational needs tailors early childhood education practices and provides a template for setting individual and program goals.

Pre-kindergarten assessment should be authentic; that is, it should be a natural, environmental extension of the classroom. Assessments should be incorporated into classroom activities whenever possible, not completed as separate, pull-out activities in which the teacher evaluates the student one-on-one. Whenever possible, assessment should evaluate children's real knowledge in the process of completing real activities. For example, observing children as they equally distribute snacks would be a better assessment of their ability to make groups than observing an exercise in which children group counters would be.

It is also important to note that assessments should be administered over time, as environmental influences can greatly impact single outcomes. If a pre-kindergarten child is tired or ill, for example, the child may not demonstrate knowledge of a skill that has actually been mastered. It is also important to consider the length of assessment for children of this age, as attention spans are still developing and can vary greatly based on environmental influences. Most assessments should be completed within half an hour.

If possible, use multiple types of assessment for the same content area when working with pre-kindergarten children. Some children may be able to demonstrate mastery kinesthetically if they are not able to use expressive language well; others may not process auditory instruction adequately, but will be able to complete an assessment after observing someone model the task. It is vital that the assessment process should never make the child anxious or scared.

Informal Assessment

INFORMAL assessments rely heavily on observational and work-sampling techniques that continually focus on child performance, processes, and product over selected periods of time and in a variety of contexts.

ANECDOTAL assessments are written descriptions that provide a short, objective account of an event or an incident. Only the facts are reported—where, what, when, and how. Anecdotal records are especially helpful when trying to understand a child's behavior or use of skills. These recordings can be used to share the progress of individual children and to develop and individualize curriculum.

The Anecdotal Observational Record Form can be used at any time to document an individual child's progress toward a goal or signs indicating the need for developmental or medical evaluation. Observations can reflect the focused skills for the week, but are not limited to those skills. You may pair the form with video or audio recordings of the child to complete an anecdotal record.

Anecdotal Observational Record Form

CHECKLISTS are lists of skills or behaviors arranged into disciplines or developmental domains and are used to determine how a child exhibits the behaviors or skills listed. Teachers can quickly and easily observe groups of children and check the behaviors or skills each child is demonstrating at the moment.

Weekly Assessment

Weekly Assessments measure progress toward specific guidelines that are addressed in the weekly curriculum. The Performance Assessment Checklist measures progress toward the guidelines of the entire curriculum. It is intended to be used three times per year.

Performance Assessment Checklist

When using either type of checklist, it is important to remember that the skills and behaviors on the list are only guidelines. Each child is unique and has his or her own developmental timetable. It is also important to remember that the checklist only documents the presence or absence of a specific skill or behavior during the time of observation. It does not necessarily mean the skill is consistently present or lacking, though consistency may be noted when the skill has been observed over time.

PORTFOLIO assessments are collections of thoughtfully selected work samples, or artifacts, and accompanying reflections indicative of the child's learning experiences, efforts, and progress toward and/or attainment of established curriculum goals. They are an authentic, performance-based method to allow teachers to analyze progress over time. As children choose work samples for their portfolios, they become involved in their own learning and assessment and begin to develop the concept of evaluating their own work.

Although early childhood activities tend to focus on processes as opposed to products, there are numerous opportunities to collect samples of children's work. Items to collect include drawings, tracings, cuttings, attempts to print their names, and paintings. You may also include informal assessments of a child's ability to recognize letters, shapes, numbers, and rhyming words.

Formal Assessment

FORMAL assessments involve the use of standardized tests. They are administered in a prescribed manner and may require completion within a specified amount of time. Standardized tests result in scores that are usually compared to the scores of a normative group. These tests generally fall into the following categories: achievement tests, readiness tests, developmental screening tests, intelligence tests, and diagnostic tests.

Assessing Children with Special Needs

Children with special needs may require a more thorough initial assessment, more frequent on-going assessments, and continuous adaptation of activities. Assessment is essentially the first task for the teacher or caregiver in developing the individualized instruction program required for children with disabilities.

Assessing Children Who Are English Language Learners

Whenever possible, assessments should be given in both the child's first language and in English.

Essential Question
What is a community?

Classroom Community Day

Build a Classroom Community Bulletin Board

- Cover a large wall bulletin board with white chart paper. With children, plan and draw roads, parks, and bodies of water on the chart paper. Gather various clean milk containers. Use quart containers for community buildings and pint and half-pint containers for houses.

- Discuss community buildings such as firehouses, schools, and so on. Elicit volunteers to paint the quart containers to represent the community buildings. Encourage them to include building features, such as windows, doors, roofs, and so on. When buildings dry, attach them with tacks to the bulletin board community. Label each building.

- Have children paint a pint or half-pint container to represent their house. Encourage them to paint it the color of their own house. Label each house. Create and add other elements of a community that you have discussed in class. Remind them to include families, neighbors, community helpers, and other elements of a community.

- Have children create invitations to invite school workers, family members, and friends to join your Classroom Community Day and share what they know about or do in the community.

- Organize the classroom into four areas. Display books, children's work, and so on in each area. Focus each area on one of the weekly themes and each week's focus question.

    - Provide art supplies and magazines in each area so children and visitors can create additions for the Community Bulletin Board.

    - Encourage families to bring in pictures or items from their community to share on Community Day.

Evaluate and Inform

☑ Review the informal observation notes you recorded for each child during the four weeks of the unit. Identify areas in which individual children will need additional support.

☑ Send a summary of your observation notes home with children. Encourage parents to respond to the summary with questions or comments.

☑ Review dated samples of children's work in their portfolios. Copy some of these samples to send home to families along with the observation summary.

☑ Send home the Unit 3 My Library Book, *In My Community,* for children to read with their families.

Celebrar la unidad

Pregunta esencial

¿Qué es una comunidad?

Día de la Comunidad en clase

Construir un tablero de avisos de la clase

- Cubra un tablero de avisos de una pared grande con una hoja de cartelón blanca. Junto con los niños, planee y dibuje calles, parques y cuerpos de agua en la hoja de cartelón. Reúna varios envases de leche vacíos y limpios. Use envases de un cuarto para los edificios de la comunidad y envases de una pinta o media pinta para las casas.

- Hablen sobre los edificios de la comunidad, como estaciones de bomberos, escuelas, etc. Solicite voluntarios para que pinten los envases de un cuarto que representan los edificios de la comunidad. Anímelos a incluir las características de los edificios, como ventanas, puertas, techos, etc. Cuando los edificios estén secos, péguelos con tachuelas al tablero de avisos de la comunidad. Rotule cada edificio.

- Pida a cada niño que pinte un envase de una pinta o de media pinta para representar su casa. Anímelo a pintar el envase del color de su propia casa. Rotule cada casa. Construya y añada otros elementos de una comunidad que hayan comentado en clase. Recuérdeles que incluyan familias, vecinos, trabajadores comunitarios y otros elementos de una comunidad.

- Pida a los niños que hagan tarjetas para invitar a los trabajadores de la escuela, familiares y amigos a participar en su Día de la Comunidad en clase y comentar lo que saben sobre la comunidad o lo que hacen en ella.

- Organice el salón de clases en cuatro áreas. Exhiba en cada área libros, el trabajo de los niños, etc. Enfoque cada área en uno de los temas semanales y en la pregunta de enfoque de cada semana.

- Coloque en cada área materiales de arte y revistas para que los niños y los visitantes pueden crear sus propios aportes para el tablero de avisos de la comunidad.

- Anime a las familias a llevar fotografías u objetos de su comunidad para mostrarlos en el Día de la Comunidad.

Evaluar e informar

- ✓ Repase las notas de la observación informal que realizó sobre cada niño durante las cuatro semanas de la unidad. Identifique las áreas en las que algunos niños en particular necesitarán apoyo adicional.

- ✓ Envíe a casa con cada niño un resumen de sus notas de observación. Anime a los padres a responderle con preguntas o comentarios.

- ✓ Revise las muestras fechadas del trabajo de los niños en sus portafolios. Haga copias de algunas de estas muestras y envíelas a las familias junto con el resumen de sus observaciones.

- ✓ Dé a los niños el librito de la Unidad 3, *Mi comunidad,* para leer con sus familias.

Appendix

About the Authors 176

Classroom Set-Up and Resources

    Opening Routines 178

    Transition Tips 180

    Center Management 182

    Teaching the English Language Learner 184

    Letter and Number Formation Guides 188

Vocabulary Development and Word Lists 192

Learning Trajectories for Mathematics 198

About the Authors

NELL K. DUKE, ED.D., is Professor of Teacher Education and Educational Psychology and Co-Director of the Literacy Achievement Research Center at Michigan State University. Nell Duke's expertise lies in early literacy development, particularly among children living in poverty, and integrating literacy into content instruction. She is the recipient of a number of awards for her research and is co-author of several books including *Literacy and the Youngest Learner: Best Practices for Educators of Children from Birth to 5* and *Beyond Bedtime Stories: A Parent's Guide to Promoting Reading, Writing, and Other Literacy Skills From Birth to 5.*

DOUG CLEMENTS is SUNY Distinguished Professor of Education at the University of Buffalo, SUNY. Previously a preschool and kindergarten teacher, Clements currently researchs the learning and teaching of early mathematics and computer applications. He has published over 100 research studies, 8 books, 50 chapters, and 250 additional publications, including co-authoring the reports of President Bush's National Mathematics Advisory Panel and the National Research Council's book on early mathematics. He has directed twenty projects funded by the National Science Foundation and Department of Education's Institute of Education Sciences.

JULIE SARAMA Associate Professor at the University at Buffalo (SUNY), has taught high school mathematics and computer science, gifted and talented classes, and early childhood mathematics. She directs several projects funded by the National Science Foundation and the Institute of Education Sciences. Author of over 50 refereed articles, 4 books, 30 chapters, 20 computer programs, and more than 70 additional publications, she helped develop the Building Blocks and Investigations curricula and the award-winning Turtle Math. Her latest book is *Early Childhood Mathematics Education Research: Learning Trajectories for Young Children.*

WILLIAM TEALE is Professor of Education at the University of Illinois at Chicago. Author of over one hundred publications on early literacy learning, the intersection of technology and literacy education, and children's literature, he helped pioneer research in emergent literacy. Dr. Teale has worked in the area of early childhood education with schools, libraries, and other organizations across the country and internationally. He has also directed three U.S. Department of Education-funded Early Reading First projects that involve developing model preschool literacy curricula for four-year-old children from urban, low-income settings in Chicago.

Contributing Authors

Kimberly Brenneman, PhD, is an Assistant Research Professor of Psychology at Rutgers University. She is also affiliated with the Rutgers Center for Cognitive Science (RuCCS) and the National Institute for Early Education Research (NIEER). Brenneman is co-author of *Preschool Pathways to Science (PrePS): Facilitating Scientific Ways of Thinking, Talking, Doing, and Understanding* and is an educational advisor for PBS's *Sid the Science Kid* television show and website. Research interests include the development of scientific reasoning and methods to improve instructional practices that support science and mathematics learning in preschool.

Peggy Cerna is an independent Early Childhood Consultant. She was a bilingual teacher for 15 years and then served as principal of the Rosita Valley Literacy Academy, a Pre-Kindergarten through Grade 1 school in Eagle Pass, Texas. Cerna then opened Lucy Read Pre-Kindergarten Demonstration School in Austin, Texas, which had 600 Pre-Kindergarten students. During her principalship at Lucy Read, Cerna built a strong parental community with the collaboration of the University of Texas, AmeriCorps, and Austin Community College. Her passion for early literacy drove her to create book clubs where parents were taught how to read books to their children.

Dan Cieloha is an educator with more than 30 years' experience in creating, implementing, and evaluating experientially based learning materials, experiences, and environments for young children. He believes that all learners must be actively and equitably involved in constructing, evaluating, and sharing what they learn. He has spearheaded the creation and field-testing of a variety of learning materials including *You & Me: Building Social Skills in Young Children*. He is also president of the Partnership for Interactive Learning, a leading nonprofit organization dedicated to the development of children's social and thinking skills.

Paula A. Jones, M.Ed., is an Early Childhood Consultant at the state and national levels. As a former Early Childhood Director for the Lubbock Independent School District, she served as the Head Start Director and co-founded three of their four Early Childhood campuses which also became a model design and Best Practices Program for the Texas Education Agency. She was a contributing author for the first Texas Prekindergarten Guidelines, served as president for the Texas Association of Administrators and Supervisors of Programs for Young Children, and is a 2010 United Way Champions for Children Award winner.

Bobbie Sparks is a retired educator who has taught biology and middle school science as well as being the K-12 district science consultant for a suburban district. At Harris County Department of Education she served as the K-12 science consultant in Professional Development. During her career as K-12 science consultant, Sparks worked with teachers at all grade levels to revamp curriculum to meet the Texas science standards. She served on Texas state committees to develop the TEKS standards as well as committees to develop items for tests for teacher certification in science.

Opening Routines

Below are a few suggested routines to use for beginning your day with your class. You can rotate through them, or use one for a while before trying a new approach. You may wish to develop your own routines by mixing and matching ideas from the suggestions given.

1. Days of the Week

Ask children what day of the week it is. When they respond, tell them that you are going to write a sentence that tells everyone what day of the week it is. Print "Today is Monday." on the board. If you have a helper chart, have children assist you in finding the name of the day's helper. Print: "Today's helper is Miguel." Ask the helper to come forward and find the Letter Tiles or ABC Picture Cards that spell his or her name.

As the year progresses, you might want to have the helper find the letters that spell the day of the week. Eventually some children may be able to copy the entire sentence with Letter Tiles or ABC Picture Cards.

2. Calendar Search

Print "Today is _____." on the board. Ask children to help you fill in the blank. Print the day of the week in the blank. Invite children to look at the calendar to determine today's date. Write the date under the sentence that tells what day of the week it is. Invite children to clap out the syllables of both the sentence and the date.

Review the days of the week and the months of the year using the "Days of the Week Song"/"Canción de los dias de la semana" and the "Months of the year"/ "Los meses del año."

Ask children what day of the week it was yesterday. When they respond, ask them what day it is today. Place a seasonal sticker on today's date. Have children follow your lead and recite "Yesterday was Monday, September 12. Today is Tuesday, September 13. Tomorrow will be Wednesday, September 14."

3. Feelings

Make happy- and sad-faced puppets for each child by cutting yellow circles from construction paper and drawing happy and sad faces on them. Laminate the faces, and glue them to tongue depressors. Cover two large coffee cans. On one can glue a happy face, and write the sentence "I feel happy today." Glue the sad face to the second can, and write the sentence "I feel sad today."

Give each child a happy- and a sad-faced puppet. Encourage children to tell how they feel today and to hold up the appropriate puppet. Encourage children to come forward and place their puppets in the can that represents their feelings. Later in the year you can add puppets to represent other emotions.

You can vary this activity by using a graph titled "How I Feel Today"/"Como me siento hoy." Have children place their puppets in the appropriate column on the graph instead of in the cans.

4. Pledge of Allegiance/ Moment of Silence

Have children locate the United States flag. Recite the Pledge of Allegiance to the U.S. flag. Then allow a minute for a moment of silence.

Discuss these activities with children, allowing them to volunteer reasons the Pledge of Allegiance is said and other places they have seen the Pledge recited.

5. Coming to Circle

Talk with children about being part of a class family. Tell children that as part of a class family they will work together, learn together, respect each other, help each other, and play together. Explain that families have rules so that jobs get done and everyone stays safe. Let children know they will learn rules for their classroom. One of those rules is how they will come together for circle. Sing "This is the Way We Come to Circle" (to the tune of "This is the Way We Wash Our Clothes").

This is the way we come to circle.
Come to circle, come to circle.
This is the way we come to circle,
So early in the morning.

This is the way we sit right down,
Sit right down, sit right down.
This is the way we sit right down,
So early in the morning.

This is the way we fold our hands,
Fold our hands, fold our hands.
This is the way we fold our hands,
So early in the morning.

Transition Tips

Sing songs or chants such as those listed below while transitioning between activities:

1. I Am Now in Pre-K

To the tune of "I'm a Little Teapot"

I am now in Pre-K,
I can learn.
I can listen. I can take a turn.
When the teacher says so,
I can play.
Choose a center and together we'll play.

2. Did You Clean Up?

To the tune of "Are You Sleeping, Are You Sleeping, Brother John?"

Did you clean up?
Did you clean up?
Please make sure.
Please make sure.
Everything is picked up.
Everything is picked up.
Please. Thank you!
Please. Thank you!

Chant: Red, Yellow, Green
Red, yellow, green
Stop, change, go
Red, yellow, green
Stop, change, go
Green says yes.
And red says no.
Yellow says everybody wait in a row.
Red, yellow, green
Stop, change, go
Red, yellow, green
Stop, change, go

3. The Five Senses Song

To the tune of "If You're Happy and You Know It"

I can see with my eyes every day (clap clap)
I can see with my eyes every day (clap clap)
I can see with my eyes
I can see with my eyes
I can see with my eyes every day (clap clap)
(Repeat with smell with my nose, hear with my ears, feel with my hands, and taste with my mouth.)

4. Eat More Vegetables

To the tune of "Row, Row, Row Your Boat"

Eat, eat, eat more,
Eat more vegetables.
Carrots, carrots, carrots, carrots
Eat more vegetables.
(Repeat with broccoli, lettuce, celery, and spinach.)

5. Circle Time

To the tune of "Here We Go 'Round the Mulberry Bush"

This is the way we come to circle
Come to circle, come to circle.
This is the way we come to circle
So early in the morning.

This is the way we sit right down,
Sit right down, sit right down.
This is the way we sit right down,
So early in the morning.

Play a short game such as one of the following to focus children's attention:

Name That Fruit!

Say: *It's red on the outside and white on the inside. It rhymes with chapel!*

Children answer, "Apple!" and then repeat twice, "Apple/Chapel."

Repeat with other fruits, such as cherry and banana.

I Spy

Use a flashlight to focus on different letters and words in the classroom. Have children identify them.

Monkey See Monkey Do

Choose one child to be the monkey leader. He or she will act out a motion such as twist, jump, clap, or raise hand, and the rest of the monkeys say the word and copy the motion.

Let's Play Pairs

Distribute one *ABC Picture Card* to each child. Draw letters from an additional set of cards. The child who has the matching letter identifies it and goes to the center of his or her choice.

That's My Friend!

Take children's name cards with their pictures from the wall and distribute making sure no one gets his or her own name. When you call a child's name, she or he has to say something positive about the child on the card and end with "That's my friend!"

Name Game

Say: *If your name begins with ____, you may choose a center.* Have the child say his or her name as he or she gets up. Repeat the child's name, emphasizing the beginning sound.

Center Management

Learning Centers provide children with additional opportunities to practice or extend each lesson's skills and concepts either individually or in small groups. The activities and materials that are explored in the centers not only promote oral language but also help develop children's social skills as they work together. The use of these Learning Centers encourage children to explore their surroundings and make their own choices.

Teacher's Role

The Learning Centers allow time for you to:

- Observe children's exploration of the centers.

- Assess children's understanding of the skills and concepts being taught.

- Provide additional support and encouragement to children who might be having difficulty with specific concepts or skills. If a child is having difficulty, model the correct approach.

Classroom Setup

The materials and activities in the centers should support what children are learning. Multiple experiences are necessary for children's comprehension. The centers should also engage them in learning by providing hands-on experiences. Every time children visit a center and practice skills or extend concepts being taught in the lessons, they are likely to broaden their understanding or discover something new.

In order to support children's learning, the materials and activities in the Learning Centers should change every week. It is important that all the children have a chance to explore every center throughout each week. Be sure they rotate to different centers and do not focus on only one activity. You might also consider adding new materials to the centers as the week progresses. This will encourage children to expand on their past work. Modify or add activities or materials based on your classroom needs.

It is crucial that children know what is expected of them in each center. To help children understand the expectation at each center, display an "I can" statement with an illustration or photograph of a student completing the activity. Discuss these expectations with children in advance, and reinforce them as needed. These discussions might include reviewing your typical classroom rules and talking about the limited number of children allowed in each center. Remind them that they may work individually or in small groups.

Library and Listening Center

Children should feel free throughout the day to explore books and other printed materials. Create a comfortable reading area in the room, and fill it with as many children's books as possible. Include a number of informational books that tell why things happen and books of rhymes, poems, and songs, as well as storybooks and simple alphabet books.

Before beginning each unit in the program, bring in books about the specific concepts or themes in a unit. Encourage children to bring in books they have enjoyed and would like to share with classmates. Even though they may not be actually reading, have children visit the area often. Here they can practice their book handling, apply their growing knowledge of print awareness, and look at pictures and talk about them. Have them read the books to you or to classmates.

Big Book literature selections from the program have been recorded and are available as part of the *Listening Library Audio CDs*. After each literature reading, encourage children to listen to the recordings. Provide CD players that work both with and without earphones. This way, individual children may listen to selections without disturbing the rest of the class. You will also be able to play the recordings for the whole class, if you choose. Encourage children to record their own stories and then share these stories with their classmates.

As you set up the Learning Centers, here are a few ideas you might want to implement in your classroom.

- Create a separate Workshop Center sign-up chart for children to use when choosing a center to explore.

- Provide an area for children who want to be alone to read or to simply reflect on the day's activities.

- Separate loud areas and quiet areas.

- Hang posters or art at eye level for the children.

- Place on shelves materials, such as books or art supplies, that are easily accessible to the children.

Teaching the English Language Learner

Stages of English-Language Proficiency

An effective learning environment is an important goal of all educators. In a supportive environment, all English learners have the opportunity to participate and to learn. The materials in this guide are designed to support children while they are acquiring English, allowing them to develop English-language reading skills and the fluency they need to achieve in the core content areas as well.

This guide provides direction in supporting children in four stages of English proficiency: Beginning, Intermediate, Advanced, and Advanced-High. While children at a beginning level by definition know little English and will probably have difficulty comprehending English, by the time they progress to the intermediate or early advanced levels of English acquisition, their skills in understanding more complex language structures will have increased. These stages can be described in general terms as follows:

BEGINNING AND INTERMEDIATE Children identified at these levels of English-language proficiency demonstrate dramatic growth. During these stages, children progress from having no receptive or productive English to possessing a basic command of English. They are learning to comprehend and produce one- or two-word responses to questions, are moving to phrases and simple sentences using concrete and immediate topics, and are learning to interact in a limited fashion with text that has been taught. They progress to responding with increasing ease to more varied communication tasks using learned material, comprehending a sequence of information on familiar topics, producing basic statements and asking questions on familiar subjects, and interacting with a variety of print. Some basic errors are found in their use of English syntax and grammar.

ADVANCED Children who have reached the Advanced level of English-language proficiency have good comprehension of overall meaning and are beginning to demonstrate increased comprehension of specific details and concepts. They are learning to respond in expanded sentences, are interacting more independently with a variety of text, and in using newly acquired English vocabulary to communicate ideas orally and in writing. They demonstrate fewer errors in English grammar and syntax than at the beginning and early intermediate levels.

ADVANCED-HIGH Children who are identified at this level of English-language proficiency demonstrate consistent comprehension of meaning, including implied and nuanced meaning, and are learning the use of idiomatic and figurative language. They are increasingly able to respond using detail in compound and complex sentences and sustain conversation in English. They are able to use standard grammar with few errors and show an understanding of conventions of formal and informal usage.

It is important to provide an instructional scaffold for phonemic awareness, phonics, words structure, language structures, comprehension strategies and skills, and grammar, usage, and mechanics so that children can successfully learn to read while advancing along the continuum of English acquisition. For example, at the Beginning level, you might ask children for *yes* or *no* answers when answering questions about selection comprehension or grammar. Children at the Advanced-High level should be asked to provide answers in complete and expanded sentences. By the time children achieve an Advanced level, their knowledge of English will be more sophisticated because they are becoming more adept at comprehending English and using techniques such as making inferences or using persuasive language.

The following charts illustrate how to use sentence stems with children at each level of English-language proficiency:

Teaching Sentence Stems

- Write the sentence stems on the board, chart paper, or sentence strips. Choose stems that are appropriate for the four general levels of English proficiency.

- Model using the sentence stem(s) for the comprehension strategy or skill.

- Read each phrase as you insert the appropriate words to express an idea. Have children repeat the sentences after you. For Beginning and Intermediate children, use the stems within the questions you ask them.

Linguistic Pattern: *I predict that* _____ .

Beginning	Intermediate	Advanced	Advanced-High
Simple questions about the text. Yes-or-no responses or responses that allow children to point to an object or picture.	Simple questions about the text which allow for one- or two-word responses or give children two options for a response to select from.	Questions that elicit a short response or a complete simple sentence using the linguistic pattern.	Have children make predictions on their own. Children should use the linguistic pattern and respond with a complete complex sentence.

Practicing Sentence Stems

- To give children multiple opportunities to generate the language they have just been taught, have them work in pairs or small groups and utilize cooperative learning participation strategies to facilitate this communicative practice.

- Pair children one level of proficiency above or below the other. For example, have Beginning children work with Intermediate level children.

- Use differentiated prompts to elicit the responses that incorporate the linguistic patterns and structures for the different proficiency levels. See the following sample of prompts and responses.

Beginning	Intermediate	Advanced	Advanced-High
Do you predict _____? *Yes/No*	Do you predict _____ or _____? *I predict* _____ .	What do you predict _____? *I predict* _____ .	Give a prediction about _____. *I predict* _____ .

- Select some common cooperative learning participation strategies to teach to children. Once they have learned some language practice activities, they can move quickly into the various routines. See the examples on the next page.

English Language Learners

My Turn, Your Turn

Children work in pairs.

1. The teacher models a sentence and the whole group repeats, or echoes it.

2. One child generates an oral phrase, and the partner echoes it.

3. Partners switch and alternate roles so that each child has a chance to both generate and repeat phrases.

Talking Stick

Children work in small groups. This strategy allows every child to have an opportunity to speak several times and encourages more reflective or reticent participants to take a turn. Children can "pass" only one time.

1. The teacher charts sentence graphic organizers and linguistic patterns children will use in their responses.

2. The teacher models use of linguistic patterns from the lesson.

3. The teacher asks a question or gives a prompt, and then passes a stick, eraser, stuffed animal, or any other designated object to one child.

4. A child speaks, everyone listens, and then the child passes the object on to the person next to him or her.

5. The next child speaks, everyone listens, and the process continues until the teacher or facilitator gives a signal to return the object.

Think-Pair-Share

This strategy allows children time for processing ideas by building in sufficient wait time to process the question and frame an answer. It is an appropriate strategy to use during small- or large-group discussions or lessons, giving all children a chance to organize their thoughts and have a turn sharing their responses with a partner. It also allows for small group verbal interaction to practice language before sharing with the larger group.

1. After reading or listening to a section of text, the teacher presents a question or task. It is helpful to guide with a specific prompt, modeling the language to be used in the response.

2. Children think about their responses for a brief, designated amount of time.

3. Partners share and discuss their responses with each other.

4. An adaptation can be to have each child share his or her partner's response within a small group to promote active listening.

Teaching Vocabulary

Building the background knowledge and a context for children to learn new words is critical in helping children understand new vocabulary. Primary language can be a valuable tool for preteaching, concept development, and vocabulary. Cognates, or words similar in English counterparts, often provide an opportunity for bridging the primary language and English. Also, children who have background knowledge about a topic can more easily connect the new information they are learning with what they already know than children without a similar context from which to work. Therefore, giving children background information and encouraging them to make as many connections as possible with the new vocabulary word they encounter will help them better understand the selection they are about to read.

In addition to building background knowledge, visual displays such as pictures, graphs, charts, maps, models, or other strategies offer unambiguous access to new content. They provide a clear and parallel correspondence between the visual objects and the new vocabulary to be learned. Thus, because the correlation is clear, the negotiation of meaning is established. Additionally, this process must be constant and reciprocal between you and each child if the child is to succeed in effectively interacting with language.

Included in this guide is a routine for teaching vocabulary words. In addition to this routine, more detailed explanations of the ways to teach vocabulary are as follows:

REAL OBJECTS AND REALIA: Because of the immediate result visuals have on learning language, when explaining a word such as *car,* the best approach is simply to show a real car. As an alternative to the real object, you can show realia. Realia are toy versions of real things, such as plastic eggs to substitute for real eggs, or in this case, a toy car to signify a real car. A large, clear picture of an automobile can also work if it is absolutely recognizable.

If, however, the child has had no experience with the item in the picture, more explanation might be needed. For example, if the word you are explaining is a zoo animal such as an *ocelot,* and children are not familiar with this animal, one picture might be insufficient. They might confuse this animal with a cat or any one of the feline species. Seeing several clear pictures, then, of each individual type of common feline and comparing their similarities and differences might help clarify meaning in this particular instance. When children make a connection between their prior knowledge of the word *cat* with the new word *ocelot,* it validates their newly acquired knowledge, and thus they process learning more quickly.

PICTURES: Supplement story illustrations with visuals such as those found in the ***Photo Library CD, ABC Picture Cards,*** magazine pictures, and picture dictionaries. Videos, especially those that demonstrate an entire setting such as a farm or zoo, or videos where different animals are highlighted in the natural habitat, for instance, might be helpful. You might also wish to turn off the soundtrack to avoid a flood of language that children might not be able to understand. This way children can concentrate on the visual-word meaning correlation.

PANTOMIME: Language is learned through modeling within a communicative context. Pantomiming is one example of such a framework of communication. Some words, such as *run* and *jump,* are appropriate for pantomiming. Throughout this guide, you will find suggestions for pantomiming words like *sick* by coughing, sneezing, and holding your stomach. If children understand what you are trying to pantomime, they will more easily engage in the task of learning.

Letter Formation Guide

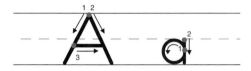

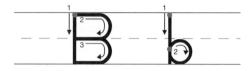

A Starting point, slanting down left
Starting point, slanting down right
Starting point, across the middle: capital *A*

a Starting point, around left all the way
Starting point, straight down,
touching the circle: small *a*

B Starting point, straight down
Starting point, around right and in
at the middle, around right and in
at the bottom: capital *B*

b Starting point, straight down, back
up, around right all the way: small *b*

C Starting point, around left to
stopping place: capital *C*

C Starting point, around left to
stopping place: small *c*

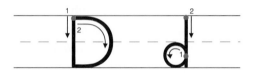

D Starting point, straight down
Starting point, around right and in
at the bottom: capital *D*

d Starting point, around left all the way
Starting point, straight down, touching
the circle: small *d*

E Starting point, straight down
Starting point, straight out
Starting point, straight out
Starting point, straight out: capital *E*

e Starting point, straight out, up and
around to the left, curving down
and around to the right: small *e*

F Starting point, straight down
Starting point, straight out
Starting point, straight out: capital *F*

f Starting point, around left and straight down
Starting point, straight across: small *f*

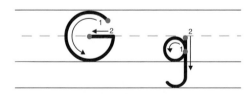

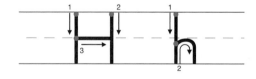

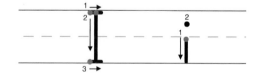

G Starting point, around left, curving up and
around
Straight in: capital *G*

g Starting point, around left all the way
Starting point, straight down, touching the
circle, around left to stopping place: small *g*

H Starting point, straight down
Starting point, straight down
Starting point, across the middle: capital *H*

h Starting point, straight down, back
up, around right, and straight down: small *h*

I Starting point, across
Starting point, straight down
Starting point, across: capital *I*

i Starting point, straight down
Dot exactly above: small *i*

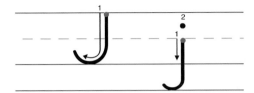 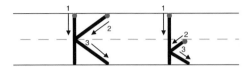 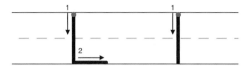

J Starting point, straight down, around left to stopping place: capital *J*

j Starting point, straight down, around left to stopping place
Dot exactly above: small *j*

K Starting point, straight down
Starting point, slanting down left, touching the line, slanting down right: capital *K*

k Starting point, straight down
Starting point, slanting down left, touching the line, slanting down right: small *k*

L Starting point, straight down, straight out: capital *L*

l Starting point, straight down: small *l*

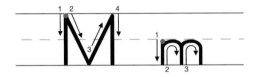 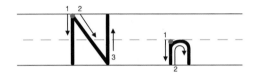 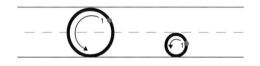

M Starting point, straight down
Starting point, slanting down right to the point, slanting back up to the right, straight down: capital *M*

m Starting point, straight down, back up, around right, straight down, back up, around right, straight down: small *m*

N Starting point, straight down
Starting point, slanting down right, straight back up: capital *N*

n Starting point, straight down, back up, around right, straight down: small *n*

O Starting point, around left all the way: capital *O*

o Starting point, around left all the way: small *o*

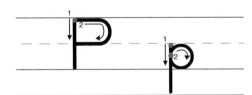 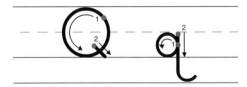 

P Starting point, straight down
Starting point, around right and in at the middle: capital *P*

p Starting point, straight down
Starting point, around right all the way, touching the line: small *p*

Q Starting point, around left all the way
Starting point, slanting down right: capital *Q*

q Starting point, around left all the way
Starting point, straight down, touching the circle, curving up right to stopping place: small *q*

R Starting point, straight down
Starting point, around right and in at the middle, touching the line, slanting down right: capital *R*

r Starting point, straight down, back up, curving around right to stopping place: small *r*

Letter Formation Guide

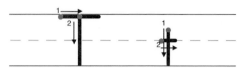

S Starting point, around left, curving right and down around right, curving left and up: capital S

s Starting point, around left, curving right and down around right, curving left and up to stopping place: small s

T Starting point, straight across
Starting point, straight down: capital T

t Starting point, straight down
Starting point, across short: small t

U Starting point, straight down, curving around right and up, straight up: capital U

u Starting point, straight down, curving around right and up, straight up, straight back down: small u

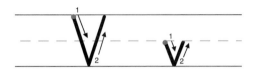

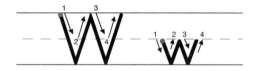

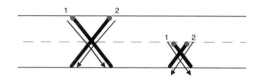

V Starting point, slanting down right, slanting up right: capital V

v Starting point, slanting down right, slanting up right: small v

W Starting point, slanting down right, slanting up right, slanting down right, slanting up right: capital W

w Starting point, slanting down right, slanting up right, slanting down right, slanting up right: small w

X Starting point, slanting down right
Starting point, slanting down left: capital X

x Starting point, slanting down right
Starting point, slanting down left: small x

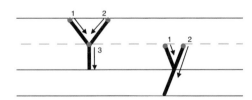

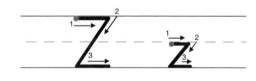

Y Starting point, slanting down right, stop
Starting point, slanting down left, stop
Starting point, straight down: capital Y

y Starting point, slanting down right Starting point, slanting down left, connecting the lines: small y

Z Starting point, straight across, slanting down left, straight across: capital Z

z Starting point, straight across, slanting down left, straight across: small z

Number Formation Guide

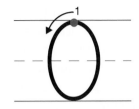

0 Starting point, curving left all the way around to starting point: *0*

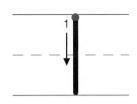

1 Starting point, straight down: *1*

2 Starting point, around right, slanting left and straight across right: *2*

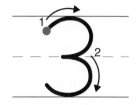

3 Starting point, around right, in at the middle, around right: *3*

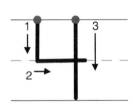

4 Starting point, straight down
Straight across right
Starting point, straight down, crossing line: *4*

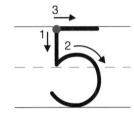

5 Starting point, straight down, curving around right and up
Starting point, straight across right: *5*

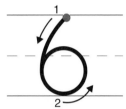

6 Starting point, slanting left, around the bottom curving up, around right and into the curve: *6*

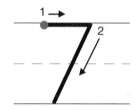

7 Starting point, straight across right, slanting down left: *7*

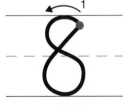

8 Starting point, curving left, curving down and around right, slanting up right to starting point: *8*

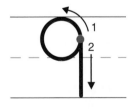

9 Starting point, curving around left all the way, straight down: *9*

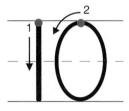

10 Starting point, straight down
Starting point, curving left all the way around to starting point: *10*

Vocabulary Development

Vocabulary development is a key part of **The DLM Early Childhood Express**. Children learn new words through exposure during reading and class discussion. They build language and vocabulary through activities using key words and phrases and by exploring selected vocabulary. After vocabulary words have been introduced, encourage children to use the words in sentences. Again, providing linguistic structures gives children a context for using new vocabulary and building oral language and gives you the opportunity to assess children's understanding of new words. For example, use sentence patterns such as the following:

- A _____ can _____.

- A _____ is a _____.
  (Use this for classification activities. *A tulip is a flower. A rabbit is an animal.*)

- The _____ is _____.
  (Use for describing. *The rabbit is soft.*)

Define words in ways children in your class can understand. When possible, show pictures of objects or actions to help clarify the meanings of words. Provide examples or comparisons to help reinforce the meanings of words and to connect new words to previously learned words. For example, say *The rabbit's FUR is soft like COTTON.* Connect words to categories. For example, say: *Pears are fruits. Are apples fruits? What else is a fruit?* Demonstrate the meaning of words when possible.

During reading, be sure children feel comfortable asking questions and sharing their reactions to what you are reading. Encourage children to share explanations, make predictions, compare and contrast ideas, sequence story events, and describe what you are reading. Encourage children's engagement by modeling reactions and responses while reading. For example, say *I like the part where _____ did _____.* or *This story is about _____.*
Support children who are reluctant to speak by using linguistic structures that encourage them to talk about stories and use vocabulary words. You might use the following linguistic structures:

- This story is about _____.

- First _____.

- Next _____.

- Last _____. (Use this for retelling stories.)

- The _____ is the same as _____.

- The _____ is different from _____.

- We read about _____.

Model asking questions before, during, and after reading:

- I wonder what this story is going to be about.

- Who is _____?

- What is _____?

- What did _____ do?

- Why did _____ do _____?

- What happened first? Middle? Last?

Be sure to ask open-ended questions. Unlike questions that simply require a *yes* or *no* or one-word answer, open-ended questions encourage children to think about responses and use new vocabulary in sentences.

Throughout the day, create opportunities for children to talk to each other as they share daily experiences, discuss and explain what they are doing, and talk abut what they are learning.

Vocabulary Words by Topic

Animals

alligator/caimán
ant/horminga
anteater/oso hormiguero
bat/murciélago
bear/oso
beaver/castor
bee/abeja
beetle/escarabajo
bobcat/lince
butterfly/mariposa
camel/camello
cat/gato
chicken/gallina/pollo
chipmunk/ardilla
cow/vaca
crab/cangrejo
deer/venado/ciervo
dog/perro
dolphin/delfin
donkey/burro
dragonfly/libélula
duck/pato
eagle/águila
elephant/elefante
flamingo/flamingo
fly/mosca
fox/zorro
frog/rana
giraffe/jirafa
goat/cabra
gorilla/
grasshopper/saltamontes
hamster/hámster
hippopotamus/hipopótamo
horse/caballo
kangaroo/canguro
koala/coala

ladybug/catarina
leopard/leopardo
lion/león
llama/llama
lobster/langosta
monkey/mono
moose/alce
mosquito/mosquito
mouse/ratón
octopus/pulpo
opossum/zarigüeya
owl/búho
panda/oso panda
parakeet/periquito
peacock/pavo real
pelican/pelicano
penguin/pingüino
pig/cerdo
polar bear/oso polar
porcupine/puerco espín
rabbit/conejo
raccoon/mapache
rhinoceros/rinoceronte
robin/petirrojo
salamander/salamandra
sea horse/caballo de mar
shark/tiburón
sheep/oveja
skunk/mofeta/zorrillo
snake/serpiente
squirrel/ardilla
starfish/estrella de mar
swan/cisne
tiger/tigre
toad/sapo
turkey/pavo
turtle/tortuga
walrus/morsa

whale/ballena
zebra/cebra

Colors and Shapes

blue/azul
green/verde
red/rojo
yellow/amarillo
circle/círculo azul
diamond/diamante
oval/óvalo
rectangle/rectángulo
square/cuadrado
triangle/triángulo

Signs

deer crossing/cruce de venado
handicapped parking/
    estacionamiento para inválidos
railroad crossing/paso del tren
school crossing/cruce escolar
speed limit/limite de velocidad
stop sign/señal de alto
traffic light/semáforo
yield sign/señal de ceder el paso

Earth

beach/playa
blizzard/tormenta de nieve
cloud/nube
coral reef/arrecife de coral
desert/desierto
dry season/temporada seca
fall/otoño
fog/niebla
forest/bosque
geyser/géiser
glacier/glaciar

hail/granizo
hurricane/huracán
ice/hielo
island/isla
lake/lago
lightning/relámpago
mountain/montaña
ocean/océano
plain/llano
rain/lluvia
rain forest/selva tropical
rainy season/temporada de lluvias
rapids/rápidos
river/río
snow/nieve
spring/primavera
stream/arroyo
summer/verano
sun/sol
tornado/tornado
tundra/tundra
volcano/volcán
waterfall/cascada
wind/viento
winter/invierno

Human Body

ankle/tobillo
arm/brazo
body/cuerpo
ear/oreja
elbow/codo
eyes/ojos
feet/pies
fingers/dedos
hair/pelo
hands/manos

Vocabulary Words by Topic

head/cabeza
hearing/oído
heel/talón
hips/caderas
knee/rodilla
legs/piernas
mouth/boca
nose/nariz
sense/sentido
shoulders/hombros
sight/vista
smell/olfato
taste/gusto
teeth/dientes
toes/dedos de los pies
touch/ tacto

Plants

cactus/cactus
carrot/zanahoria
clover/trébol
cornstalk/planta de maíz
dandelion/diente de león
fern/helecho
grapevine/parra
grass/hierba
lettuce/lechuga
lilac bush/lila de monte
marigold/caléndula
moss/musgo
oak tree/árbol de roble
onion/cebolla
orange tree/naranjo
palm tree/palma
pine tree/pino
poison ivy/hiedra venenosa
rice/arroz
rose/rosa

seaweed/alga marina
sunflower/girasol
tomato/tomate
tulip/tulipán
water lily/nenúfar
wheat/trigo

Clothing

belt/cinturón
blouse/blusa
boots/botas
boy's swimsuit/traje de baño para
    niños
coat/abrigo
dress/vestido
earmuffs/orejeras
girl's swimsuit/traje de baño para
    niñas
gloves/guantes
hat/sombrero
jacket/chaqueta
jeans/pantalones vaqueros
mittens/manoplas
pajamas/pijama
pants/pantalones
raincoat/impermeable
robe/bata
scarf/bufanda
shirt/camisa
shoes/zapatos
shorts/pantalones cortos
skirt/falda
slippers/pantuflas
socks/calcetines
sweat suit/chandal
sweater/suéter
tie/corbata
vest/chaleco

Food

apples/manzanas
bacon/tocino
bagels/roscas de pan
bananas/plátanos
beans/frijoles
beef/carne
beets/betabel
blueberries/arándanos
bread/pan
broccoli/brécol
butter/mantequilla
cake/pastel
cantaloupe/cantalupo
carrots/zanahoria
cauliflower/coliflor
celery/apio
cereal/cereal
cheese/queso
cherries/cerezas
chicken/pollo
clams/almejas
cookies/galletas
corn/maíz
cottage cheese/requesón
crackers/galletas saladas
cream cheese/queso crema
cucumbers/pepinos
eggs/huevos
figs/higos
fish/pescado
grapefruit/toronja
grapes/uvas
green peppers/pimientos verdes
ham/jamón
ice-cream cone/cono de helado
jelly/gelatina
lemons/limones

lettuce/lechuga
limes/limas
macaroni/macarrones
milk/leche
mushrooms/champiñones
nuts/nueces
onions/cebollas
orange juice/jugo de naranja
oranges/naranjas
peaches/duraznos
peanut butter/crema de cacahuete
pears/peras
peas/guisantes
pie/tarta
pineapples/piñas
plums/ciruelas
pork chop/chuleta de puerco
potatoes/papas
radishes/rábanos
raisins/pasas
rice/arroz
rolls/panecillos
salad/ensalada
sausage/salchicha
shrimp/camarón
soup/sopa
spaghetti/espaguetis
squash/calabaza
strawberries/fresas
sweet potatoes/camotes
tomatoes/tomates
watermelon/sandía
yogurt/yogur

Recreation

archery/tiro el arco
badminton/bádminton
baseball/béisbol
basketball/baloncesto
biking/ciclismo
boating/paseo en bote
bowling/boliche
canoeing/piragüismo
climbing/montañismo
croquet/croquet
discus/disco
diving/buceo
fishing/pesca
football/fútbol
golf/golf
gymnastics/gimnasia
hiking/excursionismo
hockey/hockey
horseback riding/equitación
ice-skating/patinaje sobre hielo
in-line skating/patines en línea
lacrosse/lacrosse
pole-vaulting/salto con pértiga
running/atletismo
scuba diving/buceo
shot put/lanzamiento de peso
skiing/esquí
soccer/fútbol
surfing/surfing
swimming/natación
T-ball/T-ball
tennis/tenis
volleyball/voleibol
walking/caminar
waterskiing/esquí acuático
weight lifting/levantamiento

School

auditorium/auditorio
book/libro
cafeteria/cafetería
cafeteria table/mesa de cafetería
calculator/calculadora
chair/silla
chalk/tiza
chalkboard/pizarrón
chart paper/rotafolio
classroom/aula
computer/omputadora
construction paper/papel para
    construir
crayons/crayones
desk/escritorio
easel/caballete
eraser/borrador
globe/globo
glue/pegamento
gym/gimnasio
hallway/vestíbulo
janitor's room/conserjería
learning center/centro de
    aprendizaje
library/biblioteca
markers/marcadores
music room/salón de música
notebook paper/papel de cuaderno
nurse's office/enfermería
paint/pintura
paintbrush/pincel
pen/pluma
pencil/lápiz
pencil sharpener/sacapuntas
playground/patio de recreo
principal's office/oficina del
    director

ruler/regla
science room/salón de ciencias
scissors/tijeras
stairs/escaleras
stapler/grapadora
supply room/almacén
tape/cinta adhesiva

Toys

ball/pelota
balloons/globos
bike/bicicleta
blocks/cubos
clay/arcilla
coloring book/libro para colorear
doll/muñeca
doll carriage/careola de muñecas
dollhouse/casa de muñecas
farm set/juego de la granja
game/juego
grocery cart/carro de compras
hats/sombreros
in-line skates/patines
instruments/instrumentos
jump rope/cuerda para saltar
kite/cometa
magnets/imanes
marbles/canicas
puppet/títere
puzzle/rompecabezas
scooter/motoneta
skateboard/patineta
slide/tobogán
stuffed animals/peluches
tape recorder/grabadora
top/trompo
toy cars/carro de juguete
toy trucks/camión de juguete

train set/juego de tren
tricycle/triciclo
wagon/vagón
yo-yo/yó-yó

Equipment

baggage cart/carro para equipaje
baseball/béisbol
bat/bate
mitt/manopla
basketball/pelota de baloncesto
basketball net/canasta
blueprints/planos
computer/computadora
drafting tools/borradores
bow/arco
arrow/flecha
bowling ball/pelota de boliche
bowling pin/bolos de boliche
bridle/freno
saddle/silla de montar
saddle pad/montura
broom/escoba
bulldozer/aplanadora
canoe/canoa
paddle/paleta
cash register/caja registradora
computer/computadora
crane/grúa
dishwasher/lavaplatos
drill/taladro
drum/tambor
drumsticks/palillos
dryer/secadora
dustpan/recogedor
figure skates/patinaje artistico

Vocabulary Words by Topic

football/balón
shoulder pads/hombreras
football helmet/casco
goggles/gafas
golf ball/pelota de golf
golf clubs/palo de golf
tee/tee
hammer/martillo
handcuffs/esposas
badge/placa
hat/gorra
hockey stick/palo de hockey
hockey puck/disco de hockey
ice skates/patines
hoe/azadón
hose/manguera
coat/chaqueta
hat/sombrero
sprinkler/rociador
iron/plancha
ironing board/tabla de planchar
lawn mower/cortacéspedes
mail pouch/bolsa de correo
mirror/espejo
probe/sonda
pick/pico
mop/estropajo
paintbrush/brocha de pintar
piano/piano
pliers/alicates
rake/rastrillo
roller skates/patines
saw/sierra
screwdriver/desarmador
scuba tank/tanque de buceo
mask/máscara
flippers/aletas
shovel/pala

sketch pad/cuaderno para dibujo
palette/paleta
skis/esquís
ski boots/botas para esquiar
poles/palos
soccer ball/balón de fútbol
shoes/zapatos de tenis
stepladder/escalera doble
stethoscope/estetoscopio
surfboard/tabla de surf
tennis ball/pelota de tenis
tennis racket/raqueta de tenis
tractor/tractor
vacuum cleaner/aspiradora
washer/lavadora
water skis/esquís acuáticos
rope/cuerda
life jacket/chaleco salvavidas
watering can/regadera
wheelbarrow/carretilla
wrench/llave inglesa

Home

basement/sótano
bathroom/baño
bathroom sink/lavabo
bathtub/bañera
bed/cama
bedroom/recámara/habitación
blanket/cobija/manta
chair/silla
circuit breaker/cortocircuito
dresser/cómoda
electrical outlet/enchufe
end table/mesa auxiliar
fireplace/chimenea
furnace/horno
kitchen/cocina

kitchen chair/silla de cocina
kitchen sink/fregadero
kitchen table/mesa de cocina
lamp/lámpara
light switch/interruptor de la luz
living room/sala
medicine cabinet/botiquín
nightstand/mesilla de noche
pillow/almohada
refrigerator/refrigerador
shower/ducha
smoke alarm/alarma de incendios
sofa/sofá
stove/estufa
thermostat/termostato
toilet/el baño
water heater/calentador de agua

Occupations

administrative assistant/asistente
    administrativo
air traffic controller/controlador
    aéreo
airline pilot/piloto
architect/arquitecto
artist/artista
astronaut/astronauta
athlete/atleta
author/autor
ballerina/bailarina
banker/banquero
bus driver/conductor de autobús
camera operator/operador de
    cámara
carpenter/carpintero
cashier/cajero
chef/jefe de cocina
computer technician/técnico en

    computación
cosmetologist/cosmetólogo
dancer/bailarín
dentist/dentista
doctor/doctor
electrician/electricista
engineer/ingeniero
farmer/granjero
firefighter/bombero
forest ranger/guardabosques
lawyer/abogado
manicurist/manicurista
musician/músico
nurse/enfermera
paramedic/paramédico
photographer/fotógrafo
police officer/policía
postal worker/empleado postal
real estate agent/corridor de
    bienes raíces
refuse collector/recolector de
    basura
reporter/reportero
school crossing guard/guarda
    escolar
server/mesero
ship captain/capitán de barco
singer/cantante
skater/patinador
teacher/maestro
truck driver/conductor de camión
veterinarian/veterinario
weaver/tejedora

Structures

adobe/casa de adobe
airplane hangar/hangar de avión
airport/aeropuerto
apartment building/edificio de
    departamentos/edificio de pisos
arena/arena
art museum/museo de arte
bakery/panadería
bank/banco
barn/granero
bridge/peunte
bus shelter/parada cubierta
city hall/ayuntamiento
clothing store/tienda de ropa
condominium/condominio
courthouse/tribunal
covered bridge/puente cubierto
dam/presa
dock/muelle
drawbridge/puente levadizo
duplex/dúplex
fire station/estación de bomberos
flower shop/floristeria
garage/garaje
gas station/gasolinera
gazebo/mirador
grain elevator/elevador de granos
grocery store/supermercado
hospital/hospital
house/casa
library/biblioteca
log cabin/cabaña de madera
marina/marina
monument/monumento
movie theater/cine
opera house/teatro de la ópera
palace/palacio

parking garage/estacionamiento
pizza shop/pizzaría
police station/estación de policía
power plant/central eléctrica
pyramid/pirámide
restaurant/restaurante
school/escuela
shelter house/albergue
shopping mall/centro comercial
skyscraper/rascacielos
stadium/estadio
swimming pool/alberca/piscina
tent/tienda
toy store/juguetería
train station/estación del tren
windmills/molino de viento

Transportation

airplane/avión
bicycle/bicicleta
bus/autobús
canoe/canoa
car/coche
four-wheel-drive vehicle/coche con
    doble tracción
helicopter/helicóptero
hot air balloon/globo de aire
    caliente
kayak/kayac
moped/ciclomotor
motor home/casa motora
motorboat/lancha motora
motorcycle/motocicleta
pickup truck/camioneta
rowboat/bote de remos
sailboat/velero
school bus/camión escolar

semitrailer truck/camión con semi-
    remolque
ship/barco
submarine/submarino
subway/metro
taxi/taxi
train/tren
van/furgoneta

Learning Trajectories for Math

Children follow natural developmental progressions in learning. Curriculum research has revealed sequences of activities that are effective in guiding children through these levels of thinking. These developmental paths are the basis for *Building Blocks* learning trajectories.

Learning Trajectories for Primary Grades Mathematics

Learning trajectories have three parts: a mathematical goal, a developmental path along which children develop to reach that goal, and a set of activities matched to each of the levels of thinking in that path that help children develop the next higher level of thinking. The **Building Blocks** learning trajectories give simple labels, descriptions, and examples of each level. Complete learning trajectories describe the goals of learning, the thinking and learning processes of children at various levels, and the learning activities in which they might engage. This document provides only the developmental levels.

The following provides the developmental levels from the first signs of development in different strands of mathematics through approximately age 8. Research shows that when teachers understand how children develop mathematics understanding, they are more effective in questioning, analyzing, and providing activities that further children's development than teachers who are unaware of the development process. Consequently, children have a much richer and more successful math experience in the primary grades.

Each of the following tables, such as "Counting," represents a main developmental progression that underlies the learning trajectory for that topic.

For some topics, there are "subtrajectories"—strands within the topic. In most cases, the names make this clear. For example, in Comparing and Ordering, some levels are "Composer" levels and others involve building a "Mental Number Line." Similarly, the related subtrajectories of "Composition" and "Decomposition" are easy to distinguish. Sometimes, for clarification, subtrajectories are indicated with a note in italics after the title. For example, Parts and Representing are subtrajectories within the Shape Trajectory.

Frequently Asked Questions (FAQ)

1. Why use learning trajectories? Learning trajectories allow teachers to build the mathematics of children—the thinking of children as it develops naturally. So, we know that all the goals and activities are within the developmental capacities of children. Finally, we know that the activities provide the mathematical building blocks for success.

2. When are children "at" a level? Children are at a certain level when most of their behaviors reflect the thinking—ideas and skills—of that level. Most levels are levels of thinking. However, some are merely "levels of attainment" and indicate a child has gained knowledge. For example, children must learn to name or write more numerals, but knowing more numerals does not require more complex thinking.

3. Can children work at more than one level at the same time? Yes, although most children work mainly at one level or in transition between two levels. Levels are not "absolute stages." They are "benchmarks" of complex growth that represent distinct ways of thinking.

4. Can children jump ahead? Yes, especially if there are separate subtopics. For example, we have combined many counting competencies into one "Counting" sequence with subtopics, such as verbal counting skills. Some children learn to count to 100 at age 6 after learning to count objects to 10 or more, some may learn that verbal skill earlier. The subtopic of verbal counting skills would still be followed.

5. How do these developmental levels support teaching and learning? The levels help teachers, as well as curriculum developers, assess, teach, and sequence activities. Through planned teaching and encouraging informal, incidental mathematics, teachers help children learn at an appropriate and deep level.

6. Should I plan to help children develop just the levels that correspond to my children's ages? No! The ages in the table are typical ages children develop these ideas. (These are rough guides only.) These are "starting levels" not goals. We have found that children who are provided high-quality mathematics experiences are capable of developing to levels one or more years beyond their peers.

Developmental Levels for Counting

The ability to count with confidence develops over the course of several years. Beginning in infancy, children show signs of understanding numbers. With instruction and number experience, most children can count fluently by age 8, with much progress in counting occurring in kindergarten and first grade. Most children follow a natural developmental progression in learning to count with recognizable stages or levels. This developmental path can be described as part of a learning trajectory.

Age Range	Level Name	Level	Description
1–2	Precounter	1	At the earliest level a child shows no verbal counting. The child may name some number words with no sequence.
1–2	Chanter	2	At this level, a child may sing-song or chant indistinguishable number words.
2	Reciter	3	At this level, the child may verbally count with separate words, but not necessarily in the correct order.
3	Reciter (10)	4	A child at this level may verbally count to 10 with some correspondence with objects. He or she may point to objects to count a few items, but then lose track.
3	Corresponder	5	At this level, a child may keep one-to-one correspondence between counting words and objects—at least for small groups of objects laid in a line. A corresponder may answer "how many" by recounting the objects.
4	Counter (Small Numbers)	6	At around 4 years of age, the child may begin to count meaningfully. He or she may accurately count objects in a line to 5 and answer the "how many" question with the last number counted. When objects are visible, and especially with small numbers, the child begins to understand cardinality (that numbers tell how many).
4	Producer (Small Numbers)	7	The next level after counting small numbers is to count out objects to 5. When asked to show four of something, for example, this child may give four objects.
4	Counter (10)	8	This child may count structured arrangements of objects to 10. He or she may be able to write or draw to represent 1–10. A child at this level may be able to tell the number just after or just before another number, but only by counting up from 1.
5	Counter and Producer—Counter to (10+)	9	Around 5 years of age, a child may begin to count out objects accurately to 10 and then beyond to 30. He or she has explicit understanding of cardinality (that numbers tell how many). The child may keep track of objects that have and have not been counted, even in different arrangements. He or she may write or draw to represent 1 to 10 and then 20 and 30, and may give the next number to 20 or 30. The child also begins to recognize errors in others' counting and is able to eliminate most errors in his or her own counting.
5	Counter Backward from 10	10	Another milestone at about age 5 is being able to count backward from 10 to 1, verbally, or when removing objects from a group.
6	Counter from N (N+1, N–1)	11	Around 6 years of age, the child may begin to count on, counting verbally and with objects from numbers other than 1. Another noticeable accomplishment is that a child may determine the number immediately before or after another number without having to start back at 1.
6	Skip Counting by 10s to 100	12	A child at this level may count by 10s to 100 or beyond with understanding.
6	Counter to 100	13	A child at this level may count by 1s to 100. He or she can make decade transitions (for example, from 29 to 30) starting at any number.
6	Counter On Using Patterns	14	At this level, a child may keep track of a few counting acts by using numerical patterns, such as tapping as he or she counts.
6	Skip Counter	15	At this level, the child can count by 5s and 2s with understanding.
6	Counter of Imagined Items	16	At this level, a child may count mental images of hidden objects to answer, for example, "how many" when 5 objects are visible and 3 are hidden.
6	Counter On Keeping Track	17	A child at this level may keep track of counting acts numerically, first with objects, then by counting counts. He or she counts up one to four more from a given number.
6	Counter of Quantitative Units	18	At this level, a child can count unusual units, such as "wholes" when shown combinations of wholes and parts. For example, when shown three whole plastic eggs and four halves, a child at this level will say there are five whole eggs.
6	Counter to 200	19	At this level, a child may count accurately to 200 and beyond, recognizing the patterns of ones, tens, and hundreds.
7	Number Conserver	20	A major milestone around age 7 is the ability to conserve number. A child who conserves number understands that a number is unchanged even if a group of objects is rearranged. For example, if there is a row of ten buttons, the child understands there are still ten without recounting, even if they are rearranged in a long row or a circle.
7	Counter Forward and Back	21	A child at this level may count in either direction and recognize that sequence of decades mirrors single-digit sequence.

Learning Trajectories for Math

Developmental Levels for Comparing and Ordering Numbers

Comparing and ordering sets is a critical skill for children as they determine whether one set is larger than another in order to make sure sets are equal and "fair." Prekindergartners can learn to use matching to compare collections or to create equivalent collections. Finding out how many more or fewer in one collection is more demanding than simply comparing two collections. The ability to compare and order sets with fluency develops over the course of several years. With instruction and number experience, most children develop foundational understanding of number relationships and place value at ages four and five. Most children follow a natural developmental progression in learning to compare and order numbers with recognizable stages or levels. This developmental path can be described as part of a learning trajectory.

Age Range	Level Name	Level	Description
2	Object Corresponder	1	At this early level, a child puts objects into one-to-one correspondence, but may not fully understand that this creates equal groups. For example, a child may know that each carton has a straw, but does not necessarily know there are the same numbers of straws and cartons.
2	Perceptual Comparer	2	At this level, a child can compare collections that are quite different in size (for example, one is at least twice the other) and know that one has more than the other. If the collections are similar, the child can compare very small collections.
3	First-Second Ordinal Counter	3	At this level the child can identify the "first" and often "second" object in a sequence.
3	Nonverbal Comparer of Similar Items	4	At this level, a child can identify that different organizations of the same number are equal and different from other sets (1–4 items). For example, a child can identify ••• and •°• as equal and different from •• or •°.
4	Nonverbal Comparer of Dissimilar Items	5	At this level, a child can match small, equal collections of dissimilar items, such as shells and dots, and show that they are the same number.
4	Matching Comparer	6	As children progress, they begin to compare groups of 1–6 by matching. For example, a child gives one toy bone to every dog and says there are the same number of dogs and bones.

Age Range	Level Name	Level	Description
4	Knows-to-Count Comparer	7	A significant step occurs when the child begins to count collections to compare. At the early levels, children are not always accurate when a larger collection's objects are smaller in size than the objects in the smaller collection. For example, a child at this level may accurately count two equal collections, but when asked, says the collection of larger blocks has more.
4	Counting Comparer (Same Size)	8	At this level, children make accurate comparisons via counting, but only when objects are about the same size and groups are small (about 1–5 items).
5	Counting Comparer (5)	9	As children develop their ability to compare sets, they compare accurately by counting, even when a larger collection's objects are smaller. A child at this level can figure out how many more or less.
5	Ordinal Counter	10	At this level, a child identifies and uses ordinal numbers from "first" to "tenth." For example, the child can identify who is "third in line."
6	Counting Comparer (10)	11	This level can be observed when the child compares sets by counting, even when a larger collection's objects are smaller, up to 10. A child at this level can accurately count two collections of 9 items each, and says they have the same number, even if one collection has larger blocks.
6	Mental Number Line to 10	12	As children move into this level, they begin to use mental images and knowledge of number relationships to determine relative size and position. For example, a child at this level can answer which number is closer to 6, 4 or 9 without counting physical objects.
6	Serial Orderer to 61	13	At this level, the child orders lengths marked into units (1–6, then beyond). For example, given towers of cubes, this child can put them in order, 1 to 6.
7	Place Value Comparer	14	Further development is made when a child begins to compare numbers with place value understanding. For example, a child at this level can explain that "63 is more than 59 because six tens is more than five tens, even if there are more than three ones."
7	Mental Number Line to 100	15	Children demonstrate the next level when they can use mental images and knowledge of number relationships, including ones embedded in tens, to determine relative size and position. For example, when asked, "Which is closer to 45, 30 or 50?" a child at this level may say "45 is right next to 50, but 30 isn't."
8+	Mental Number Line to 1,000s	16	At about age 8, children may begin to use mental images of numbers up to 1,000 and knowledge of number relationships, including place value, to determine relative size and position. For example, when asked, "Which is closer to 3,500—2,000 or 7,000?" a child at this level may say "70 is double 35, but 20 is only fifteen from 35, so twenty hundreds, 2,000, is closer."

Developmental Levels for Recognizing Number and Subitizing (Instantly Recognizing)

The ability to recognize number values develops over the course of several years and is a foundational part of number sense. Beginning at about age two, children begin to name groups of objects. The ability to instantly know how many are in a group, called *subitizing*, begins at about age three. By age eight, with instruction and number experience, most children can identify groups of items and use place values and multiplication skills to count them. Most children follow a natural developmental progression in learning to count with recognizable stages or levels. This developmental path can be described as part of a learning trajectory.

Age Range	Level Name	Level	Description
2	Small Collection Namer	1	The first sign occurs when the child can name groups of 1 to 2, sometimes 3. For example, when shown a pair of shoes, this young child says, "two shoes."
3	Maker of Small Collections	2	At this level, a child can nonverbally make a small collection (no more than 4, usually 1 to 3) with the same number as another collection. For example, when shown a collection of 3, the child makes another collection of 3.
4	Perceptual Subitizer to 4	3	Progress is made when a child instantly recognizes collections up to 4 and verbally names the number of items. For example, when shown 4 objects briefly, the child says "4."
5	Perceptual Subitizer to 5	4	This level is the ability to instantly recognize collections up to 5 and verbally name the number of items. For example, when shown 5 objects briefly, the child says "5."
5	Conceptual Subitizer to 51	5	At this level, the child can verbally label all arrangements to about 5, when shown only briefly. For example, a child at this level might say, "I saw 2 and 2, and so I saw 4."
5	Conceptual Subitizer to 10	6	This step is when the child can verbally label most arrangements to 6 shown briefly, then up to 10, using groups. For example, a child at this level might say, "In my mind, I made 2 groups of 3 and 1 more, so 7."
6	Conceptual Subitizer to 20	7	Next, a child can verbally label structured arrangements up to 20 shown briefly, using groups. For example, the child may say, "I saw 3 fives, so 5, 10, 15."
7	Conceptual Subitizer with Place Value and Skip Counting	8	At this level, a child is able to use groups, skip counting, and place value to verbally label structured arrangements shown briefly. For example, the child may say, "I saw groups of tens and twos, so 10, 20, 30, 40, 42, 44, 46…46!"
8+	Conceptual Subitizer with Place Value and Multiplication	9	As children develop their ability to subitize, they use groups, multiplication, and place value to verbally label structured arrangements shown briefly. At this level, a child may say, "I saw groups of tens and threes, so I thought, 5 tens is 50 and 4 threes is 12, so 62 in all."

Learning Trajectories for Math

Developmental Levels for Composing (Knowing Combinations of Numbers)

Composing and decomposing are combining and separating operations that allow children to build concepts of "parts" and "wholes." Most prekindergartners can "see" that two items and one item make three items. Later, children learn to separate a group into parts in various ways and then to count to produce all of the number "partners" of a given number. Eventually children think of a number and know the different addition facts that make that number. Most children follow a natural developmental progression in learning to compose and decompose numbers with recognizable stages or levels. This developmental path can be described as part of a learning trajectory.

Age Range	Level Name	Level	Description
4	Pre-Part-Whole Recognizer	1	At the earliest levels of composing, a child only nonverbally recognizes parts and wholes. For example, when shown 4 red blocks and 2 blue blocks, a young child may intuitively appreciate that "all the blocks" includes the red and blue blocks, but when asked how many there are in all, the child may name a small number, such as 1.
5	Inexact Part-Whole Recognizer	2	A sign of development is that the child knows a whole is bigger than parts, but does not accurately quantify. For example, when shown 4 red blocks and 2 blue blocks and asked how many there are in all, the child may name a "large number," such as 5 or 10.
5	Composer to 4, then 5	3	At this level, a child knows number combinations. A child at this level quickly names parts of any whole, or the whole given the parts. For example, when shown 4, then 1 is secretly hidden, and then shown the 3 remaining, the child may quickly say "1" is hidden.
6	Composer to 7	4	The next sign of development is when a child knows number combinations to totals of 7. A child at this level quickly names parts of any whole, or the whole when given parts, and can double numbers to 10. For example, when shown 6, then 4 are secretly hidden, and then shown the 2 remaining, the child may quickly say "4" are hidden.
6	Composer to 10	5	This level is when a child knows number combinations to totals of 10. A child at this level may quickly name parts of any whole, or the whole when given parts, and can double numbers to 20. For example, this child would be able to say "9 and 9 is 18."
7	Composer with Tens and Ones	6	At this level, the child understands two-digit numbers as tens and ones, can count with dimes and pennies, and can perform two-digit addition with regrouping. For example, a child at this level may explain, "17 and 36 is like 17 and 3, which is 20, and 33, which is 53."

Developmental Levels for Adding and Subtracting

Single-digit addition and subtraction are generally characterized as "math facts." It is assumed children must memorize these facts, yet research has shown that addition and subtraction have their roots in counting, counting on, number sense, the ability to compose and decompose numbers, and place value. Research has also shown that learning methods for addition and subtraction with understanding is much more effective than rote memorization of seemingly isolated facts. Most children follow an observable developmental progression in learning to add and subtract numbers with recognizable stages or levels. This developmental path can be described as part of a learning trajectory.

Age Range	Level Name	Level	Description
1	Pre +/−	1	At the earliest level, a child shows no sign of being able to add or subtract.
3	Nonverbal +/−	2	The first sign is when a child can add and subtract very small collections nonverbally. For example, when shown 2 objects, then 1 object being hidden under a napkin, the child identifies or makes a set of 3 objects to "match."
4	Small Number +/−	3	This level is when a child can find sums for joining problems up to 3 1 2 by counting with objects. For example, when asked, "You have 2 balls and get 1 more. How many in all?" the child may count out 2, then count out 1 more, then count all 3: "1, 2, 3, 3!"
5	Find Result +/−	4	**Addition** Evidence of this level in addition is when a child can find sums for joining (you had 3 apples and get 3 more; how many do you have in all?) and part-part-whole (there are 6 girls and 5 boys on the playground; how many children were there in all?) problems by direct modeling, counting all, with objects. For example, when asked, "You have 2 red balls and 3 blue balls. How many in all?" the child may count out 2 red, then count out 3 blue, then count all 5. **Subtraction** In subtraction, a child can also solve take-away problems by separating with objects. For example, when asked, "You have 5 balls and give 2 to Tom. How many do you have left?" the child may count out 5 balls, then take away 2, and then count the remaining 3.

Age Range	Level Name	Level	Description
5	Find Change +/−	5	**Addition** At this level, a child can find the missing addend (5 + _ =7) by adding on objects. For example, when asked, "You have 5 balls and then get some more. Now you have 7 in all. How many did you get?" The child may count out 5, then count those 5 again starting at 1, then add more, counting "6, 7," then count the balls added to find the answer, 2. **Subtraction** A child can compare by matching in simple situations. For example, when asked, "Here are 6 dogs and 4 balls. If we give a ball to each dog, how many dogs will not get a ball?" a child at this level may count out 6 dogs, match 4 balls to 4 of them, then count the 2 dogs that have no ball.
5	Make It +/−	6	A significant advancement occurs when a child is able to count on. This child can add on objects to make one number into another without counting from 1. For example, when told, "This puppet has 4 balls, but she should have 6. Make it 6," the child may put up 4 fingers on one hand, immediately count up from 4 while putting up 2 fingers on the other hand, saying, "5, 6," and then count or recognize the 2 fingers.
6	Counting Strategies +/−	7	This level occurs when a child can find sums for joining (you had 8 apples and get 3 more…) and part-part-whole (6 girls and 5 boys…) problems with finger patterns or by adding on objects or counting on. For example, when asked "How much is 4 and 3 more?" the child may answer "4…5, 6, 7. 7!" Children at this level can also solve missing addend (3 + _ = 7) or compare problems by counting on. When asked, for example, "You have 6 balls. How many more would you need to have 8?" the child may say, "6, 7 [puts up first finger], 8 [puts up second finger]. 2!"
6	Part-Whole +/−	8	Further development has occurred when the child has part-whole understanding. This child can solve problems using flexible strategies and some derived facts (for example, "5 + 5 is 10, so 5 + 6 is 11"), can sometimes do start-unknown problems (_ + 6 = 11), but only by trial and error. When asked, "You had some balls. Then you get 6 more. Now you have 11 balls. How many did you start with?" this child may lay out 6, then 3, count, and get 9. The child may put 1 more, say 10, then put 1 more. The child may count up from 6 to 11, then recount the group added, and say, "5!"

Age Range	Level Name	Level	Description
6	Numbers-in-Numbers +/−	9	Evidence of this level is when a child recognizes that a number is part of a whole and can solve problems when the start is unknown (_ + 4 = 9) with counting strategies. For example, when asked, "You have some balls, then you get 4 more balls, now you have 9. How many did you have to start with?" this child may count, putting up fingers, "5, 6, 7, 8, 9." The child may then look at his or her fingers and say, "5!"
7	Deriver +/−	10	At this level, a child can use flexible strategies and derived combinations (for example, "7 + 7 is 14, so 7 + 8 is 15") to solve all types of problems. For example, when asked, "What's 7 plus 8?" this child thinks: 7 + 8 = 7 [7 + 1] = [7 +7] + 1 = 14 + 1 = 15. The child can also solve multidigit problems by incrementing or combining 10s and 1s. For example, when asked "What's 28 + 35?" this child may think: 20 + 30 = 50; + 8 = 58; 2 more is 60, and 3 more is 63. He or she can also combine 10s and 1s: 20 + 30 = 50. 8 + 5 is like 8 plus 2 and 3 more, so it is 13. 50 and 13 is 63.
8+	Problem Solver +/−	11	As children develop their addition and subtraction abilities, they can solve by using flexible strategies and many known combinations. For example, when asked, "If I have 13 and you have 9, how could we have the same number?" this child may say, "9 and 1 is 10, then 3 more makes 13. 1 and 3 is 4. I need 4 more!"
8+	Multidigit +/−	12	Further development is shown when children can use composition of 10s and all previous strategies to solve multidigit +/− problems. For example, when asked, "What's 37 − 18?" this child may say, "Take 1 ten off the 3 tens; that's 2 tens. Take 7 off the 7. That's 2 tens and 0…20. I have one more to take off. That's 19." Or, when asked, "What's 28 + 35?" this child may think, 30 + 35 would be 65. But it's 28, so it's 2 less…63.

Developmental Levels for Multiplying and Dividing

Multiplication and division build on addition and subtraction understanding and are dependent upon counting and place-value concepts. As children begin to learn to multiply, they make equal groups and count them all. They then learn skip counting and derive related products from products they know. Finding and using patterns aid in learning multiplication and division facts with understanding. Children typically follow an observable developmental progression in learning to multiply and divide numbers with recognizable stages or levels. This developmental path can be described as part of a learning trajectory.

Age Range	Level Name	Level	Description
2	Non-quantitative Sharer "Dumper"	1	Multiplication and division concepts begin very early with the problem of sharing. Early evidence of these concepts can be observed when a child dumps out blocks and gives some (not an equal number) to each person.
3	Beginning Grouper and Distributive Sharer	2	Progression to this level can be observed when a child is able to make small groups (fewer than 5). This child can share by "dealing out," but often only between 2 people, although he or she may not appreciate the numerical result. For example, to share 4 blocks, this child may give each person a block, check that each person has one, and repeat this.
4	Grouper and Distributive Sharer	3	The next level occurs when a child makes small equal groups (fewer than 6). This child can deal out equally between 2 or more recipients, but may not understand that equal quantities are produced. For example, the child may share 6 blocks by dealing out blocks to herself and a friend one at a time.
5	Concrete Modeler ×/÷	4	As children develop, they are able to solve small-number multiplying problems by grouping—making each group and counting all. At this level, a child can solve division/sharing problems with informal strategies, using concrete objects—up to 20 objects and 2 to 5 people—although the child may not understand equivalence of groups. For example, the child may distribute 20 objects by dealing out 2 blocks to each of 5 people, then 1 to each, until the blocks are gone.
6	Parts and Wholes ×/÷	5	A new level is evidenced when the child understands the inverse relation between divisor and quotient. For example, this child may understand "If you share with more people, each person gets fewer."

Age Range	Level Name	Level	Description
7	Skip Counter ×/÷	6	As children develop understanding in multiplication and division, they begin to use skip counting for multiplication and for measurement division (finding out how many groups). For example, given 20 blocks, 4 to each person, and asked how many people, the children may skip count by 4, holding up 1 finger for each count of 4. A child at this level may also use trial and error for partitive division (finding out how many in each group). For example, given 20 blocks, 5 people, and asked how many each should get, this child may give 3 to each, and then 1 more.
8+	Deriver ×/÷	7	At this level, children use strategies and derived combinations to solve multidigit problems by operating on tens and ones separately. For example, a child at this level may explain "7 × 6, five 7s is 35, so 7 more is 42."
8+	Array Quantifier	8	Further development can be observed when a child begins to work with arrays. For example, given 7 × 4 with most of 5 × 4 covered, a child at this level may say, "There are 8 in these 2 rows, and 5 rows of 4 is 20, so 28 in all."
8+	Partitive Divisor	9	This level can be observed when a child is able to figure out how many are in each group. For example, given 20 blocks, 5 people, and asked how many each should get, a child at this level may say, "4, because 5 groups of 4 is 20."
8+	Multidigit ×/÷	10	As children progress, they begin to use multiple strategies for multiplication and division, from compensating to paper-and-pencil procedures. For example, a child becoming fluent in multiplication might explain that "19 times 5 is 95, because 20 fives is 100, and 1 less five is 95."

Developmental Levels for Measuring

Measurement is one of the main real-world applications of mathematics. Counting is a type of measurement which determines how many items are in a collection. Measurement also involves assigning a number to attributes of length, area, and weight. Prekindergarten children know that mass, weight, and length exist, but they do not know how to reason about these or to accurately measure them. As children develop their understanding of measurement, they begin to use tools to measure and understand the need for standard units of measure. Children typically follow an observable developmental progression in learning to measure with recognizable stages or levels. This developmental path can be described as part of a learning trajectory.

Age Range	Level Name	Level	Description
3	Length Quantity Recognizer	1	At the earliest level, children can identify length as an attribute. For example, they might say, "I'm tall, see?"
4	Length Direct Comparer	2	In this level, children can physically align 2 objects to determine which is longer or if they are the same length. For example, they can stand 2 sticks up next to each other on a table and say, "This one's bigger."
5	Indirect Length Comparer	3	A sign of further development is when a child can compare the length of 2 objects by representing them with a third object. For example, a child might compare the length of 2 objects with a piece of string. Additional evidence of this level is that when asked to measure, the child may assign a length by guessing or moving along a length while counting (without equal-length units). For example, the child may move a finger along a line segment, saying 10, 20, 30, 31, 32.
6	Serial Orderer to 6+	4	At this level, a child can order lengths, marked in 1 to 6 units. For example, given towers of cubes, a child at this level may put them in order, 1 to 6.
6	End-to-End Length Measurer	5	At this level, the child can lay units end-to-end, although he or she may not see the need for equal-length units. For example, a child might lay 9-inch cubes in a line beside a book to measure how long it is.
7	Length Unit Iterater	6	A significant change occurs when a child iterates a single unit to measure. He or she sees the need for identical units. The child uses rulers with help.
7	Length Unit Relater	7	At this level, a child can relate size and number of units. For example, the child may explain, "If you measure with centimeters instead of inches, you'll need more of them because each one is smaller."
8+	Length Measurer	8	As a child develops measurement ability, they begin to measure, knowing the need for identical units, the relationships between different units, partitions of unit, and the zero point on rulers. At this level, the child also begins to estimate. The children may explain, "I used a meterstick 3 times, then there was a little left over. So, I lined it up from 0 and found 14 centimeters. So, it's 3 meters, 14 centimeters in all."
8+	Conceptual Ruler Measurer	9	Further development in measurement is evidenced when a child possesses an "internal" measurement tool. At this level, the child mentally moves along an object, segmenting it, and counting the segments. This child also uses arithmetic to measure and estimates with accuracy. For example, a child at this level may explain, "I imagine one meterstick after another along the edge of the room. That's how I estimated the room's length to be 9 meters."

Learning Trajectories for Math

Developmental Levels for Recognizing Geometric Shapes

Geometric shapes can be used to represent and understand objects. Analyzing, comparing, and classifying shapes help create new knowledge of shapes and their relationships. Shapes can be decomposed or composed into other shapes. Through their everyday activities, children build both intuitive and explicit knowledge of geometric figures. Most children can recognize and name basic two-dimensional shapes at four years of age. However, young children can learn richer concepts about shape if they have varied examples and nonexamples of shape, discussions about shapes and their characteristics, a wide variety of shape classes, and interesting tasks. Children typically follow an observable developmental progression in learning about shapes with recognizable stages or levels. This developmental path can be described as part of a learning trajectory.

Age Range	Level Name	Level	Description
2	Shape Matcher—Identical	1	The earliest sign of understanding shape is when a child can match basic shapes (circle, square, typical triangle) with the same size and orientation.
2	Shape Matcher—Sizes	2	A sign of development is when a child can match basic shapes with different sizes.
2	Shape Matcher—Orientations	3	This level of development is when a child can match basic shapes with different orientations.
3	Shape Recognizer—Typical	4	A sign of development is when a child can recognize and name a prototypical circle, square, and, less often, a typical triangle. For example, the child names this a square. ☐ Some children may name different sizes, shapes, and orientations of rectangles, but also accept some shapes that look rectangular but are not rectangles. Children name these shapes "rectangles" (including the nonrectangular parallelogram).
3	Shape Matcher—More Shapes	5	As children develop understanding of shape, they can match a wider variety of shapes with the same size and orientation.
3	Shape Matcher—Sizes and Orientations	6	The child matches a wider variety of shapes with different sizes and orientations.
3	Shape Matcher—Combinations	7	The child matches combinations of shapes to each other.
4	Shape Recognizer—Circles, Squares, and Triangles	8	This sign of development is when a child can recognize some nonprototypical squares and triangles and may recognize some rectangles, but usually not rhombi (diamonds). Often, the child does not differentiate sides/corners. The child at this level may name these as triangles.
4	Constructor of Shapes from Parts—Looks Like *Representing*	9	A significant sign of development is when a child represents a shape by making a shape "look like" a goal shape. For example, when asked to make a triangle with sticks, the child may create the following: △.

Age Range	Level Name	Level	Description
5	Shape Recognizer— All Rectangles	10	As children develop understanding of shape, they recognize more rectangle sizes, shapes, and orientations of rectangles. For example, a child at this level may correctly name these shapes "rectangles."
5	Side Recognizer *Parts*	11	A sign of development is when a child recognizes parts of shapes and identifies sides as distinct geometric objects. For example, when asked what this shape is, the child may say it is a quadrilateral (or has 4 sides) after counting and running a finger along the length of each side.
5	Angle Recognizer *Parts*	12	At this level, a child can recognize angles as separate geometric objects. For example, when asked, "Why is this a triangle," the child may say, "It has three angles" and count them, pointing clearly to each vertex (point at the corner).
5	Shape Recognizer— More Shapes	13	As children develop, they are able to recognize most basic shapes and prototypical examples of other shapes, such as hexagon, rhombus (diamond), and trapezoid. For example, a child can correctly identify and name all the following shapes:
6	Shape Identifier	14	At this level, the child can name most common shapes, including rhombi, without making mistakes such as calling ovals circles. A child at this level implicitly recognizes right angles, so distinguishes between a rectangle and a parallelogram without right angles. A child may correctly name all the following shapes:
6	Angle Matcher *Parts*	15	A sign of development is when the child can match angles concretely. For example, given several triangles, the child may find two with the same angles by laying the angles on top of one another.

Age Range	Level Name	Level	Description
7	Parts of Shapes Identifier	16	At this level, the child can identify shapes in terms of their components. For example, the child may say, "No matter how skinny it looks, that's a triangle because it has 3 sides and 3 angles."
7	Constructor of Shapes from Parts—Exact Representing	17	A significant step is when the child can represent a shape with completely correct construction, based on knowledge of components and relationships. For example, when asked to make a triangle with sticks, the child may create the following:
8	Shape Class Identifier	18	As children develop, they begin to use class membership (for example, to sort) not explicitly based on properties. For example, a child at this level may say, "I put the triangles over here, and the quadrilaterals, including squares, rectangles, rhombi, and trapezoids, over there."
8	Shape Property Identifier	19	At this level, a child can use properties explicitly. For example, a child may say, "I put the shapes with opposite sides that are parallel over here, and those with 4 sides but not both pairs of sides parallel over there."
8	Angle Size Comparer	20	The next sign of development is when a child can separate and compare angle sizes. For example, the child may say, "I put all the shapes that have right angles here, and all the ones that have bigger or smaller angles over there."
8	Angle Measurer	21	A significant step in development is when a child can use a protractor to measure angles.
8	Property Class Identifier	22	The next sign of development is when a child can use class membership for shapes (for example, to sort or consider shapes "similar") explicitly based on properties, including angle measure. For example, the child may say, "I put the equilateral triangles over here, and the right triangles over here."
8	Angle Synthesizer	23	As children develop understanding of shape, they can combine various meanings of angle (turn, corner, slant). For example, a child at this level could explain, "This ramp is at a 45° angle to the ground."

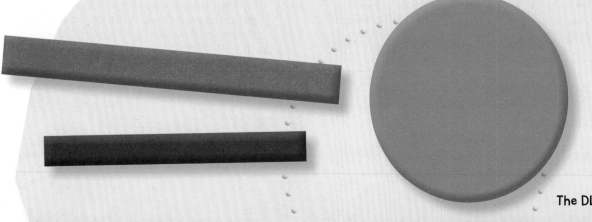

Developmental Levels for Composing Geometric Shapes

Children move through levels in the composition and decomposition of two-dimensional figures. Very young children cannot compose shapes but then gain ability to combine shapes into pictures, synthesize combinations of shapes into new shapes, and eventually substitute and build different kinds of shapes. Children typically follow an observable developmental progression in learning to compose shapes with recognizable stages or levels. This developmental path can be described as part of a learning trajectory.

Age Range	Level Name	Level	Description
2	Pre-Composer	1	The earliest sign of development is when a child can manipulate shapes as individuals, but is unable to combine them to compose a larger shape.
3	Pre-Decomposer	2	At this level, a child can decompose shapes, but only by trial and error.
4	Piece Assembler	3	Around age 4, a child can begin to make pictures in which each shape represents a unique role (for example, one shape for each body part) and shapes touch. A child at this level can fill simple outline puzzles using trial and error.
5	Picture Maker	4	As children develop, they are able to put several shapes together to make one part of a picture (for example, 2 shapes for 1 arm). A child at this level uses trial and error and does not anticipate creation of the new geometric shape. The children can choose shapes using "general shape" or side length, and fill "easy" outline puzzles that suggest the placement of each shape (but note that the child is trying to put a square in the puzzle where its right angles will not fit).
5	Simple Decomposer	5	A significant step occurs when the child is able to decompose ("take apart" into smaller shapes) simple shapes that have obvious clues as to their decomposition.

Age Range	Level Name	Level	Description
5	Shape Composer	6	A sign of development is when a child composes shapes with anticipation ("I know what will fit!"). A child at this level chooses shapes using angles as well as side lengths. Rotation and flipping are used intentionally to select and place shapes.
6	Substitution Composer	7	A sign of development is when a child is able to make new shapes out of smaller shapes and uses trial and error to substitute groups of shapes for other shapes in order to create new shapes in different ways. For example, the child can substitute shapes to fill outline puzzles in different ways.
6	Shape Decomposer (with Help)	8	As children develop, they can decompose shapes by using imagery that is suggested and supported by the task or environment.
7	Shape Composite Repeater	9	This level is demonstrated when the child can construct and duplicate units of units (shapes made from other shapes) intentionally, and understands each as being both multiple, small shapes and one larger shape. For example, the child may continue a pattern of shapes that leads to tiling.
7	Shape Decomposer with Imagery	10	A significant sign of development is when a child is able to decompose shapes flexibly by using independently generated imagery.
8	Shape Composer—Units of Units	11	Children demonstrate further understanding when they are able to build and apply units of units (shapes made from other shapes). For example, in constructing spatial patterns, the child can extend patterning activity to create a tiling with a new unit shape—a unit of unit shapes that he or she recognizes and consciously constructs. For example, the child may build Ts out of 4 squares, use 4 Ts to build squares, and use squares to tile a rectangle.
8	Shape Decomposer — Units of Units	12	As children develop understanding of shape, they can decompose shapes flexibly by using independently generated imagery and planned decompositions of shapes that themselves are decompositions.

Developmental Levels for Comparing Geometric Shapes

As early as four years of age, children can create and use strategies, such as moving shapes to compare their parts or to place one on top of the other, for judging whether two figures are the same shape. From Pre-K to Grade 2, they can develop sophisticated and accurate mathematical procedures for comparing geometric shapes. Children typically follow an observable developmental progression in learning about how shapes are the same and different with recognizable stages or levels. This developmental path can be described as part of a learning trajectory.

Age Range	Level Name	Level	Description
3	"Same Thing" Comparer	1	The first sign of understanding is when the child can compare real-world objects. For example, the children may say two pictures of houses are the same or different.
4	"Similar" Comparer	2	This sign of development occurs when the child judges two shapes to be the same if they are more visually similar than different. For example, the child may say, "These are the same. They are pointy at the top."
4	Part Comparer	3	At this level, a child can say that two shapes are the same after matching one side on each. For example, a child may say, "These are the same" (matching the two sides).
4	Some Attributes Comparer	4	As children develop, they look for differences in attributes, but may examine only part of a shape. For example, a child at this level may say, "These are the same" (indicating the top halves of the shapes are similar by laying them on top of each other).
5	Most Attributes Comparer	5	At this level, the child looks for differences in attributes, examining full shapes, but may ignore some spatial relationships. For example, a child may say, "These are the same."
7	Congruence Determiner	6	A sign of development is when a child determines congruence by comparing all attributes and all spatial relationships. For example, a child at this level may say that two shapes are the same shape and the same size after comparing every one of their sides and angles.
7	Congruence Superposer	7	As children develop understanding, they can move and place objects on top of each other to determine congruence. For example, a child at this level may say that two shapes are the same shape and the same size after laying them on top of each other.
8+	Congruence Representer	8	Continued development is evidenced as children refer to geometric properties and explain with transformations. For example, a child at this level may say, "These must be congruent because they have equal sides, all square corners, and I can move them on top of each other exactly."

Developmental Levels for Spatial Sense and Motions

Infants and toddlers spend a great deal of time learning about the properties and relations of objects in space. Very young children know and use the shape of their environment in navigation activities. With guidance they can learn to "mathematize" this knowledge. They can learn about direction, perspective, distance, symbolization, location, and coordinates. Children typically follow an observable developmental progression in developing spatial sense with recognizable stages or levels. This developmental path can be described as part of a learning trajectory.

Age Range	Level Name	Level	Description
4	Simple Turner	1	An early sign of spatial sense is when a child mentally turns an object to perform easy tasks. For example, given a shape with the top marked with color, the child may correctly identify which of three shapes it would look like if it were turned "like this" (90 degree turn demonstrated), before physically moving the shape.
5	Beginning Slider, Flipper, Turner	2	This sign of development occurs when a child can use the correct motions, but is not always accurate in direction and amount. For example, a child at this level may know a shape has to be flipped to match another shape, but flips it in the wrong direction.
6	Slider, Flipper, Turner	3	As children develop spatial sense, they can perform slides and flips, often only horizontal and vertical, by using manipulatives. For example, a child at this level may perform turns of 45, 90, and 180 degrees. For example, a child knows a shape must be turned 90 degrees to the right to fit into a puzzle.
7	Diagonal Mover	4	A sign of development is when a child can perform diagonal slides and flips. For example, children at this level may know a shape must be turned or flipped over an oblique line (45 degree orientation) to fit into a puzzle.
8	Mental Mover	5	Further signs of development occur when a child can predict results of moving shapes using mental images. A child at this level may say, "If you turned this 120 degrees, it would be just like this one."

Learning Trajectories for Math

Developmental Levels for Patterning and Early Algebra

Algebra begins with a search for patterns. Identifying patterns helps bring order, cohesion, and predictability to seemingly unorganized situations and allows one to make generalizations beyond the information directly available. The recognition and analysis of patterns are important components of young children's intellectual development because they provide a foundation for the development of algebraic thinking. Although prekindergarten children engage in pattern-related activities and recognize patterns in their everyday environment, research has revealed that an abstract understanding of patterns develops gradually during the early childhood years. Children typically follow an observable developmental progression in learning about patterns with recognizable stages or levels. This developmental path can be described as part of a learning trajectory.

Age Range	Level Name	Level	Description
2	Pre-Patterner	1	A child at the earliest level does not recognize patterns. For example, a child may name a striped shirt with no repeating unit a "pattern."
3	Pattern Recognizer	2	At this level, the child can recognize a simple pattern. For example, a child at this level may say, "I'm wearing a pattern" about a shirt with black and white stripes.
4	Pattern Fixer	3	At this level the child fills in missing elements of a pattern, first with ABABAB patterns. When given items in a row with an item missing, such as ABAB_BAB, the child identifies and fills in the missing element (A).
4	Pattern Duplicator AB	4	A sign of development is when the child can duplicate an ABABAB pattern, although the children may have to work alongside the model pattern. For example, given objects in a row, ABABAB, the child may make his or her own ABABAB row in a different location.
4	Pattern Extender AB	5	At this level the child extends AB repeating patterns. For example, given items in a row—ABABAB—the child adds ABAB to the end of the row.
4	Pattern Duplicator	6	At this level, the child is able to duplicate simple patterns (not just alongside the model pattern). For example, given objects in a row, ABBABBABB, the child may make his or her own ABBABBABB row in a different location.
5	Pattern Extender	7	A sign of development is when the child can extend simple patterns. For example, given objects in a row, ABBABBABB, he or she may add ABBABB to the end of the row.
7	Pattern Unit Recognizer	8	At this level, a child can identify the smallest unit of a pattern. For example, given objects in a row with one missing, ABBAB_ABB, he or she may identify and fill in the missing element.

Developmental Levels for Classifying and Analyzing Data

Data analysis contains one big idea: classifying, organizing, representing, and using information to ask and answer questions. The developmental continuum for data analysis includes growth in classifying and counting to sort objects and quantify their groups. Children eventually become capable of simultaneously classifying and counting; for example, counting the number of colors in a group of objects. Children typically follow an observable developmental progression in learning about patterns with recognizable stages or levels. This developmental path can be described as part of a learning trajectory.

Age Range	Level Name	Level	Description
2	Similarity Recognizer	1	The first sign that a child can classify is when he or she recognizes, intuitively, two or more objects as "similar" in some way. For example, "that's another doggie."
2	Informal Sorter	2	A sign of development is when a child places objects that are alike in some attribute together, but switches criteria and may use functional relationships as the basis for sorting. A child at this level might stack blocks of the same shape or put a cup with its saucer.
3	Attribute Identifier	3	The next level is when the child names attributes of objects and places objects together with a given attribute, but cannot then move to sorting by a new rule. For example, the child may say, "These are both red."
4	Attribute Sorter	4	At the next level the child sorts objects according to given attributes, forming categories, but may switch attributes during the sorting. A child at this stage can switch rules for sorting if guided. For example, the child might start putting red beads on a string, but switches to spheres of different colors.
5	Consistent Sorter	5	A sign of development is when the child can sort consistently by a given attribute. For example, the child might put several identical blocks together.
6	Exhaustive Sorter	6	At the next level, the child can sort consistently and exhaustively by an attribute, given or created. This child can use terms "some" and "all" meaningfully. For example, a child at this stage would be able to find all the attribute blocks of a certain size and color.

Age Range	Level Name	Level	Description
6	Multiple Attribute Sorter	7	A sign of development is when the child can sort consistently and exhaustively by more than one attribute, sequentially. For example, a child at this level can put all the attribute blocks together by color, then by shape.
7	Classifier and Counter	8	At the next level, the child is capable of simultaneously classifying and counting. For example, the child counts the number of colors in a group of objects.
7	List Grapher	9	In the early stage of graphing, the child graphs by simply listing all cases. For example, the child may list each child in the class and each child's response to a question.
8+	Multiple Attribute Classifier	10	A sign of development is when the child can intentionally sort according to multiple attributes, naming and relating the attributes. This child understands that objects could belong to more than one group. For example, the child can complete a two-dimensional classification matrix or form subgroups within groups.
8+	Classifying Grapher	11	At the next level the child can graph by classifying data (e.g., responses) and represent it according to categories. For example, the child can take a survey, classify the responses, and graph the result.
8+	Classifier	12	A sign of development is when the child creates complete, conscious classifications logically connected to a specific property. For example, a child at this level gives a definition of a class in terms of a more general class and one or more specific differences and begins to understand the inclusion relation.
8+	Hierarchical Classifier	13	At the next level, the child can perform hierarchical classifications. For example, the child recognizes that all squares are rectangles, but not all rectangles are squares.
8+	Data Representer	14	Signs of development are when the child organizes and displays data through both simple numerical summaries such as counts, tables, and tallies, and graphical displays, including picture graphs, line plots, and bar graphs. At this level the child creates graphs and tables, compares parts of the data, makes statements about the data as a whole, and determines whether the graphs answer the questions posed initially.